SENSING THE PAST

Also by Jim Cullen

———

The Civil War in Popular Culture: A Reusable Past (1995)

*The Art of Democracy: A Concise History of Popular Culture
in the United States (1996)*

Born in the U.S.A.: Bruce Springsteen and the American Tradition (1997)

Popular Culture in American History (2001) (Editor)

Restless in the Promised Land: Catholics and the American Dream (2001)

The American Dream: A Short History of an Idea That Shaped a Nation (2003)

*The Fieldston Guide to American History for Cynical Beginners:
Impractical Lessons for Everyday Life (2005)*

*The Civil War Era: An Anthology of Sources (2005)
(Editor, with Lyde Cullen Sizer)*

Imperfect Presidents: Tales of Misadventure and Triumph (2007)

Essaying the Past: How to Read, Write, and Think About History (2009)

SENSING THE PAST

HOLLYWOOD STARS AND HISTORICAL VISIONS

JIM CULLEN

OXFORD
UNIVERSITY PRESS

OXFORD
UNIVERSITY PRESS

Oxford University Press is a department of the University of Oxford.
It furthers the University's objective of excellence in research,
scholarship, and education by publishing worldwide.

Oxford   New York

Auckland   Cape Town   Dar es Salaam   Hong Kong   Karachi
Kuala Lumpur   Madrid   Melbourne   Mexico City   Nairobi
New Delhi   Shanghai   Taipei   Toronto

With offices in

Argentina   Austria   Brazil   Chile   Czech Republic   France   Greece
Guatemala   Hungary   Italy   Japan   Poland   Portugal   Singapore
South Korea   Switzerland   Thailand   Turkey   Ukraine   Vietnam

Oxford is a registered trademark of Oxford University Press
in the UK and certain other countries.

Published in the United States of America by
Oxford University Press
198 Madison Avenue, New York, NY 10016

Library of Congress Cataloging-in-Publication Data
Cullen, Jim, 1962–
Sensing the past: Hollywood stars and historical visions / Jim Cullen.
p.   cm.
Includes bibliographical references and index.
ISBN 978-0-19-992764-7 — ISBN 978-0-19-992766-1 (pbk.)
1. Historical films—United States—History and criticism.
2. Motion pictures and history.   3. United States—In motion pictures.   I. Title.
PN1995.9.H5C85 2013
791.43'658—dc23   2012014442

1 3 5 7 9 8 6 4 2

Printed in the United States of America
on acid-free paper

To the memory, and friendship,
of William G. McLoughlin (1922–1992)
and John L. Thomas (1927–2005),
American Civilization faculty, Brown University

"*A teacher affects eternity;*
he can never tell where his influence stops."
        —*The Education of Henry Adams (1907)*

"Someday I will look back and muse about the curiosities of history: acting and politics all mixed up together."

—Jodie Foster, 1982

CONTENTS

———

ACKNOWLEDGMENTS

A dozen years ago, with some misgivings, I left a position teaching fresh-man composition at Harvard University and began working at the Ethical Culture Fieldston School in New York City. I reckoned that my liking for the job would correlate directly to the degree it resembled college teaching. Instead, I've found that many of the things I've loved most about working at Fieldston are those that don't, among them the opportunity for sustained participation in the lives of remarkable young people at the most impres-sionable moment of their lives. So it is that I begin by expressing my thanks for the privilege of sharing this institution with its students.

I have also been deeply fortunate in my colleagues and the administra-tion at Fieldston, who have treated me with a rare combination of benign neglect and active support. In particular, former principal John Love, former dean of faculty Hugo Mahabir, director of special projects Marga-ret Johnson, and my teammates in the History Department, especially Andy Meyers, have provided me with assets that include good conversa-tion, research resources, and substantial financial support in the form of a 2011–12 Southwind Grant for professional development.

Two other institutions were also pivotal. The Westchester County library system was invaluable for getting my hands on movies. And the good baristas of Starbucks, particularly its Dobbs Ferry and Ardsley, New York, locations, provided relief from the solitude of reading and writing with an atmosphere of quiet bonhomie.

Invaluable editorial advice came from old friends and dedicated pro-fessionals. Among the most important guidance I received came from the anonymous readers provided by Oxford University Press. I am espe-cially indebted to my graduate school classmate Woody Register for his exceptionally acute critique of the manuscript. I'm also grateful to Mark Simpson-Vos of the University of North Carolina Press for his generos-ity. Thanks too to Jim Sparrow at the University of Chicago, Leah Olson of Sarah Lawrence College, freelance writer Dan Greenberg, and psychiatrist Beth Haase for their insights. My colleague in the Visual Arts Department, Larry Buskey, helped me with illustrations; my colleague in the Performing Arts Department, William Norman, was a font of information who saved me from many errors of fact and judgment.

I'd like to say a few words here about the ongoing influence of Greil Marcus. Many years ago, I encountered his book *Mystery Train: Images of America in Rock 'n' Roll Music* (1975), which played a significant role in my decision to become a cultural historian. It was only when I was completing this project that I realized its shape—case studies of six artists still in the prime of their careers—is patterned on *Mystery Train*. I've never met Marcus, but his fingerprints are all over this book. (I suspect Bruce Springsteen's are, too—another hero of mine I've never met.)

It is one of the curiosities of my career that I've enjoyed the most success with British-based publishers, only one reason I'm an Anglophile. This is the second book I've published with Oxford, and I feel profoundly indebted to Susan Ferber, whose enthusiasm and kindness have been durable. Shannon McLachlan acquired the manuscript; Brendan O'Neill exercised tact and good editorial judgment in steering it into print. Copy editor India Cooper and senior production editor Joellyn Ausanka have once again graced my work with their talents, and Alana Podolsky has been a spirited publicist; it was a great privilege to work with these people.

The bedrock for this work is my family, which has tolerated my excesses and provided me with refuge from my obsessions. My parents and sister remain cherished company on my lifelong journey. My in-laws, Nancy Sizer and the late Ted Sizer, remain role models, as do their four children. My oldest son, Jay, was a valuable sounding board, a role I found bittersweet, as he played it most actively in the weeks leading up to his departure for the University of Chicago. His absence, in turn, has led me to experience a new wave of appreciation for the company of my sons Grayson and Ryland as well as my daughter, Nancy. But of course their tenure with me will also be temporary. The keystone of my arch remains Lyde Cullen Sizer.

—Jim Cullen
Hastings-on Hudson, New York
August 2012

SENSING THE PAST

Introduction

John Wayne's Threshold

The story of this book begins in 2001, when I left academe and began working as a high school teacher. In the process of trying to plan the first semester of a U.S. history survey, I made a curious discovery after generating a slate of movies I planned to show over the course of the fall semester: every one of them starred Daniel Day-Lewis. There was *The Crucible*. And *Last of the Mohicans*. And *The Age of Innocence*. Later I added *Gangs of New York* and *There Will Be Blood*. All told, there were nine times I ran an annual event I dubbed "the Daniel Day-Lewis Film Festival."

Maybe it's not surprising that my predilections would express themselves without conscious effort. But keep in mind that we're talking about *Daniel Day-Lewis* here. As anyone vaguely familiar with his work knows, Day-Lewis is legendary for the extraordinary variety of characters he has played, and the vertiginous psychological depth with which he has played them. I first became aware of Day-Lewis in early 1985, when, in the space of a week, I watched him portray the priggish Cecil Vyse in the tony Merchant-Ivory film adaptation of E. M. Forster's *Room with a View* and then saw him play Johnny, the punk East End homosexual, in Stephen Frears's brilliantly brash *My Beautiful Laundrette*. Day-Lewis went on to have a distinguished career, winning an Academy Award for his portrayal of the handicapped Irish poet Christy Brown in *My Left Foot* in 1989, but between 1988 and 2007 he played a string of American figures that ranged from a seventeenth-century Puritan to a twentieth-century art collector.

What could this mean, I wondered? Every year like clockwork, I watched these films again with my students, marveling at the inexhaustible nuances of Day-Lewis's performances. Gradually I discerned a thread that connected the Puritan to the gangster, the pioneer, and the lawyer.[1] But perhaps the more important outcome of the experience is that it got me thinking: Could it make sense to think of actors as historians? That people, in the process of doing a job whose primary focus was *not* thinking in terms of an interpretation of the past, were nevertheless performing one? And that in doing so repeatedly over the course of a career they would articulate an interpretive version of American history as a whole?

Of course, such people are aware of when they're dealing with historical situations (or contemporary situations with historical resonances), and may make real effort to exercise historical imagination as part of their work. But that's the point: it's *part* of their work. We all understand that there are many people out there who "do" history without writing books—archivists, curators, and, of course, filmmakers, including documentarians as well as writers and directors of feature films, who work consciously and conceptually to craft an interpretive experience for their audiences. What intrigues me about actors, though, is the obvious limitations and obstacles to executing a purely historical function. Their work is always embedded in a larger context in which their control of the material is limited—actors do not typically write their own lines—and their craft is collaborative, part of enterprises that will always be as much aesthetic and commercial as they will be historical.

Now I must acknowledge that there is less to the distinction I'm making than meets the eye. Archivists, curators, and documentary filmmakers also labor under limitations of various kinds; they collaborate; they embark on enterprises that are very often aesthetic and commercial, too: they can't afford not to. So do academic historians. But there's a powerful mythology surrounding academic work—a mythology that extends, for example, to procedures for hiring and promotion at research universities—that suggests scholarship should exist outside such considerations.[2] That it has its own intrinsic value and should be pursued independently of them. This is a powerful proposition, and it has led to work of enormous value that has enriched our understanding of the past. I'd never want to see it go away and understand it cannot be taken for granted in a society under great financial pressure and long-standing anti-intellectual influences.

But I'm after something a little different: to apprehend the way history is absorbed into the fabric of everyday life—messy, fragmented, more suggestive than direct. In the words of one scholar who has compared cinematic history with more traditional kinds, "its point is not to have a point but to point."[3] In the ensuing pages I follow such cues, tracing sometimes faint, and always contestable, master narratives as they emerge in bodies of work.

———

All works of art essentially say the same thing: *this is the way the world works.* They usually say it implicitly rather than explicitly (in modes of harmony or dissonance; optimism or pessimism; naturalism or artifice), and as often as not point toward an alternative to the set of arrangements they depict. In the process of such a search, works of art will refer directly or indirectly to other works of art—they will say, in effect, *the world doesn't work* that *way; instead, it works* this *way*. Or they will say, *yes, the world works* that *way, but with* this *caveat or corollary*. But all works of art must start, if not end, with an assertion about the world as it is. No work of art claims to represent reality in its totality—it could not, for then it would be life and not art—but every work of art claims to capture something essential, which is to say something shared.

The lifeblood of art is choices. To create is to edit, and editing is a process (usually conscious, but sometimes not) of making decisions about what to include, which inevitably means decisions about what to exclude. Representing reality—which is to say using one thing to stand for another—is at least as much a matter of subtraction as it is addition. And, if you will permit one more theoretical statement here, representation is a matter of abstraction, the transubstantiation of substance and concept.

Works of art vary in their degree of abstraction (think of the difference between a Michelangelo and a Picasso painting), and I think it's fair to say that some forms of art tend to be more abstract than others (think of the difference between a symphony and a building). If you were to somehow chart a spectrum of verisimilitude from the abstract to the concrete, the medium of film would fall on the latter end. Though, even more than the other arts, it rests on an illusion (namely a neurological quirk of the human brain in which images shown in rapid succession create a perception of motion), film is regarded as among the most mimetic of the arts. At the same time, because film is typically experienced in finite segments of time—unlike media such as television, which is a more open-ended enterprise measured in seasons—we tend to think of films as finite, fully realized worlds in themselves we experience in a sitting.

For all their perceived transparency, however, we all understand that movies—I'm going to make a semantic switch now, both because in a digital age the word *film* is on the way to losing its precision, and because the word *movie* has a vernacular immediacy that corresponds to the larger point I'm about to make—have traditionally been expensive and complicated to produce. Every year at the Oscars, the Motion Picture Academy of Arts and Sciences (note the double plural) hands out a bevy of rewards to remind us of this fact. One reason they have to remind us is that for all our increasing cultural sophistication about the film industry—the attention to box office grosses, for example, or the celebrity status of directors or producers like Steven Spielberg, who typically work behind the camera—is that there are few things in life that immerse one to the degree a good movie does. We watch what's before us. And what's before us, the overwhelming majority of the time, is the people we call "actors." Movies are among the most mimetic of the arts, and actors are among the most mimetic aspects of the movies.

I so love that word: *actor*. To act is to pretend, to *make* believe. But it's also to commit, to execute. As we have been reminded since the time of the ancient Greek philosopher Heraclitus, character is destiny: an actor embodies a set of ideas, the value of which is very often bound up in the fate of the character that actor plays. (A case when this is not so—when the good guy gets punished, when the bad gal literally or figuratively gets away with murder—becomes a statement in its own right.) The immediacy and clarity of this widely available performance art, an art that slices across linguistic lines and educational levels, make it—paradoxically, given the vast sums and hierarchies with which it has always been associated—thrillingly democratic.

Actors vividly display the act of choice central to the artistic process. Putting aside the fact that any acting performance includes countless renditions that are shot out of sequence or discarded on the cutting room floor, watching a movie involves witnessing an inexhaustible array of choices in language, posture, expression, and setting. A century of experience has taught us that some people make these choices so strikingly that we will watch them repeatedly not only in the same movie, but in movie after movie. One is reminded of the words of F. Scott Fitzgerald's narrator Nick Carraway, who, in the process of explaining what made his friend Jay Gatsby great, defined personality as "an unbroken series of successful gestures."[4] Writing almost a century later, the rock critic Greil Marcus, in a characteristically roaming exegesis of the rock band The Doors, notes that "when actors migrate from movie to movie, traces of their characters travel with them, until, regardless of the script, the setup, the director's instructions, it's partly the old characters speaking out of the mouths of the new ones, guiding a new character's hand into a gesture you remember from two or twenty years before."[5]

This is what the best actors do—or at any rate, a certain kind of successful actor does. In his now-classic study *Acting in the Cinema*, James Naremore defines acting as "the transposition of everyday behavior into the theatrical realm." Acknowledging the surprisingly thin line between acting done on a stage or in a studio and the roles—with varying degrees of staginess—we all play in everyday life, Naremore notes that the key challenge for people in television and movies, who often must move and act in highly artificial ways in order to appear "natural" in front of a camera, involves "a compromise between 'obviousness' and 'doing nothing.'" Some actors (Naremore cites Spencer Tracy as a quintessential example) are so deft at manipulating this duality that we have a hard time distinguishing the difference between an onscreen and offscreen persona, even as we know there must be one, and we find ourselves fascinated in the attempt to do so.[6]

We have a term for such people: we call them movie stars. More so than other artists, movie stars intrigue us because they exhibit a series of intriguing frictions. One set of frictions involves the relationships between the actual person, the character that person plays in a given movie, and the variations on that character in a career of movie roles. All but a child recognizes that each of these is distinct, but a star wouldn't be a star if there weren't *some* connection between them. Moreover, such connections are perceived to *matter*. In addition to connecting the star to the role, they also connect the star to the fan—which in turn creates another set of frictions, because the fan experiences something shared with the movie star while at the same time experiencing a sense of awe-inspiring distance; hence the metaphor of an astronomical object in the sky. Bruce Springsteen, a cinematic songwriter if ever there was one, captures this friction in his classic song "Backstreets": "Remember all the movies, Terry, we'd go see/Trying to learn how to walk like the heroes we thought we had to be." Seeking liberation through, and yet being oppressed by, the set of choices made by a movie star (who in turn can feel oppressed by all the attention of fans) is among the great conundrums of cinematic life.

And here's one more friction that's particularly germane: the tension between the power of choice at the heart of acting and the limits of control intrinsic to appearing in a movie. For, as any veteran will tell you, acting is also *re*acting—to your co-star, to the director, and to the technical demands of the immediate task at hand, not to mention the professional apparatus of agents, managers, studios, and the like. This sense of obvious as well as subtle enmeshment (we know what *that's* like!) helps explain the intensity of identification the public sometimes has with actors, a kinship of enmeshment fostered by other media.

Here we must return to the distinction between actors and the subset of that species we know as movie stars, acknowledging that the line is porous. Actors need *work*, and although they may have standards or priorities about the jobs they take, a professional's code very often includes a commitment to flexibility and variety. Movie stars, by contrast, tend to think in terms of *roles*. They have more power than actors to choose the parts they play—which in its most potent form is the power to say no repeatedly—and to convert that power into other kinds, like directing or producing.

Our democratic impulses lead us to honor actors, whose work ethic (typically exhibited on a daily basis in theaters, as opposed to episodic stints on sets) we admire. But it's stars that capture our imaginations.

That said, my decision to focus on movie stars is to a great degree a utilitarian one. In the way their work is embedded in a web of considerations, they mimic the manifold complications and compromises of everyday life. But to the extent that they have more power over the conditions of their work than most people, they make it possible to discern, even isolate, strands in their thinking that are powerful because they are widely shared—very often at the level of presumption more than explicit argument. Indeed, it's precisely their uncanny capacity to project these shared presumptions and put them in a new light that allows such people to become stars in the first place.

Perhaps a small example will help illustrate my point. Consider one of the most famous images in Hollywood cinematic history: the final shot of John Ford's classic 1956 Western *The Searchers*, which shows John Wayne standing in a doorway. Wayne's character, Ethan Edwards, is an unreconstructed Confederate soldier who has returned to Texas in 1868 and visits his brother's family shortly before most of that family, sans

PAST MASTER: John Wayne in a characteristically liminal pose at the end of the 1956 film *The Searchers*. (His clutched arm is an act of homage to a cherished predecessor, Harry Carey.) Wayne's cinematic history is also historiography: not merely a specimen or a symptom but also an interpretation available for multiple uses, factual and otherwise, laudable or not. *(Warner Bros.)*

Ethan's niece Debbie, gets massacred by Comanche Indians. An avowed racist, Ethan spends the next five years trying to avenge this atrocity, assisted, much to his dismay, by Debbie's adoptive—and part-Cherokee—brother. When Ethan learns that she has been married to a Comanche chief and wants to live as a Native American, he tries to kill her: better dead than red. Ultimately, however, he seizes her and returns her to "civilized" life with an adoptive white family. His self-appointed mission complete, Ethan remains at the threshold of the house, seemingly unwilling or unable to enter. And then he turns and walks away, with that much imitated, but never equaled, loping walk that Wayne made famous.

Now, there's much that has been, and still can be, said about *The Searchers*. Some commentary focuses on the accuracy of the film's scenario, based on the 1954 novel by Alan Le May, with a screenplay by Frank S. Nugent. It looks at the story's resonances with a long tradition of captivity narratives dating back to Mary Rowlandson's 1682 account of her time with the Narragansett Indians during King Philip's War; it views *The Searchers* as a document of American racism, and so on. A variant on this approach traces the morphology of the film: what did Le May do with the factual events on which his novel is loosely based, and what in turn did director John Ford do with Le May? Still another line of inquiry looks at the internal cinematic logic of *The Searchers*. It's worth noting, for example, that the final shot of the movie is the culmination of a whole string of threshold sequences, from doorways to tepees to caves, that runs through the film.[7]

While I'm interested in such questions, and have pursued them myself at different points in my career—as indeed I do in the pages that follow—my real interest here is in *The Searchers* as a *John Wayne* movie. Definitive as his performance is for generations of film fans, there was nothing ordained about casting him in the film; indeed, at different points in his career Ford kept Wayne at arm's length. It's possible to imagine, say, Clark Gable or Gary Cooper playing a tortured soul like Ethan Edwards, even as most of us would say this by way of a concession—Wayne just seems so right for the part. But one reason *why* Wayne seems so right for the part is that he had already literally and figuratively established himself as the man on the threshold. He did it in *Red River* (1948), and he would do it again in *The Man Who Shot Liberty Valance* (1962), among other pictures. Far more than Gable or Cooper, Wayne repeatedly portrayed tortured souls who do dirty work, and yet in the process of doing so create or preserve a life of decency for others, even if they cannot cross over into the promised land themselves. This is not just a statement that John Wayne made about John Wayne's world; it's a statement John Wayne is making about the world he and the rest of us live in as well.

There's a long history of film criticism that analyzes the choices of directors or film moguls in terms of such patterns, going back to the auteur theory that dominated cinematic studies in the second half of the twentieth century. Less common, for some of the reasons I've suggested, is thinking about a body of work on the part of an actor as something more than the embodiment of a personal archetype. But that may be changing. "There is a slowly developing vocabulary adequate to an accurate and objective discussion about film acting: what it is and how it affects the film and its audience, how an individual creates a presence on the screen, what the presence is, and what the viewer's relationship is to it," veteran critic Robert Kolker notes in the most recent edition of his classic study, A Cinema of Loneliness. Kolker doesn't cite any examples of such emerging scholarship, however. I will cite Garry Wills's 1997 book, John Wayne's America, as a pioneering example of the kind of work I'm pursuing here.[8]

Of course, directors remain major, even decisive influences on these people, especially in their early work. But in the last third of the twentieth century movie stars increasingly became important shapers of an overall cinematic product themselves; in many cases it was their decision to participate that decided whether a particular project was made or not. Stars also often shape scripts and casting, and it's no accident that many stars (including four of the subjects of this book) became directors themselves. Moreover, many—consider the relationship between Steven Spielberg and Tom Hanks, for example, or Clint Eastwood and Don Siegel—related to each other as peers.[9]

Whatever the relationship, I'm looking at a specific kind of statement a star makes in amassing a body of work that consists of a series of roles: historical ones. Whether in a Western like The Searchers or a World War II movie like The Sands of Iwo Jima (1949), Wayne repeatedly chose to depict restless, isolated men who must effectively become Moses figures. Wayne hardly invented this line of interpretation; indeed, its very power and influence derive from the way he tapped a vein of thought that runs back through the scholarship of Frederick Jackson Turner, the novels of James Fenimore Cooper, and the religious testimony of Mary Rowlandson. But if Wayne offered his viewers a specific master narrative of American history, it was never the only one available. Actually, by the end of his life in 1979 its influence was fading fast, supplanted by a younger generation who viewed the Moses figures he portrayed as having little redemptive character, and who questioned the decency or efficacy of those "Israelites" for whom Wayne characters made sacrifices. But Wayne's persona lingers—and, more importantly, so does his point of view. His history is also historiography: not merely a specimen or a symptom, but also an interpretation available for multiple uses, factual and otherwise, laudable or not.

Do people like Wayne *consciously* make such historical statements? Do they really think of themselves as historians? The answer, for the most part, is no—which is precisely why they're so interesting. To paraphrase an old John Lennon song, history is what happens when you're making other plans. These plans, when realized, become movies that are in effect "chapters" in which the body of work as a whole is the "book." When you analyze a literary text, you're very likely to care what formative influences shaped it, and the analogy here would be the other players in the filmmaking process: a production designer or a screenwriter is to an actor what a real person or a historical event is to a novelist. These influences matter, but they're not central: the text itself is. Similarly, you're likely to care what the author of a text may have had to say about her work, but at the end of the day it is what's between the covers (or on the screen) that matters, not what the author (or actor) says on a talk show. When artists assert, as they often do, that work "speaks for itself," this is what they mean: that a finished piece offers its audience a proposition that can be accepted, rejected, revised, or whatever as a discrete statement in its own right, whatever the creator(s) may think, or whatever others may say about the creator(s). Think of this as the "literary" side of my (old-fashioned) American Studies equation.

The "historical" side of the equation rests on a different proposition: that what actors do comes closer than what historians do to capturing the ways ordinary people actually think and feel about the past. For most of us, history is a series of propositions that from an academic standpoint can seem disconcertingly primitive: of progress; of decline; of cycles; of the rich foiling the poor; of a break that occurred when X happened. The stories that get told on the basis of these ideas prove nothing, and are almost always imaginary. But the most successful of them embody mythic truths that bear *some* relationship to fact, and to a shared collective memory, even if there is much to disagree with in the particulars. Movies give us a sometimes hopelessly jumbled collage that most people don't even begin to untangle unless they're somehow provoked into doing so, either by having an unexpected experience at a place like a movie theater, or being coaxed into articulating its contours in a place like a classroom. But it's nevertheless a part of their everyday lives—a sense of time comparable to those of sight and sound that also orient us. I mean "sense" in another way as well: as an experience that's not quite conscious—or, to the degree that it is, is ineffable. To sense the past is to feel in time.

———

The entity we know as the United States of America has had a four-century-long ambivalence about the role of institutions—religious, economic, military, and political, among others—in everyday life.[10] All societies do. But what has always made this one relatively unusual is the degree to which an anti-institutional disposition has been the default setting of our history. Recall that English North America was colonized by people who were, to greater or lesser degrees, misfits in the mother country. In *religious* terms, this was doubly true, in the sense that British North America was Protestant terrain (anti-institutional by definition), and in the way American evangelicalism to this day is often a matter of its distance from, even hostility toward, mainline churches.[11] In *economic* terms, colonial merchants spent a century routinely flouting laws to channel their economic development—and got furious when the British government finally got serious about enforcing those laws when it came time to pay for the French and Indian War.[12] In *military* terms, colonial subjects regarded standing armies with great suspicion, even in those cases when they were presumably sent to protect them from imperial enemies, and remained partial to armed militias even when the need for a continental army was apparent.[13] And *politically* speaking, the American Revolution was a matter of the colonists fighting at least as much to prevent losing their existing freedom as to embrace a clearly articulated alternative.[14] Ever since, the United States has had a noticeably more libertarian cast to its society than other countries, even the mother country from which so much of its heritage derived.

This of course is not the whole story. There is another tradition in American history, of moments—relatively brief, intense, and long remembered—of institutional innovation and assertion. The years leading up to and following the adoption of the Constitution; the decades culminating in the Civil War; the Progressive Era: these were periods of strong social reform, reform boosted by assertive government as well as nongovernmental institutions that sought to manage social behavior. Whether because of strong resistance, overweening excess, or the real but mysterious underlying rhythms of history, these moments of institutional energy ran their course. But they left behind legacies, ranging from the emancipation of slaves to the creation of a national income tax, that proved durable.

The last such period of institutional vigor occurred in the middle third of the twentieth century, in response to the twin crises of the Great Depression and World War II, which fostered the creation of a powerful consensus about the need for a strong institutional presence in everyday life.[15] Some kinds of institutions prospered more than others (the military tended to grow more obviously powerful than mainline religious denominations did), and all these institutions had vocal critics. But the tenor of that criticism was typically self-consciously iconoclastic: those who rejected the value of strong institutions, whether that criticism originated on the left or the right, correctly saw themselves as outsiders.

To a great degree, the institutional tenor of the nation's artistic life reflected these sensibilities. Nowhere was this truer than in U.S. cinematic culture, dominated as it was by a regime that went by the name of "the studio system." This vertically controlled oligopoly, which crested during World War II, allowed a small group of people with still familiar names like Warner and Fox and Disney to efficiently produce a large number of movies in assembly line fashion, using skilled workers in crafts that ranged from set construction to publicity. These studios were quintessentially institutional in their outlook, and, notwithstanding occasional questions their products asked, or problems they posed, they (or their censors) typically saw to it that Hollywood movies affirmed the efficacy, even necessity, of what was often called "the American Way of Life."[16] To be sure, such a phrase was widely considered synonymous with private enterprise, and as such was ritualistically contrasted with the totalitarian institutionalism of Communist societies. But American capitalism of this period was *managerial* capitalism, more corporate than entrepreneurial in outlook, with a social utility that was largely, though never completely, taken for granted.

With the culmination of the demographic bulge known as the Baby Boom in the mid-1960s, which coincided with the zenith of American geopolitical power, this institutional regime was, unbeknown to most Americans, nearing its end. Ironically, many of those most inclined to question it, like the idealists at the University of Michigan who founded the Students for a Democratic Society, were beneficiaries of it. Others, like African Americans of the mainstream civil rights movement, sought to realign rather than destroy it: they needed strong institutions, whether legal, political, or religious, to protect them. Still others, like Wall Street financiers and leaders of the feminist movement, promoted an avowedly libertarian approach that enshrined private power and choice, challenging the efficacy and even the legitimacy of long-standing bastions of church and state.[17]

In both structure and content, Hollywood reflected these changes. A combination of legal challenges, technological alternatives (notably television), and the growing power of agents and artists precipitated the collapse of the studio system.[18] Pathbreaking movies like *Bonnie and Clyde* (1967) and *Easy Rider* (1969) upended social conventions. And a growing unease about the reality of a sometimes denied American empire—and, simultaneously, anxiety about the supremacy of the empire—increasingly shaped the moviegoing habits of Americans, even those thousands of miles away from Asian or Latin American battlefields.

This is, in its broadest sense, the inheritance of those of us born in the second half of what was famously dubbed "the American Century." Like it, hate it, or something in between, the works of art we've reacted to most strongly have been those that engage the consequences of this anti-institutional turn and our collective memory of what preceded it, a collective memory so powerful that it continues to shape the consciousness of those born long after it held sway. We sometimes marvel at the unself-conscious confidence of the gunslinger in the old Western or the glamour of the mid-century bombshell. But whether in relief or disappointment, we cannot ignore the irony, skepticism, and ambivalence of our age. Or, more accurately, our fallible belief that these cultural traits are more common to our time than to earlier ones.

For all their differences, differences that justify a set of discrete treatments, the movie stars I examine here are alike in that they embody the historical transition from institutionalism to anti-institutionalism that I'm sketching. Their master narratives reflect that transition in varying, overlapping, and often surprising ways. I'll take a moment for a brief overview.

The oldest figure in this study, Clint Eastwood, was a child during the New Deal and rose to stardom in the heyday of the Great Society. He was too old to be a part of the counterculture of the 1960s, which he observed with bemused detachment. Eastwood became a cultural icon in the seventies and eighties because his iconic character, Dirty Harry, was emblematic of a quickening libertarian conservative current in American society. But while Eastwood was widely considered the apogee of the rugged individualist lionized by Ronald Reagan—who turned Eastwood's Dirty Harry line "Make my day" into a slogan with which to challenge his political opponents—his body of work always affirmed the value of community, albeit of loose, improvised kinds. While Eastwood was always a skeptic about formal institutions, his career was premised on trying to capture the best of what they had to offer by other means. I call this a "Jeffersonian" sensibility (in contrast to the more centralized approach of his great opponent, Alexander Hamilton). I use the pastoral image of him as "tending to the flock," using the word *tending* to suggest this counterintuitive notion of him as a nurturing figure as well as to denote a tendency rather than an avowed principle or practice.

If a close look at Clint Eastwood's career suggests surprisingly communitarian tendencies, the second figure of this book, Daniel Day-Lewis, outdoes even Wayne in his rugged individualism—and, even more importantly, his fatalism. The quintessential Day-Lewis character is a frontiersman, even when that frontiersman is disguised as a gang member (or an elite lawyer) on a New York City street. Day-Lewis's work reveals the degree to which the great American historian of the frontier, Frederick Jackson Turner—whose scholarship is now regarded by academic historians as more of an artifact of its time than a viable version of the past—is nevertheless alive and well in contemporary popular culture. But while Turner, an avowed Progressive, fashioned his famous theory of the frontier as living metaphor that could find a new meaning in virtual realms, the arc of Day-Lewis's frontiersman is tragic, strangled by institutional forces that depend upon yet finally destroy him (if he doesn't first destroy himself).

Not all the figures I look at in this book embrace the anti-institutional currents of our time. The great social movement we know as feminism is a house with many rooms, so one must be careful not to overgeneralize. But one of those rooms—a rather large one, by my reckoning—has anti-institutional dimensions, if for no other reason than that formal authority in most societies has a patriarchal foundation. So the staging ground for emancipation tends to be personal: feminism has a libertarian cast, albeit a libertarianism that leans left rather than right. One can see these tendencies vividly on display in the work of Meryl Streep, especially in movies like *Kramer vs. Kramer* and *Silkwood*. But over the course of an exceptionally long and productive career, Streep's body of work has gradually taken on a decisively more public profile, as her characters grasp and exercise levers of power in institutions that range from national governments to the Roman Catholic Church. As such, she represents a realization of—and, in some crucial respects, an improvement over—the historical vision first codified by Betty Friedan in her now-classic manifesto, *The Feminine Mystique* (1963).

It was formal institutions—legal, political, religious—that made slavery possible in the United States. Paradoxically, it was also formal institutions that destroyed slavery (and provided ways to combat it through the long night of segregation). This understanding of history comes instinctively to many African Americans. Certainly it does to Denzel Washington, who both dramatizes the emancipatory power of institutions in movies like *Glory* and chronicles their ongoing power to oppress in others like *The Hurricane*. There is, however, one institution that consistently has served as Washington's lodestar: the family. The families of Clint Eastwood—and there are many—always have a makeshift quality. But Washington's tend to be rock-solid, even when they're symbolic. One of the oldest tropes in women's history is that of republican motherhood: the idea (sometimes challenged in its contours or viability) that the success of American society depends on producing good women so that they in turn can raise good men. Washington's career, by contrast, is an affirmation of republican fatherhood: good fathers make good sons, and good sons make history. (In recent years, some of Washington's "sons" turn out to be daughters.)

The last two figures in this book have far more straightforward, if antithetical, stances toward institutional commitment. Tom Hanks is the arch-institutionalist. Again and again, he has shown himself to be the quintessential team player, whether the team in question is a government agency like NASA, a family business, or a women's baseball club. Hanks's genial Everyman persona has made him a uniquely compelling vehicle for liberal values in a conservative age. As such, he represents the curious dominance of the Left in the realm of popular culture, even as it has been repeatedly repudiated in the realm of electoral politics.

In a way, my final subject, Jodie Foster, is an outlier. The youngest of this set, she's demonstrated the least interest in American history in her body of work. Perhaps this is because Foster has also shown herself to be deeply skeptical about both the intentions and capacity of formal institutions to function as forces for good in American life. (No less than those of Daniel Day-Lewis, her characters are loners.) In ways that I have found both elusive and arresting, however, Foster is an important figure in suggesting the limits of collective identity in a time when the institutional foundations of our national life seem increasingly fragile.

In the process of pursuing a manifold set of personal and professional goals, these six artists reveal, directly or indirectly, what they understand about the world that preceded them. They dramatize the consequences of accepting or rejecting those lessons in their master narratives of American history. As such, they have much to teach us, whether we happen to be professional historians or not.

CHAPTER I

———

Tending to the Flock

Clint Eastwood, Ambivalent Wanderer

Master narrative: U.S. history as a struggle
over—and for—small communities

> Man was destined for society. His morality therefore was to be
> formed to this object. He was endowed with a sense of right and
> wrong merely relative to this.
> > —Thomas Jefferson, letter to (his nephew)
> > Peter Carr, August 10, 1787

I'm one of those people—and I think I can safely extrapolate that there are, by a conservative estimate, tens of millions of us—who grew up with Clint Eastwood in the background of our lives. I do want to emphasize *background*. While Eastwood has long enjoyed a durable fan base, he's also long been a household name. (This status was reinforced in 2012 when Eastwood appeared in a politically ambiguous television advertisement for Chrysler that premiered during the Super Bowl.)[1] To some degree, this status is a simple matter of marketing muscle; with his movies promoted across media platforms that have ranged from newspapers to Facebook, his presence has been unavoidable. To some degree, too, Eastwood's choice of roles has made him a kind of cultural shorthand for the perennially popular, if not universally admired, gunslinger. Finally, there's Eastwood's sheer longevity, a longevity that has now spanned generations. This was true even four decades ago, as Eastwood himself slyly indicated in *Breezy*, a 1973 movie about a May-December romance that he directed but in which he did not act. At one point, the unlikely pair (William Holden and Kay Lenz) go on a date to see *High Plains Drifter*, a 1973 Western starring none other than Clint Eastwood, one of the few movies at the time that could plausibly bridge what was then a rather large generation gap, in part because of his combination of masculine toughness

and sex appeal. Eastwood's durability became apparent again a generation later in *Back to the Future Part III* (1990), when Michael J. Fox's character, Marty McFly, time-travels to 1885 and identifies himself to the residents of the fictive California town as "Clint Eastwood."

After knocking around Hollywood for a few years in the mid-1950s,
when he appeared in a series of small movie roles, Eastwood first became
famous for his role as Rowdy Yates on the long-running television series
Rawhide (1959–66), where he was a largely unremarkable heartthrob of
the kind those of us over the age of twenty-five or so have seen come and
go many times. He became a genuine pop culture phenomenon with the
release of *Dirty Harry* (1971), the first of five films in which he played a
strong, silent, and violent San Francisco policeman who practiced rough
justice by his own lights. These films made Eastwood a rich and powerful
man in Hollywood. He quietly leveraged that power, often extending it
by continuing to make crowd-pleasing thrillers—years before his greatest
commercial successes, film critic and biographer Richard Schickel estimated that Eastwood had made $1.5 *billion* for Warner Bros. alone[2]—and
alternating these blockbusters with more personal projects.

For anyone born after 1985 or so, the terms "spaghetti Western" and
"Dirty Harry" constitute relatively arcane pop culture references.[3] Yet
for the moment, these people are as likely to recognize Eastwood's name
as their elders. With the 1992 release of the Academy Award–winning

LONE GUNMAN: Eastwood in *Dirty Harry* (1971). His San Francisco
policeman Harry Callahan represented the apogee of his anti-institutional
sensibility in the 1970s and 1980s. *(Malpaso Productions)*

Unforgiven, Eastwood began one of the most remarkable second leases on life in film history. This run, which included a second Best Picture Oscar for *Million Dollar Baby* (2004), cannot help but inspire awe, and hope, in anyone with a fear of aging. Eastwood gave a widely acclaimed performance as an irascible racist in *Gran Torino* in 2008, which he claimed would be the last acting he would do (though as of this writing he's slated to appear with Amy Adams in *Trouble with the Curve*, a movie about an aging baseball scout, in late 2012). In the fall of 2011, at age eighty-one, he released the thirty-third feature film he directed, *J. Edgar*, a biopic of the notorious FBI director J. Edgar Hoover.

Over the course of the fifty years, there have been two main narratives in Eastwood's career. For the most part, they are successive and divergent, though not completely so. The first one might be summarized as "Clint Eastwood, action hero," which defined his persona from the 1960s straight through the 1980s. While its appeal was considerable at the box office, critical opinion was tepid at best. "Clint Eastwood isn't offensive; he isn't an actor, so one can't call him offensive," legendary *New Yorker* critic Pauline Kael said of the second Dirty Harry movie, *Magnum Force*, in 1974. "He'd have to do something before we could consider him bad at it."[4]

Beginning in the 1980s, however, a gradual wave of revisionism began to build in Eastwood's favor. A new narrative, which might be termed "Clint Eastwood, major artist," took shape. The Museum of Modern Art hosted a one-day retrospective of his work in 1980, and some feminists began taking note of the strong female figures in some of his movies (often played by his paramour of the time, Sondra Locke). The turning point was *Unforgiven* (1992), widely considered a "revisionist" Western, ostensibly because of its relative amorality and willingness to depict violence in a more tawdry light than traditional Western fare like *The Magnificent Seven* (1960). *Unforgiven*, by contrast, was widely seen in terms of the way it ruthlessly undercut traditional notions of Western heroism.

While the first storyline of "Clint Eastwood, action hero" continued to linger in the popular imagination long after critical opinion began to shift, many of those who adopted the "Clint Eastwood, major artist" narrative believed that Eastwood himself had changed identities. Sometimes this shift was understood in political terms. Both in the tough stance on urban crime that marks the Dirty Harry movies, and in Eastwood's avowed Republicanism—he voted for Dwight Eisenhower and Richard Nixon—he was considered the property of the Right. Yet by the 1990s, Eastwood was attacked by conservative critics for his portrayal of an ineffective sheriff in *A Perfect World* (1993) and a sympathetic stance toward euthanasia in *Million Dollar Baby* nine years later. *Letters from Iwo Jima* (2006) and

Gran Torino are downright multicultural in their attempt to represent an Asian point of view. Spike Lee criticized the lack of black characters in Eastwood's other movie about the Battle of Iwo Jima, *Flags of Our Fathers* (2006). But any fair reading of Eastwood's career would have to acknowledge bona fide diversity in his treatment of African American characters as an actor and director, particularly in the string of films that runs from his biopic about Charlier Parker, *Bird* (1988), to that about Nelson Mandela and the South African rugby team, *Invictus* (2009).[5]

But what I find interesting in his career is the degree of continuity that marks it. One thing that never changes, for example, is the strong sense of rugged individualism that runs through Eastwood's work. In and of itself, that's hardly surprising or even all that interesting, given the centrality of this trope in the Western tradition with which he is widely associated. But the *ambivalence* about that individualism, the nagging persistence, even need, for *social* connection and *social* order: that's not something people tend to associate with, much less profess to want from, a Clint Eastwood movie.

Indeed, if I were making this assertion in the last quarter of the twentieth century instead of the first quarter of the twenty-first, it might well seem myopic. It seems to overlook the hard-hat Nixonian hostility toward the liberal establishment so central to the appeal of the Dirty Harry movies, for example. "Eastwood can do no wrong," the president reputedly said of *Dirty Harry* in 1971, lifting his policy against showing R-rated films in the White House. "Let's see the picture."[6]

In retrospect, however, Eastwood's characters come off more strongly than they did at the time as team players. The issue has always been the *kind* of team. Eastwood has never made his peace with formally structured organizations, but he has never given up trying to achieve the sense of purpose and cohesion they afford by other means. His libertarian leanings have never entirely overridden his communitarian longings.

In trying to make sense of this seeming contradiction, I found myself thinking about another figure of ideological complexity and popular appeal: Thomas Jefferson. Eastwood never references Jefferson in his work. Jefferson, of course, has little of obvious relevance to say about cinematic Westerns, notwithstanding the fact that he made the genre possible with the Louisiana Purchase, and that the West had, in the words of one historian, "an almost mystical place" in Jefferson's thinking.[7] But many questions that preoccupied Jefferson—the freedom of the individual in a democratic republic; the proper basis of social life and the role of institutions in civil society; the extent to which popular participation in civic life can be extended across demographic lines—are also questions that preoccupy Eastwood.

Of course, these are questions that have preoccupied a lot of people since 1776. But the answers Jefferson gave—at their core an emphasis on limited government, coupled with confidence that ordinary Americans could collaborate pragmatically in addressing social problems—have proven both distinctive and durable. They are not the same answers rendered by, say, Abraham Lincoln and Franklin Roosevelt (who had similar confidence in ordinary people, but not in limited government), or Alexander Hamilton and Theodore Roosevelt (who placed more emphasis on the role of elite leadership, and had less confidence in ordinary people, than Lincoln or FDR did). In many important respects Eastwood came of age in a world decisively shaped by these figures; certainly the size and scope of the national state, and the role it plays in everyday life, are patently obvious.

But as historians have been observing at least since the end of World War II, it is one of the curious aspects of the Jeffersonian sensibility that it has lived on long after it would seem to have become irrelevant—long after, for example, the agrarian world that was the foundation of his worldview has been thoroughly supplanted by industrial society.[8] Many, myself included, had long since written Jefferson off as one of the more notably hypocritical, inconsistent, and counterproductive figures in American national life, a figure either sentimentalized by those unhappy with the realities of the modern world, or invoked by those who would justify excessive privilege in the name of freedom. Eastwood has forced me to reconsider that.

———

To a truly striking degree, Clint Eastwood is a transitional figure in the history of the U.S. cinema. Born in 1930, he is almost a full generation older than the Baby Boomers on whom his work has had the greatest impact. While this doesn't explain everything—one can find all kinds in any generation—it does appear that to some degree, demography was destiny, in both the projects Eastwood chose and the way he executed them. Having experienced the full force of institutional confidence in American life (the welfare state, the military industrial complex, et al.) well into adulthood, he knew both its strengths and weaknesses, and proved to be a skillful surfer in the coming wave of social change.

Eastwood was a child of the Great Depression. While his biographers sometimes exaggerate the degree of privation in a family that was at heart middle-class in outlook, there's little question that the Eastwoods were subject to fluctuating economic fortunes. They were also notably itinerant;

Eastwood was born in San Francisco, but his parents moved regularly up and down the length of the West Coast to take jobs that ranged from gas station attendant to office work at IBM. Eastwood's father, Clinton Sr., had briefly attended college at the University of California; both he and his wife, Ruth, were musically literate and passed this passion on to their son and younger daughter. Regular, if not passionate, attendees of whatever Protestant church was nearby, Eastwood's parents voted for Franklin Delano Roosevelt twice before switching their allegiance to Republican Wendell Willkie in 1940. The elder Eastwood did not serve in the armed forces during the Second World War but took a job as a pipe fitter in a shipyard.[9]

Such experiences seem to have inculcated a kind of low-key pragmatism that marked Eastwood's youth, and to some extent his adulthood. The family eventually settled in the Bay Area suburb of Glenview, a town that was affluent but on the Oakland border; it was the latter that Eastwood would give as his hometown. He was an indifferent student and switched from the more upscale high school in Glenview to Oakland Tech, a trade school. Upon his graduation in 1949, he moved with his family to Seattle and held a series of odd jobs that included work at lumber mills (it was in these years he acquired a taste for country music). By 1951 he knew he did not wish to lead a working-class life and planned to study music at Seattle University. But with the Korean War on, he was drafted. He managed to spend most of his time in the army working as a lifeguard, happy to avoid going overseas.

Mingled within this hybrid middle-class and plebeian youth was what might be termed an incipient countercultural sensibility. Years before the Beach Boys made the sport a Baby Boom symbol of the California good life, Eastwood was a surfer. He had a love of nature—"You looked down into that valley [at Yosemite National Park], without too many people around, and boy, that was to me a religious experience"—that biographer Richard Schickel usefully encapsulates as "Pacific Rim Transcendentalism."[10] Above all, Eastwood was a deeply passionate jazz fan, and more specifically a bop fan.[11] As many in the next generation would, he had a tremendous appetite for African American culture, one he was in a geographic position to sate by virtue of his location in Oakland, a major black metropolis. Able to sing, play piano, and write music, Eastwood composed the soundtracks for a number of his movies, notably *Bird* and *Mystic River*. Eastwood also recorded an album of country standards during his television years (reissued in 2010),[12] sang a duet with Ray Charles in his 1980 hit movie *Any Which Way You Can,* and had a No. 1 country hit, "Bar Room Buddies," a duet with Merle Haggard from *Bronco Billy*, also in 1980.

But nothing reveals the degree to which Eastwood successfully rode a wave of generational transition more than the way he ended up becoming an actor. After finishing his tour in the army (and surviving a near-death experience in a plane crash off the California coast), he continued to work odd jobs that included pumping gas and digging swimming pools. He also got married and enrolled in a business administration program at Los Angeles City College. But his inchoate professional ambitions were finally beginning to coalesce: He began taking acting classes and in 1954 got his first big break when he landed a job as a contract player for Universal Studios.

Eastwood thus became one of the final products of the studio system, a system crucial to what is widely regarded as the golden age of Hollywood, which took shape in the late 1920s and was now lurching toward collapse. To use a sports metaphor, he was a farm-team prospect in a big-league franchise. The studios in this system, whose membership varied but always included major players like Paramount and Fox, were vertically controlled operations in which everyone from electricians to directors was a salaried employee who worked at the direction of studio executives. Those executives—legendary figures like Jack Warner, Louis B. Mayer, or David Selznick—would swap talent in their stable as part of their empire-building. The program in which Eastwood was employed for two years was not considered a major pipeline to stardom, but he did win a string of bit parts in Universal movies, no doubt in part on the strength of his striking good looks. After his contract was terminated in 1955, he continued to dwell on the fringes of Hollywood, but by 1958 his career as an actor was dangerously close to ending.

The turning point came with his casting as Rowdy Yates, a young, impetuous, but nevertheless impressive young cowboy on the CBS television series *Rawhide*. Though it ran for eight seasons, *Rawhide* never had the profile or prestige of better-remembered shows like *Bonanza* (1959–73) or *Gunsmoke* (1955–75), and for most of the series, Eastwood's character played second fiddle to Eric Fleming, who starred in the role of Gil Favor, the boss of what proved to be a never-ending cattle drive. Though Eastwood got bored with the show, it proved to be pivotal for his career in a number of ways. For one thing, it gave him an economic foundation that allowed him to invest in more ambitious projects. For another, the show made him a minor celebrity and allowed him to make a series of professional contacts that would be fruitful for decades. For a third, it established a lasting relationship with the Western genre that would become important to his artistic development.

Finally, in a less obvious but still important fashion, working in that genre—becoming comfortable in the very *concept* of a genre and experiencing the rhythms of steady production—would later become a hallmark of Eastwood's career. His younger contemporaries, whether directors like George Lucas, Francis Ford Coppola, and Martin Scorsese or actors like Robert De Niro, Al Pacino, or Dustin Hoffman, were far more self-conscious artists who would work to an almost obsessive degree on projects that emulated or alluded to the work of their cinematic predecessors. Though they came of age in a world of television, their primary influences were nevertheless cinematic.[13] Eastwood admired pioneering directors such as William Wyler and John Ford, too. Like Lucas and Coppola, he set up a production company, and like De Niro and Scorsese, he had a set of regular collaborators. But Eastwood would go on to have a much more workaday approach to his art that can make some of these figures seem downright self-indulgent by comparison.[14] Temperament had something to do with this. But so did class background, ethnicity, and generational experience.

Eastwood nevertheless had something important in common with all these people, something common to a lot of people in Hollywood: a thirst for control over the terms of his work. To a great degree, this is a male thirst, and while it's certainly widespread across the globe, it has a distinctively American cast, largely because the United States has long been viewed as a place where such a thirst could get slaked. Clint Eastwood's career since the mid-1960s is a case study in how such control was attained. More importantly, he built this career by rendering a gallery of characters engaged in such an enterprise—and the conflicts and ambiguities that resulted. Eastwood became an international star because he made the fantasy of the autonomous individual seem realistic. He showed it as plausible in the nineteenth-century past, as well as the twentieth- and the twenty-first-century present.

And yet, even as he's done this, he's never quite repudiated the values of personal connection and institutional affiliation, albeit affiliation of a relatively small scale. Even as he's given us fantasies of control, the self-abnegation at the heart of concepts like love, loyalty, and principle has remained in the picture. We shouldn't overlook it. In fact, we can't. This is an American dilemma.

"A guy sits in the audience, he's twenty-five years old, and he's scared stiff about what he's going to do with his life," Eastwood told Richard Schickel, as part of a series of interviews that formed the core of Schickel's highly regarded 1996 biography. "He wants to have that self-sufficient thing he sees up there on the screen." And then, Schickel reports, "to this thought he appended somewhat surprisingly, somewhat gratuitously, another, darker one: 'But it will never happen that way. Man is always dreaming of being an individual, but man is really a flock animal.' "[15] Actually, such a remark goes to the heart of a crucial truth about Eastwood. Not the whole truth, but an overlooked one that's important to his appeal and his artistry.

Of course, one of the reasons why this truth *is* overlooked is precisely that it's not especially obvious. As the above comment makes clear, Eastwood understands very well that a major source of his appeal is the way in which he embodies a vision of autonomy that has great allure. Eastwood understands that allure, because he experienced it, and he acted on it. Once he did, it took a while for countercurrents to emerge. But not *that* long.

Eastwood's opportunity to break free from the confining strictures of *Rawhide* came from an unlikely direction: Italy. Director Sergio Leone, who had worked on a series of American films with major directors like Mervyn LeRoy and William Wyler, offered Eastwood the lead in a Western he was calling *The Magnificent Stranger*, based on *Yojimbo*, the 1961 Japanese film directed by Akira Kurosawa, itself based on the Westerns of John Ford. Leone offered the job to Eastwood because he couldn't afford top-level Hollywood talent. Eastwood accepted it because he could do it on his summer hiatus from *Rawhide*.

This wasn't an especially risky move on Eastwood's part—if the results proved embarrassing, no one he cared about would be likely to see them—but it was a shrewd one. The character he was to play (named Joe, but eventually marketed as "the Man with No Name") was a far remove from Rowdy Yates: tougher, more worldly, and decidedly a man, not a boy. In a lot of ways, Leone's spaghetti Westerns were deeply conventional (they were hardly paragons of racial enlightenment in their portrayal of Mexicans, for example). But they marked a sharp departure from traditional Westerns in ways that ranged from the amorality of the characters to his distinctive interplay of long shots and close-ups.

Leone is justly celebrated for injecting new life into the Western; his tendency to situate characters in vast landscapes and his dry sense of humor are two reasons why. But Eastwood made important contributions of his own to the movie that became *A Fistful of Dollars* in 1964, followed by *For a Few Dollars More* (1965) and *The Good, the Bad and the Ugly* (1966). Before leaving for Italy and Spain to shoot the first of these movies, he put together the distinctive wardrobe for his character, including the poncho and the signature cigar that proved iconic. He also convinced

Leone to greatly winnow the dialogue and backstory. In what would prove to be a recurrent pattern in Eastwood movies, we are introduced to a protagonist who comes out of nowhere. Such collaboration, which would also mark Eastwood's later work with Don Siegel, suggests the degree to which an actor, no less than a director, can play a decisive role in shaping a cinematic work of art.

The hallmark of Eastwood's characters in this trilogy is a lack of attachment. In a weird way, the figure he plays is detached even from himself; though he has a different name in each (Joe in *Fistful*, Manco in *For a Few Dollars More*, and Blondie in *The Good, the Bad and the Ugly*), he's essentially the same person, notably in that wardrobe. This sense of jarringly loose connection extends to his characters' relationships with other people. In *Fistful*, Eastwood's Joe forms an alliance with Colonel Douglas Mortimer, the character played by Lee Van Cleef; in the final movie, he kills Van Cleef's Angel Eyes (again, different names, essentially same person). In *The Good, the Bad and the Ugly,* "the good" Blondie has a twisted buddy relationship with "the ugly" Tuco (Eli Wallach); united in greed, they abuse each other in a jocular way.

This sense of radical libertarianism is perhaps most obvious in *The Good, the Bad and the Ugly.* The final installment of Leone's trilogy, it has an antiheroic message embedded in an epic sense of scale, one made possible by the surprise success of its predecessors, which gave him major studio funding from United Artists. Once again we're given a cast of grasping characters who are trying to swindle established authorities and each other. But the backdrop this time is the U.S. Civil War, portrayed as an exercise in brutality that dwarfs anything the characters do to each other. Slavery is never named, much less seen, which is perhaps not entirely surprising given that the setting of the movie is the New Mexico Territory (where there was some fighting in the early months of the war). At different points, for purely functional reasons, the three main characters present themselves as Yanks or Rebels as part of an effort to capture a cache of Confederate gold. But insofar as they register any opinion about the war that rages around them, it's to profess amazement—and disgust. Eastwood's character, witnessing a futile struggle over a largely inconsequential bridge, observes, "I've never seen so many men wasted so badly." At a couple of other points, he provides comfort to dying men in the form of whiskey or a cigar, private acts of charity independent of, perhaps even in defiance of, any larger design.

Though each of the films was instantly popular upon release in 1964–66, Leone's trilogy was not widely shown in the United States until 1967; they were first exhibited as part of a triple bill in 1969.[16] It's intriguing to consider this fact in light of what was happening in Hollywood in these pivotal years. This was the moment of *Bonnie and Clyde*, *The Graduate* (both 1967), and *Easy Rider* (1969). All of these movies thrilled their young audiences with their avowedly countercultural sensibilities. Eastwood's Leone Westerns shared the skeptical spirit of such films, and a comparably unflinching attitude toward violence. In this protean moment, Eastwood might well have seemed to some hippies as someone over thirty who could be trusted. For Eastwood, in any case, the Leone Westerns were less important as a platform for any statement he may have wished to make—at this point, he wasn't really in a position to be making statements, nor do his comments then or since suggest he particularly wanted to—than as a vehicle for professional liberation.

By 1968 he was in a position to say what he would do and how he would do it. He declined to appear in another Leone movie, established his own production company—Malpaso, or "bad step," a play on his agent's assertion that taking the role of the Man with No Name would be a bad career move, as well as the name of a creek near Eastwood's home—and began looking for scripts. He did not yet have the clout to direct, and Eastwood never wrote his own material. But under the terms of the deal he cut with his old studio, Universal, he did have the power to name his own director and to shape the material to his own satisfaction. It is in this sense that the resulting picture, *Hang 'em High*, can be said to be the first Clint Eastwood movie—and as such also serves as a telling document of Eastwood's emerging Jeffersonian vision of history and politics.

That Clint Eastwood would choose a Western as the first movie on which to make a distinctive mark is hardly surprising. Eastwood had come to national attention in a television Western; he made his cinematic breakthrough in spaghetti Westerns. As a matter of marketing it made sense to build on this success as part of a long-term strategy of achieving professional autonomy. It's also clear, in any case, that Eastwood has always liked Westerns, and his movies are filled with allusions that come from the Western tradition. The name of Eastwood's character in *Hang 'em High*, Jed Cooper, is a nod toward Gary Cooper, who starred memorably in *High Noon* (a film Eastwood would reference a number of times in his movies, including *High Plains Drifter* and the personally fraught ending of *Dirty Harry*).

Over the course of his career, Eastwood has appeared in over a dozen movies that can be classified as Westerns, from his cameo appearance in

Star in the Dust (1956) to his culminating statement on the genre, *Unfor-given*, thirty-six years later. Along the way, he appeared in many more movies with contemporary settings, though it takes no great leap of imag-ination to consider the (urban) Dirty Harry movies as part of what the great film historian Robert Ray would call "disguised Westerns,"[17] or to understand the appeal of his 2000 movie *Space Cowboys* in terms of the Western baggage that the movie's stars (Tommy Lee Jones, James Garner, Donald Sutherland, and Eastwood himself) brought to their roles as as-tronauts.

Occasionally, Eastwood has made movies with other historical settings. He's made a few World War II movies and revisited the Great Depres-sion in *Honkytonk Man* (1982), a movie about a country singer that East-wood considers among his best work, and in a forgettable caper with Burt Reynolds, *City Heat* (1984), that is among his worst. As a director, East-wood seems to have taken an interest in making movies about real people and events, among them the 1920s crime drama *Changeling* (2008) and *J. Edgar* (2011). But the locus of his work is the Western.

So what do we see when we watch an Eastwood Western? Naturally, we get wide-open landscapes; indeed, panoramic establishing shots are fixtures of almost all Eastwood movies. We also see a diversity of char-acters along a moral spectrum and a frequent resort to violence. All this is typical of the genre. What's more particular to Eastwood is that his typical character is a loner in temperament but not in practice. He often appears, like the characters of the spaghetti Westerns, *High Plains Drifter* (1973), and *Pale Rider* (1985), out of nowhere. In their actions— and, in particular, in the lack of a backstory that is very common in Eastwood movies—these people *deny* history.[18] Yet they become en-gaged in the life of a community and change it. Even when, as in the case of *High Plains Drifter*, the character rides, *Shane*-style, off into the sunset, he typically restores (or imposes) order in the name of estab-lished authority.

I don't want to go overboard here. I'm not suggesting that Eastwood's character is a bourgeois banker at heart. Nor do I deny that there are cases, like *Pale Rider*, where the character disappears into the ether with no strings attached. Moreover, the established authorities in Eastwood movies are often corrupt, sometimes irredeemably. But these facts, taken as a whole, never constitute a wholesale—or, in any case, permanent— rejection of the need for the social and legal institutions that constitute a tenable society.

Besides being the first film over which he exercised decisive power, *Hang 'em High* is significant in the way in which it lays down a durable pattern of tracks along the lines I'm describing. After a moment of pastoralism in which Eastwood's Jed Cooper leads his cattle with a gentle but firm hand, he is accosted by an angry posse that incorrectly thinks he's a poacher. After briefly deliberating, they decide to lynch him. This opening sequence encapsulates the plot of the 1943 film *The Ox-Bow Incident*, a childhood favorite of Eastwood's. But while that film focuses on the miscarriage of justice resulting from the absence of effective legal authority, *Hang 'em High* uses it as a point of departure for a journey in a more complex and ambiguous direction.

The first sign of a different direction is the means of Cooper's rescue: the rope he's been left swinging on is cut loose by a marshal's bullet. The marshal brings Cooper to town in his paddy wagon; investigation into the matter demonstrates that Cooper is innocent of theft, and he is released by Adam Fenton (Pat Hingle), known in the Oklahoma county in which the movie is set as a hanging judge. Cooper thirsts for revenge—this primal instinct fuels the rest of the movie—a desire the judge understands and sanctions by hiring Cooper as a second marshal and insisting that any vengeance he wreaks be conducted under official auspices.

But as Cooper systematically tracks down his assailants, he begins to understand that the judge's motives are in part political: apprehending the lynch mob helps demonstrate that Oklahoma is ready for statehood, with all the power and privilege this will bring the territory—and, presumably, the judge himself. Cooper's disgust deepens when one of the men involved in his lynching confesses and apologizes, which is good enough for Cooper but not the judge. Cooper threatens to quit unless this assailant is pardoned. He is—and the movie ends with Cooper riding off, still wearing the badge he will use in tracking down his remaining adversaries.

Hang 'em High is a movie with a number of narrative loose ends and interpretive ambiguities. In fact, it was subject to diametrically opposing interpretations. Reviewing it (generally positively) for the *New York Times*, Howard Thompson asserted that "the movie not only makes sense, but actually promotes good old-fashioned law abidance," contrasting *Hang 'em High* with what he considered the "sado-masochistic exercises" of the Leone films. *Variety*, by contrast, called it "an episodic, rambling tale which glorifies personal justice."[19] Part of the confusion, I think, is attributable to this moment of cultural transition I've been describing. As Edward Gallafent notes, what you would traditionally expect in a Western of this type is a resolution of the revenge plot, combined with a romance in which a couple settles down into heterosexual monogamy (Cooper has relationships with two women, neither of which is permanent). But as Gallafent points out, this is 1968, not 1958, and a traditional outcome was less credible in this moment of exceptional social turmoil.[20]

At the same time, *Hang 'em High* is effectively a *Clint Eastwood* movie, directed by the handpicked Ted Post, not a Sergio Leone movie. The fact that Eastwood's character rides off wearing a badge means something. The *Times* reviewer was right: that badge legitimates Cooper's quest for personal justice, and it also gives him (limited) power to moderate it from within. The decision to keep the badge is a conscious one, and a concluding one, which gives it decisive weight in the moral calculus of the movie. Jed decides that working within a corrupt system is ultimately less problematic than resorting to the same vigilantism that endangered him in the first place.

An even murkier critique of vigilantism can be seen in another Eastwood Western, *Joe Kidd* (1972), helmed by master director John Sturges of *Magnificent Seven* fame. Once again, Eastwood, the title character, is a bystander unwittingly drawn into a dispute, this time between a Mexican leader named Louis Chama angry about U.S. government indifference about land claims and a judge who does little to help. When the Mexicans take matters into their own hands, Kidd stands aside except to help the judge escape. When Chama attempts retribution for this intervention, Kidd joins forces with a posse led by Frank Harlan (Robert Duvall), who sees Chama as a threat to his mining empire. But as Kidd begins to realize that the ruthless Harlan is a bad seed, he also begins to make a distinction between the vigilantism of Chama, based on a real grievance, and that of Harlan, based on greed. Improbably, Kidd insists—and even more improbably, he gets Chama's consent—that the Mexican seek vindication through the legal process. Insofar as any logic emerges in what is finally an ideologically murky film, it's clear that a) the movie shows sympathy for minority rights, b) it gropes toward allegiance to traditional political institutions, and c) it evinces what is, given Eastwood's well-known Republican politics, a surprisingly strong and consistent critique of capitalism.[21] In all these ways, the movie suggests a Jeffersonian sensibility.

Such skeptical, often uneasy, decisions to forge alliances, cooperate, and even defer to traditional authority are conveyed more clearly in other Eastwood movies of the time. The World War II armed forces of *Where Eagles Dare* (1968) and *Kelly's Heroes* (1970) are laced with venality and double-dealing—the sardonic mood of the latter prefigures that of *M*A*S*H* two years later—but there's never any doubt who the real (Nazi) enemy is. In *Two Mules for Sister Sara* (1970), Eastwood's character is a mercenary operating for Juarista Mexican nationalists against French imperialists. At the start of the movie he impulsively allows himself to get involved with a woman (Shirley MacLaine in an unlikely role) he incorrectly thinks is a nun. But he grudgingly respects her "vocation" and her genuine commitment to the nationalist cause, and casts his lot with a headstrong nationalist colonel. In *Coogan's Bluff* (1968), a fish-out-of-water story about an Arizona lawman who comes to New York City to apprehend a fugitive, Eastwood's protagonist butts heads with the NYPD detective played by Lee J. Cobb. Eastwood's Coogan will ultimately have to make a citizen's arrest in the quest to get his man, but the story will end with him on terms of mutual respect with his adversarial police ally.

Before going further, some caveats and clarifications. First, I understand I'm reading against the grain of these movies, where the iconoclasm and independence of these characters were surely seen as the most obvious, relevant, and attractive things about them. Certainly in the short run—the string of movies that runs from *Dirty Harry* in 1971 through *High Plains Drifter* two years later—Eastwood exhibits a bleakness about social arrangements that was consonant with the larger mood of the Vietnam/Watergate/post-civil-rights era.

Yet this was never the whole story. Actually, there's less difference than there seemed to be between Eastwood and the man who is often considered, sometimes by Eastwood himself, his foil: John Wayne. "I do all the stuff Wayne would never do," Eastwood has famously said. "I play bigger-than-life characters, but I'll shoot a guy in the back. I go by the

ODD COUPLE: Eastwood and Shirley MacLaine in *Two Mules for Sister Sara* (1970). This Western was paradigmatic of Eastwood characters entering unlikely partnerships. *(Universal Pictures)*

expediency of the moment." Eastwood also noted that Wayne sent him a letter objecting to *High Plains Drifter*, because he felt the fecklessness of the community it depicts did not reflect American values. Richard Schickel adds that "the West has always been a location for Clint, not a passion. He has never identified the region or its people as the font of American virtues."[22] True. But for all their obvious differences, Eastwood and Wayne portrayed people on legal or psychological margins who nevertheless got involved with people in the middle of things—sometimes reluctantly, sometimes temporarily, but almost always in the service of social good, even when they decried such motives. The perceived difference is less *what* they do than *how* they do it, and the different times in which they acted.

Which brings me to a second clarification. We sometimes think about institutional commitment in terms of the political spectrum—the Right avoids it, the Left embraces it—but it's never been that simple. American partisan politics has always been an argument over the *configuration* of institutional commitment. The Right likes liberty when it comes to things like the market but values solidarity when it comes to things like collective defense. The Left values solidarity when it comes to social welfare but privileges autonomy when it comes to matters like personal expression. A big part of Eastwood's success, particularly in the early going, is the way in which he sidestepped, even blurred, such distinctions. As Robert Mazzocco has noted, many of Eastwood's epigrammatic lines, like "You see, in this world there's two kinds of people, my friend: those with a loaded gun and those who dig" (from *The Good, the Bad and the Ugly*), work as well for the Social Darwinist as they do for the Marxist.[23] What you had in the early seventies was an unusual period of double disenchantment: people didn't trust the government, but they were more disenchanted than they'd been just a few years before about the possibilities of personal freedom, too.

This sense of libertarian double despair was relatively brief but intense. Eastwood both captured it in contemporary movies and retroactively projected it back into the past in his Westerns. In the case of *The Beguiled*, his second collaboration with Don Siegel (the first was *Coogan's Bluff*), Eastwood plays John McBurney, an injured Civil War soldier rescued by a child and brought to a remote all-girl boarding school in rural Louisiana. The residents of the school, no less than McBurney himself, greet this turn of events as promising a sense of liberation, sexual and otherwise, from their stultifying environment. But their interactions prove increasingly toxic—literally so for McBurney, in one of the few films where an Eastwood character dies. Nothing about this world affirms the value of cooperation, much less solidarity. As with *The Good, the Bad and the Ugly*, the social and political questions of the Civil War are marginal, if not irrelevant. McBurney tries to use emancipation as the functional equivalent of a pickup line with a slave at the school, who essentially responds by saying that she'd rather stick with the devils she knows, an expression of skepticism consonant with the disillusioned spirit of the civil rights movement of the early 1970s.

A second Eastwood movie released in 1971, *Play Misty for Me*, marked his directorial debut and was similarly grim. There's plenty to be said about this foray into the horror genre in terms of Eastwood's gender politics; for the moment the key point is that Eastwood's protagonist, a disk jockey named Dave Garver, is entirely on his own in grappling with the stalker who takes over his life. He not only lacks friends with whom he can talk about it but finds the police impotent to prevent her from ravaging his life—or that of the girlfriend with whom he is grappling with long-term commitment. Eastwood's character lives (and almost dies) solely by his own wits.

But the film that most obviously captures the public mood of the time is the third Eastwood movie of 1971, *Dirty Harry,* again directed by Siegel with substantial input from Eastwood. This is an important movie in the Eastwood canon, principally because it launched him into the rarefied firmament of stardom. Harry Callahan became an iconic figure and Clint Eastwood a household name. The movie is also important because in a series of ways that were obvious at the time, its cinematic coding leans right. That Callahan is a renegade cop in liberal *San Francisco*, ground zero of the counterculture, is one indication of this. So it is fitting both that Callahan's serial killer antagonist has the decidedly New Age name of Scorpio and that in the most celebrated scene in the movie, Eastwood utters his most famous line—" 'Do I feel lucky?' Well, do ya, punk?"—to a black man. In the law-and-order mentality of the Nixon era, where "urban crime" was synonymous with "black crime," the resonances were both obvious and visceral.

Eastwood and Siegel disavowed such political valences, a stance that seems naive if it isn't mendacious. They hedged their ideological bets by having one scene where Eastwood banters comfortably with an African American doctor (a moment Siegel had to fight the studio to keep in the movie) and a subplot in which his genial racism toward his new Puerto Rican partner proves misplaced when that partner saves his life. (He later gets killed, and the mortality rate of Harry's partners becomes a silent joke in the series.) Certainly a perspective on minority crime that focuses on the cost to the victims, most of whom, as we know, are minorities, is not a simple matter of retrograde hard-hat conservatism.[24]

In an important respect, Eastwood was accurate in a meaningful way when he described the essence of the film as an allegory of the autonomous individual forced to function "in a world of bureaucratic corruption and ineffectiveness."[25] This indictment climaxes at the end of the movie, where Eastwood's character commits an act—throwing away his badge—that gave the actor a good deal of trouble. In his memoirs, Don Siegel recounted a conversation with a fretful Eastwood not happy with the implications of Harry quitting his job ("he kept kicking the carpet like a stallion kicking turds"). Siegel countered by saying that Harry is only rejecting the bureaucratic straitjacket of the police department.[26] But Eastwood is right: quitting is quitting. Perhaps that's why Siegel agreed to a script change so that, at the last moment, Harry hears police sirens in the distance and pulls back from the brink. When it came time to shoot the scene, however, Eastwood changed his mind and went with the scene as originally written. As such, the badge tossing, in the willfulness of the actor as well as the characters he plays, is the most defiant act in Eastwood's entire body of work, exceeding even the anarchic spirit of the spaghetti Westerns.

That said, there may be less to the act than meets the eye. To understand why, it's useful to point out that the badge toss is an allusion to the ending of *High Noon* (1952). In that classic Western, Gary Cooper plays Will Kane, the longtime marshal of Hadleyville (itself an allusion to the Mark Twain story "The Man Who Corrupted Hadleyville," about yet another feckless community),[27] in New Mexico Territory, who plans to retire and marry his Quaker wife, played by Grace Kelly. But at the very moment he's about to leave, the notorious Frank Miller gang arrives. A sense of duty forces Kane to remain, and he seeks to mobilize the town to respond to the threat. But no one comes forward to help him, forcing him to confront the gang alone. At the end of the movie, he too tosses his badge to the ground. *High Noon* was written by Carl Foreman, a blacklisted screenwriter during the McCarthy era, and many people at the time and since have read the film as a parable of liberal fecklessness in the face of cynical conservative character assassination. Kane's rejection of the civic compact is so potent precisely because he's so strongly associated with notions of the common good. Yet his act is an indictment less of the idea of community itself than of this particular community. One could plausibly say the same of Harry Callahan's San Francisco.

A similar logic arguably appears to underline *High Plains Drifter*.[28] John Wayne, who told Eastwood he disliked the movie, saw it in terms of *High Noon*, another movie he hated.[29] Wayne apparently believed that the dysfunctional communities portrayed in *Drifter* and *Noon* implied a rejection of American life generally. Though some have considered this a mindless reading of these films, it strikes me as plausible: certainly Eastwood has never made a grimmer one. His nameless protagonist (echoes of Leone here) has supernatural qualities—he seems to have flashbacks to a fatal beating that appears to be his own—and comes to town to avenge the death of a sheriff. The lawman was murdered by hired assassins because he was about to reveal that the local mining company was poaching on federal land. When those assassins, convicted for a different crime, return from jail, the townspeople hire Eastwood's protagonist to protect them. He does, after a fashion, but not before administering a form of rough justice to all.

High Plains Drifter marked the low point in Eastwood's disenchantment with the social order. From here on out, however, the winds begin to blow the other way. While Eastwood never entirely loses the anti-institutional character of these early films, his communitarian tendencies grow increasingly stronger.

You can see them resurfacing as early as the first sequel to Dirty Harry, *Magnum Force* (1973). Whether or not, as some have speculated, Eastwood responded to the politically minded criticism he received from the Left, the villains this time are different. Instead of anarchists, we're given subversive authoritarians on the Right, namely a renegade cell of the San Francisco police that wants to become a law unto itself. As Eastwood later explained, the movie "tried to show that he [Callahan] was a police officer who didn't dislike the laws and the set-up the way it was. He just disliked how it had disintegrated into a bureaucratic nightmare. But he wasn't contesting the Constitution of the United States."[30] His adversaries, by contrast, *are* contesting it. These people, who begin as great admirers of Harry, feel betrayed by his unwillingness to sanction their activities. As the leader of the renegades tells him, "You've got a chance to join the team, but you'd rather stick with the system." Harry's response: "I hate the goddamned system, but until someone comes along with some changes that make sense I'll stick with it." Through three more movies and another fifteen years, no one ever does.

This is, in its way, a remarkable fact. American popular culture in these years was studded with characters, ranging from Robert B. Parker's Spenser to Sue Grafton's Kinsey Millhone, who began their careers as cops, felt too hemmed in by police work, and left the force to work as private detectives. Indeed, the entire genre, dating at least back to Sam Spade, depends on the existence of people who work outside the system, even if they affirm many of its values. But Dirty Harry, in his way as much a rebel as any of these people, nevertheless decides to remain in the fold, even when, as in the case of the otherwise forgettable final install-ment, *The Dead Pool* (1988), his celebrity status as a cop creates serious complications in his ability to do his job.

In short, the Clint Eastwood we see at the movies, once he's firmly in the saddle of his career, is a paradox: a loner who is, despite himself, also a team player. It's important to make clear what *kind* of team player he is, though—or more accurately, to make clear what kind of team he plays *for*: small ones. Eastwood may affirm the need for government, but in art as in life, he has little use for *big* government, one reason why he was em-braced by no less than Ronald Reagan, who appropriated the famous Dirty Harry line from *Sudden Impact* (1983) "Go ahead, make my day." Like Reagan, Eastwood entered the political realm: he ran for, and won, the mayoralty of his adopted hometown of Carmel, California, in 1986, on a platform of less regulation. But Eastwood did not serve more than a single term and has sought no political office since. This emphasis on the local, on the importance of the West, and on temporary voluntary service makes Eastwood a surprisingly vivid exemplar of a lingering Jeffersonian strand in American political culture.

There's an irony here. A twentieth-century man whose vision of his-tory comes into focus with movies set in the nineteenth century is the heir of a vision of history that came into focus in the late eighteenth century. It was Jefferson more than any other American who codified a philosophic skepticism about the role of government institutions in American life, as well as a small-scale, voluntaristic vision of a society grounded in a loose association of autonomous individuals. Though he was no anarchist, Jefferson had great confidence in the power of individuals to read and follow an inner moral compass to do that which they knew was right. In his famous formulation: "State a moral case to a ploughman and a profes-sor: the farmer will decide it as well, and often better than the latter, be-cause he has not been led astray by artificial rules."[31]

Of course, there are no ploughmen in the San Francisco of Dirty Harry. But the impatience with "artificial rules" has only intensified since the time Jefferson codified it. "Jefferson would have fully understood the Western world's recent interest in devolution and localist democracy," Gordon Wood, a scholar not prone to presentist pronouncements, recently wrote. "He believed in nationhood but not in the modern idea of the state. He hated all bureaucracy."[32]

Writing about a half century earlier than Wood, historian Daniel Boorstin captured the psychological nuances of Jeffersonianism in ways that can also easily be applied to Eastwood's characters. "The genius of

Jeffersonian philosophy was intuitive and practical; reflection, speculation, and contemplation were given second place," Boorstin wrote in *The
Lost World of Thomas Jefferson*. In contrast to the Puritan, "overwhelmed
by the intensity of inward struggle," the Jeffersonian "thoroughly exter-
nalized his struggle." This lack of inner self-doubt is the hallmark of early
Eastwood—and, to a great degree, a source of criticism of his work, notably Pauline Kael's.[33]

Is this Jeffersonian vision a realistic one? Even in Jefferson's own time,
he had his critics, and in a great many respects they proved right. Among
other things, Jefferson never quite worked out, even to his own satisfaction, if or how slavery would fit into this picture, precisely because he was
unwilling to use the power of the state to address what he himself regarded as a great moral evil. Observers at the time and since have also
pointed out that Jefferson's faith in democratic will could result in due
process being considered just another "artificial rule" and lead, ironically,
to tyrannical behavior, evident in the way Jefferson sought to remove
judges he didn't like. (We may like the idea of Dirty Harry as a renegade
cop; we may not like the idea of him as police chief.)

Nevertheless, the Jeffersonian strand in American political culture has
proven remarkably resilient—incorporated into the worldview of the
hippie of the Left no less than that of the tax-cutter of the Right—and has
proven impervious to the rise of an urban industrial society that was
Jefferson's worst nightmare. Clint Eastwood lives a life far removed from
that Jefferson envisaged. And yet it is one he, and his millions of fans,
continue to embrace in the twenty-first century. It seems like a fantasy,
but histories made by those with whom we disagree often do. For a great
many people it certainly *seems* real.

And in some respects, it *is* real. This becomes clear when one shifts
one's gaze from the most formal institutions like a government to the
smallest and arguably most pivotal one: the family. Very few of Eastwood's movies are explicitly about the role of the government in American life (though this has begun to change in recent years). But movies
about family—and the different ways a family can be defined—are very
much at the center of what he and others have understood his work to
mean. More specifically still, domestic politics, in both the national and
familial sense of the term, is to a great extent *gender* politics. Jefferson's
own gender politics were fairly conventional for a man of his time, notwithstanding a nominal assent to the proposition that a successful republic depends on republican-minded women to produce good men.[34] But
there is nevertheless a Jeffersonian accent in the gradual emergence of an
informal, voluntary, egalitarian vision of gender relations in Eastwood's

work. Coincidentally, that crystallized in a Western that Eastwood released in the bicentennial year of 1976.

Long before he fell under the critical gaze of academic feminists, Clint Eastwood was teaching millions of American boys how to be men. Of course, much of what made Eastwood such an arresting figure was inimitable: we're not all blessed with his chiseled good looks, his outsized stature, his unique walk, or the distinctive expression of skepticism one writer has described as "the Clint glint."[35] But the even temper, the poker face, the disciplined minimalism of speech: these *could* be emulated. Even now, a half century later, Eastwood's grace is stunning and exerts a magnetic pull on those who have presumably long since worked out their notion of manhood.

Such distinctive features notwithstanding, Eastwood is decidedly a man of his time, which is to say that he's a male who came of age before feminism and who has struggled to come to terms with it ever since. In his early interviews, he referred to women as "chicks," and he had a reputation in some quarters as a ladies' man. While none of this is prima facie proof of sexism, it does suggest the behavior of a traditional alpha male who puts his own gratification first. At the same time, there has been growing recognition, one that has quickened in recent years, that Eastwood has shown an unusual and increasing sensitivity to issues of gender in his work and has, especially recently, made real efforts to integrate a female point of view.[36]

In terms of his portrayal of women, one could say there's not much tension in Eastwood's early work, because essentially there aren't any. With the exception of a rare act of kindness in defending a young woman in *A Fistful of Dollars* ("I knew someone like you once and there was no one there to help," he explains), women are largely beside the point in all the Leone movies, which reconstruct a version of manhood independent of shopworn ideals, one that rests on a notion of stoic competence. And while there's a little more room for women in major Eastwood works such as *Hang 'em High*, *High Plains Drifter*, or *Two Mules for Sister Sara,* his characters typically arrive, and leave, alone. (The ending of *Two Mules* is an exception to this rule, though it's safe to say that we're not looking at an orthodox romance in this couple's future.) Dirty Harry, a widower, has a tryst with an Asian woman in *Magnum Force*, but he never forms a permanent attachment.[37]

As a result, some academic critics have seen Eastwood's work as symptomatic of a broader misogyny in American society. "To young men of the sixties who remained unaffected by any of the protest movements, yet felt anxious about their maleness, the authoritarian Eastwood hero suggested that the traditional superiority of the strong, silent male, could be recovered," Joan Mellen wrote in her 1977 book, *Big Bad Wolves*. She went on to note, in language typical of the time, that Eastwood's allure was so strong that "he even appealed to some women before the women's movement exposed the neurosis of the male so incapable of seeing anyone female as equal to himself or as a human being at all." A generation later, this line of reasoning was retrofitted with the feminist-theory prose of the 1990s in the words of a male scholar who wrote that "Eastwood's 1960s and 1970s films construct a solipsistic order organized around the phallus, and in the service of an imaginary projection of the self." Such a sentence is a model of clarity when juxtaposed with that of the regrettably typical Paul Smith, who writes of the voyeuristic male audiences of Dirty Harry movies, "The gender power relations that subvent a masculinist culture produce male subjects who are misogynist and sexually violent in their urge to accede to the transcendent power of ideal masculine subjectivity" (and we're only halfway through the sentence at that point).[38]

Indeed, in the late sixties and early seventies, the gender politics of Eastwood's movies go from bad to worse, perhaps reflecting the same nihilistic turn in his work discernible in his stance toward civilizing institutions (which, it should be noted, have long been coded as female). In *The Beguiled*, the war between the sexes is far more obvious and damaging than the War Between the States. In *Play Misty for Me*, there's never any suggestion that disk jockey Dave Garver has brought chaos upon himself as a result of his freewheeling sexual ways.[39] Instead, his ordeal reflects a broader Eastwood theme that violence is a pervasive force in society at large that can be fought but never contained. This makes sense; as feminists have long been apt to point out, it's wrong to blame the victim.

In what is surely the low point in his body of work, the main character of *High Plains Drifter* rapes a woman who repeatedly insults him near the start of the movie (in an outcome some will perceive as adding insult to injury, she ends up enjoying it). Is the suggestion that this woman had it coming? It may not be clear at first, but as the movie proceeds we come to understand that she is deeply enmeshed in the town's corruption. The logical conclusion, then, part of the movie's larger theme of vengeance, is that she does indeed deserve what she gets. "I might do it differently if I were making it now," Eastwood said of the rape scene, somewhat lamely, two decades later. "I might omit that."[40]

Beginning in the mid-seventies, however, we begin to see signs of some active reevaluation on Eastwood's part. The first sign of this is the third installment of the Dirty Harry saga, *The Enforcer* (1976), in which Callahan is saddled with a female partner (Tyne Daly) as part of an affirmative action initiative by the San Francisco Police Department. Callahan is aggressively scornful of this character, though over the course of the movie she gains his grudging and finally avowed respect for a toughness that, along with a sharp learning curve, makes her a good cop—and one who saves Callahan's life. The fact that the two partners become friends, not lovers, indicates respect. Yet by a feminist calculus *The Enforcer* nevertheless comes up short, partly because Daly's character effectively has to pay for this respect with her life and, more decisively, she can only win it on Callahan's terms: a woman will be considered an equal when she's as good as a man is at the things *he* thinks matter.

In *The Gauntlet*, released the following year, one can discern further realignment in Eastwood's gender politics. This is another detective movie, though Eastwood's (alcoholic) character is far less competent than Dirty Harry; indeed, he's sent by his boss to escort a police witness (Sondra Locke) from Las Vegas to Phoenix precisely because he's considered not too bright. Locke's character is sharper in figuring out what's going on than her putative protector, and it's to Eastwood's credit that he would venture out from the protective persona of the invincible characters he had ridden to stardom over the course of the preceding decade. The most memorable moment in *The Gauntlet* occurs when Eastwood's character is in danger of being overwhelmed by a group of armed adversaries, and Locke's character prevents this by baiting them to gang-rape her. This courageous stratagem is a remarkable act of toughness, a willingness to risk what has sometimes been considered a fate worse than death. There is a sense in which this toughness is defined in a specifically female way, though it is perhaps still in terms of a traditionally male measure of physicality. Locke, who would prove to be a versatile performer in a half-dozen Eastwood movies, would again demonstrate a form of feminism-by-male-logic in the fourth Dirty Harry movie, *Sudden Impact*, in which she avenges her sister's and her own rapes by serially murdering her adversaries, shooting them in the genitals. It's enough to soften Harry Callahan's hard heart—and lead him to temporarily suspend official rules of law.

In some important sense, however, these shifts in the way Eastwood depicts women and heterosexual relationships are less important than the way in which he is actively reconsidering the sense of isolation on the part of his male characters and his tentative engagement with the concepts of connection and family. Perhaps not surprisingly, some early moves in this direction are cast in terms of men's relationships with each other rather than with women. Even in this regard, Eastwood's characters had a long way to go. Feminists have long argued that the strong, silent male archetype carries with it more than a hint of homophobia, a notion that finds credence in *Magnum Force*, for instance, in which Callahan compliments his soon-to-be adversaries, who might be gay, at a firing range by saying, "If everybody could shoot like that, I wouldn't care if the whole damn department was queer." (It's possible to interpret this as a statement of tolerance, but again, as with his partner in *The Enforcer*, it's strictly on his terms.) *Thunderbolt and Lightfoot,* an overlooked 1974 buddy movie about two crooks on the lam, shows an Eastwood character—with great difficulty—forming an emotional bond with another person, though one has to wonder whether *anyone* could resist the charm of the young Jeff Bridges, his co-star who steals the movie.[41] (Many years later, Eastwood would engage with gay life in a much more sympathetic way by directing *J. Edgar*, in which Leonardo DiCaprio portrays the politically monstrous FBI director who nevertheless forges a durable bond with longtime lover Clyde Tolson, played by Armie Hammer.)

The key turning point in terms of Eastwood's stance toward personal connection, one that intersects with his stance toward more impersonal institutions, is *The Outlaw Josey Wales* (1976). As many observers of Eastwood's career have noted, this project originated with a problematic source. The 1973 novel on which it is based, *Gone to Texas*, was written by Forrest Carter, a.k.a. Asa Carter, who in writing this book (and the subsequent *The Education of Little Tree* three years later) was trying to erase his past as a speechwriter for George Wallace, the segregationist governor of Alabama—and author of his famous slogan "Segregation now, segregation tomorrow, segregation forever!"[42] Eastwood made the movie unaware of Carter's background, though the DNA of his ideology is not far from the surface. The author describes Josey Wales as "free, unfettered by law and the irritating hypocrisy of organized society." Later, Wales finds common cause with the Comanche chief Ten Bears by noting that "Guv'mints don't live together...men live together."[43] In the world of the book, libertarian ideology transcends race.

Or so Carter would have us believe. But the preoccupations of the novel, and subsequent movie, are much closer to home. At the start of the film, Josey Wales is a farmer in Civil War Missouri, living the Jeffersonian idyll of a family man tilling his own soil. That idyll is shattered when a Union-based militia attacks his farm, killing his wife and son. Quietly seething, Wales joins a Confederate militia and becomes a minor legend.

When the war ends, his compatriots have nowhere to go and decide to surrender. Josey and a young colleague do not; the core question in the movie is whether Wales will find his way to freedom.

The road to freedom, as it turns out, is littered with baggage. Wales loses his young compatriot early on but wanders into Cherokee territory and befriends an old man named Lone Watie (apparently related to Stand Watie, a Cherokee chief and Confederate general). Watie decides to travel with Wales, and the two in turn encounter an abused Navajo woman at a trading post, who joins them. Later in the story, they encounter an old woman and her granddaughter (played by Locke; the two characters fall in love) and subsequently rescue them when they are captured by Comanches. The old woman is trying to find her way to the farm that her son, a dead Union veteran, left to the family. These people establish a household there.

The problem is that the old woman's farm lies squarely in Comanche territory. This prompts Wales, in an act of bravery, to ride alone right into their camp, where he presents himself to the aforementioned Ten Bears as a fellow victim of government oppression, asking simply, but not humbly, for a life of coexistence—and offering an acknowledgment in the form of annual tribute that the territory in question is indeed Comanche. Ten Bears, impressed with the courage and honesty of this paleface, grants his wish, and the two exchange a blood bond. But Wales remains a fugitive, and the U.S. Army inevitably closes in. After a climactic showdown, the movie ends on a surprisingly hopeful note (one whose outcome is facilitated by nearby townspeople). Wales just might settle down and start his life anew. "The irony is that Josey Wales inherits a family," Eastwood

MAN IN THE MIDDLE: Eastwood in *The Outlaw Josey Wales* (1976). His nuclear family destroyed in the Civil War, Wales gradually reconstructs a surrogate one with himself at the center. *(Warner Bros.)*

later explained to a French interviewer. Later in the same interview, he noted, "You can only do so much with the lone hero. If you give him some family ties, you give him a new dimension."[44]

The Outlaw Josey Wales was a landmark for Eastwood. For the rest of his career, he would return repeatedly to the problem of broken families and the attempt—sometimes successful, sometimes not—to reconstruct alternative ones.[45] (Interestingly, with the notable exception of *The Bridges of Madison County*, Eastwood has never told a story about an intact nuclear family.)

One can certainly see the family theme at work in one of Eastwood's most personal projects, *Bronco Billy* (1980). This willfully sentimental movie focuses on a set of willfully naive characters who work for an old-fashioned traveling Wild West show that winds its way to contemporary Idaho. This is where Locke, this time playing a pampered socialite fleeing the prospect of a loveless marriage, comes into the picture. Like the audience watching the film, she can't quite believe these people are for real. And they're not. The troupe is a collection of ex-cons and alcoholics; Eastwood's Billy is a former shoe salesman from New Jersey who served time for killing his wife when she slept with his best friend. Despite mishaps and misunderstandings that lead them at one point to attempt a comically absurd train robbery, all these people hang together, enduring various forms of humiliation for each other.

You get the idea: families come in all shapes and sizes. In Eastwood's world, however, they tend to be patriarchal: in one way or another, he's the father figure. This is true even when the man in question is a shambling wreck and by any conventional standards a poor role model, as is Eastwood's character in *Honkytonk Man* (1982), his paean to country music set in the thirties. In this road movie, he plays a consumptive alcoholic making his way from rural Oklahoma to Nashville for an audition at the Grand Ole Opry. Along the way, his sheltered nephew and the not-so-sheltered young woman who joins them experience the world and carry on his legacy.

Three years later, *Pale Rider* fuses sexual and paternal notions of manhood, but in an ethereal way. Here Eastwood plays another one of his mystical characters in the vein of *High Plains Drifter*, the so-called Preacher who appears out of nowhere to help a town challenge the depredations of a greedy mining corporation. The twist in this variation on *Shane* is that the child who looks up to him is a girl, not a boy, and that he intervenes more directly to bolster the confidence of her father than Alan Ladd did for the father in the 1953 classic. In a less high-minded departure from the original, the Preacher also avails himself of the man's fiancée so that she can have a single night of passion she's unlikely to enjoy in a life with her reliable, if unexciting, man.

The pivotal movie in the evolution of Eastwood's gender politics is *Tightrope* (1984). This is another cop drama, but one with Eastwood's most flawed protagonist to date. This time he plays a divorcé trying to raise two daughters—the first time we see Eastwood playing a family man—who's also trying to solve a serial murder case involving the death of a string of prostitutes. The complication is that this character has many of the kinky sexual predilections of the criminal he's pursuing. Into this situation comes a rape crisis counselor, played by Genevieve Bujold, with whom the Eastwood character has a series of intellectually as well as sexually provocative exchanges. Many analysts, particularly feminist critics, have seen this movie as a decisive departure for Eastwood. Perhaps the most influential, Judith Mayne, notes that Bujold's character "is distinctly 'other' than [Eastwood's] Block, yet she represents a set of values that, however strange or foreign they may seem to him, are values to be contended with." Such a perspective is important not only in terms of Eastwood's career but also in American cinema generally. As philosopher Drucilla Cornell, in her study of the moral dimensions of Eastwood's masculinity, notes, "Rarely does Hollywood portray a sexy, witty feminist, who runs women's self-defense classes, as a desirable sex object expressly *because* of her strength and *because* of her feminism."[46]

FAMILY GUY: Eastwood as New Orleans detective Harry Block with his two daughters in *Tightrope* (1984). Some observers see the film as a turning point in Eastwood's gender politics. *(Warner Bros.)*

Eastwood also demonstrated a sense of humor about such issues, and cast them in generational terms, in *Heartbreak Ridge* (1986), in which he plays a decorated Korean War veteran approaching retirement, who returns to his old base on a last tour of duty to whip some recruits into shape on the eve of the invasion of Grenada. The movie unconvincingly inflates this unimpressive chapter of the Cold War. But the scene where Eastwood—now approaching senior citizenship and starting to look (and sound) like it—tries to win back his ex-wife by using language he picks up in women's magazines is priceless.

All this said, there were signs that Eastwood was running out of commercial, artistic, and ideological steam by the end of the eighties. He's simply too old to be credibly paired with Bernadette Peters in *Pink Cadillac* (1989)—or, for that matter, as the partner for Charlie Sheen in *The Rookie* (1990), a movie with an odd moment in that Eastwood's character is raped at knifepoint by a female villain (while an old Eastwood movie plays in the background). This is the kind of moment that arrives sooner or later for a great many movie stars, and had Eastwood's career ended here, any fair-minded person would have to say that he had enjoyed an extraordinarily productive, and surprisingly successful, run as a screen icon.

And then came *Unforgiven*.

The 1992 release of *Unforgiven* marked Eastwood's entry into mass consciousness as a major artist: he won an Academy Award for Best Director and took home a Best Picture Oscar as the producer of the movie. So it's remarkable to consider that since then he's had a whole other career's worth of output, making more than a dozen movies of notable variety, gradually phasing out his work as an actor while focusing more on directing.

In fact, *Unforgiven* is notable as much for the sense of continuity it shows in Eastwood's thinking as it is for being a radical departure.[47] Take, for example, its stance—or, more accurately, the ambiguity of its stance—toward vigilantism, an issue that has preoccupied him since *Hang 'em High*. Remember that in *Hang 'em High*, Eastwood's character is a victim of those who take the law into their own hands, and while he seeks vengeance, he does so by donning a badge, even though the system he represents is itself unjust. In *High Plains Drifter*, it's the state that is the victim, in two senses: townspeople have been illegally mining on federal property, and the sheriff of the town is killed when he tries to do something about it as a government representative. Eastwood's character comes to the town to avenge the murder, but it's never really clear who it is that metes out the extralegal justice—whether he is the brother of the sheriff, the reincarnated spirit of the sheriff, or a retributive angel (or devil) whose code transcends human law.

A comparable sense of ambiguity characterizes *Unforgiven* as well. The plot, set mostly in the town of Big Whiskey, Wyoming, in 1881, is put in motion at the start of the movie when a prostitute with the tellingly biblical name of Delilah diminishes the manhood of a customer by laughing at his small penis, getting her face disfigured with a knife as a result. When the sheriff of Big Whiskey, Little Bill Daggett (Gene Hackman), reacts with indifference, the prostitutes of the town pool their resources to put a $1,000 bounty on the head of the perpetrator and his confederate. A young-would be gunfighter calling himself "the Schofield Kid" (Jaimz Woolvett) responds to this call and seeks to recruit the once legendary outlaw William Munny (Eastwood), a grieving widower with two children and a failing pig farm. Munny resists the Schofield Kid's entreaties—he says his wife has reformed him of his drunken and murderous ways—but in good Western fashion he changes his mind. He in turn then recruits his old friend Ned Logan (Morgan Freeman), whose Indian wife disapproves.

A good deal happens after all this, but the main point for the moment is that nobody in this story comes out ahead. While the government, in the form of Little Bill—played by Hackman with a wonderfully disorienting cheerful menace—is guilty of gross negligence in his failure to address the women's grievance, their extralegal solution proves no better. There has been a good deal of debate about whether the climactic shoot-out at the end affirms or subverts the iconoclasm of the movie.[48] It's hard

DOMESTICATED ANIMAL: Eastwood as Bill Munny in *Unforgiven* (1992). A bad man, he's also a dedicated parent. *(Warner Bros.)*

not to experience a sense of visceral satisfaction when Munny finally returns to form after the violence gets personal, even as it's hard to ignore the nagging ambiguities in his brutal acts.

What may finally be most striking about *Unforgiven* is the way deals it with gender. Take, for instance, the role of the prostitutes in the movie—who for the first time in an Eastwood film show gender solidarity you don't often see in Hollywood. As noted, their attempt to act collectively proves problematic. But the movie never fails to take the women's grievances seriously and does not resort to the kind of gratuitous contrast of "good" girls against "bad" ones typical of Westerns. The only other woman we see in the film is a housewife, but she's Native American, married to a black man; this cinematic decision effectively upends the racially coded gender assumptions common to the Western tradition. The matter-of-fact handling of this interracial sexual relationship, combined with the muted way Ned Logan's friendship with Munny is never explicitly addressed, is itself a form of intellectual provocation. To what degree is Logan's later whipping by Little Bill, whose sadism has already been demonstrated, a specifically racist act?

A similar set of provocations characterizes the movie's depiction of masculinity. From the start, we repeatedly see Munny show incompetence; an embarrassingly awkward farmer, he can no longer shoot straight, either. In what may well be a first, we have two cowboys talk about masturbation, with Munny saying (to a black man, no less) that his sex drive is largely gone. Upon his arrival in Big Whiskey, Munny falls ill, and his feverishness renders him helpless when Little Bill kicks him around. Neither Munny nor Logan proves to be a particularly good gunman; their inability to hit their first target directly prolongs his agony (in a tragicomic moment, an exasperated Munny tells the victim's friends to answer his cries for water; he promises not to shoot them). And Schofield, who commits the second execution, does so when his victim is unarmed in an outhouse, later failing to maintain his bravado and emotionally crumpling with remorse. Munny eventually gets his mojo back, but his doing so never entirely erases our memories of these earlier moments.

Perhaps the most striking fact about Munny, though, is that his story both begins and ends with him as a single father. Westerns typically pay lip service to domesticity, though their heroes never embrace it. Here we see the reverse: Munny clearly hates domestic life, yet just as clearly is committed to it, symbolized by the laundry we see drying in the final shot of the film. We blanch early in the movie when he tells his young children that he'll be leaving for a couple of weeks, and that they should check with the neighbor if there's a problem. But there's never any doubt about his ultimate fidelity to his wife's memory and the lives they made, even if he will yield momentarily to murderous impulses that got unleashed in part over concern for their (economic) welfare. Insofar as there's any hope here, it's that a father's love will prove redemptive.

It's this dynamic—a man's growing awareness of his vulnerability, coupled with a growing awareness of other people and the challenges *they're* facing—that unifies Eastwood's post-*Unforgiven* career. His frame of reference widens dramatically; we have a string of movies, like *In the Line of Fire* (1993) and *Absolute Power* (1997), with settings or scenes in the nation's capital; in the case of *Hereafter* (2010), a movie about life after death, Eastwood crosses the oceans for settings around the world. But the hugest leap is imaginative. In *The Bridges of Madison County* (1995), director Eastwood used Richard LaGravenese's adaptation of James Robert Waller's 1992 novel, shifting the point of view from the man (Eastwood) to the woman (Meryl Streep) with whom he had a four-day affair. In a pointed reversal of the Eastwood Western tradition, the real story is not that of the drifter who comes and goes, but rather that of the housewife with a strong sense of duty who leaves a vibrant legacy in the form of children who ponder her choices and who are influenced by them. In *Changeling*, a movie Eastwood directed but did not appear in, Angelina Jolie endures the disappearance of her child as well a grotesque involuntary commitment to a mental institution. The movie honors her strength, not so much in the literal way of Sondra Locke's willingness to risk rape in *The Gauntlet*, but rather in her emotional resilience and the courageousness of her undying hope that her boy will return to her.

A similar focus on the fate of children, this time surrogate fathers and sons, is apparent in *A Perfect World* (1993). Here an escaped convict (Kevin Costner) shows increasingly paternal concern for the boy he has taken hostage, while a Texas Ranger (Eastwood) shows increasingly paternal concern for the convict. This is partially due to the influence of a female FBI profiler played by Laura Dern. The film is set in the days before the Kennedy assassination, and the fallibility of Eastwood's character is symbolically consonant with the imminent puncturing of masculine confidence and competence so vividly embodied by the assassinated president.

In no movie Eastwood has ever made has a man's paternal love been more heartbreakingly fervent than in *Million Dollar Baby* (2004), in which he plays a crusty trainer who reluctantly takes on a female boxer played by Hilary Swank. Estranged from his own daughter, who refuses to communicate with him, Eastwood's character fills a paternal void for Swank. When she is catastrophically injured, he faces an excruciating moral dilemma, one made more acute by his Catholic faith. In what can be interpreted as an avowed sacrifice of his soul, he honors her wishes (once again demonstrating Eastwood's skepticism about institutions, this time religious ones, which have never fared particularly well with him.) It's worth noting that even at this late date, Eastwood does hang on to vestiges of his receding masculine virility in executing her wishes.[49]

A similar pattern is at work in Eastwood's handling of race. Race relations have always been important for Eastwood protagonists, since their aura of mastery requires a sense of ease in dealing with minorities. In the early going, race relations were not entirely under their control. One subplot of *The Enforcer* concerns Harry Callahan's relations with a black separatist leader that he regards as more trustworthy than his superiors in the SFPD. "You're on the wrong side," the militant tells him. "You go out there and put your ass on the line for a bunch of dudes who'd no sooner let you in the front door than they would me." Harry's answer: "I'm not doing it for them." When asked who he is doing it for, Callahan responds, "You wouldn't believe me if I told you"—the implication being that this white man fights to protect a social order on behalf of all races. We've already seen how the ex-Confederate Josey Wales feels a tribal kinship with Ten Bears in their shared hatred of the federal government; a similar hard-bitten moment of solidarity occurs in *Escape from Alcatraz* when Eastwood, who plays a convict, responds to a taunting question from a black inmate as to why he won't sit on his turf. Is it because he's scared? "I just hate niggers" is the puckish reply, as he sits down on that turf.[50]

In the post-*Unforgiven* era, these racial circles radiate outward, and Eastwood's characters become less central in them. Even though he's the marquee name in such pictures, the locus of attention subtly shifts to other characters. In *True Crime* (1999), he plays a crusading reporter who fights to save an African American inmate condemned to death, but the movie increasingly focuses on the black man's family; by the end, Eastwood's character, though decent, is a diminished figure. In *Blood Work* (2002), Eastwood is an FBI agent who gets a heart transplant from a murdered Mexican woman and subsequently begins a relationship with the woman's sister and her surviving son while tracking down the killer (all the while squabbling with a Mexican policeman who detests him, suggesting a sense of intraracial diversity in a story about a man who literally gets racially integrated). In 2006 Eastwood directed *Flags of Our Fathers*, a movie about the Battle of Iwo Jima and the false mythology the U.S. Marines manufactured around it—and then followed it up less than two months later with *Letters from Iwo Jima*, a film that looked at the same campaign from a Japanese point of view, featuring a marvelous performance from Ken Wantanabe as the tragically dutiful General Nagaru Kuribayshi.

Perhaps the most vivid example of this pattern is Eastwood's performance turn in *Gran Torino* (2008). Here he plays Walt Kowalski, a bigoted Korean War veteran and widower in Detroit who is dismayed when a Hmong family moves in next door. As some observers have noted, Kowalski is a little like the man Dirty Harry might have become—still an impressive physical specimen well into his seventies, but a dinosaur nonetheless. Naturally, an increasingly intimate cultural exchange takes place between Kowalski and his neighbors, and just as naturally, evil forces lurk in the form of gangs who threaten their safety. A well-meaning, but largely ineffectual, young Catholic priest is in the mix, though he's more of a stand-up guy than the clerics of *Million Dollar Baby* and the more effective, but oddly more oily, Protestant minister played by John Malkovich in *Changeling*. These religious referents are worth making, because *Gran Torino*, even more so than most Eastwood movies, even the mystical *Pale Rider*, has a strong spiritual dimension. While the representatives of organized religion are useless at best— echoes here of Jefferson's spiritual skepticism[51]—Walt Kowalski is a Christ figure who sacrifices himself for the good of others. The shoot-first, ask-questions-later persona that once defined Eastwood's own persona has passed away.

———

I've made some effort along the way in this discussion to suggest that for all their obvious differences, Clint Eastwood has a few things in common with Thomas Jefferson. As I've noted, both men lavished great attention on the West and saw it as the great proving ground of American society. Both men believed in the efficacy of individual autonomy and placed most of their confidence in middling men with a stake in their communities, be they farmers or policemen. And both were skeptical of large institutions of any kind, whether religious, commercial, military, or, especially, governmental. Yet this last skepticism was always the source of a tugging ambivalence. Jefferson the revolutionary was also the president of the United States—and the author of the Kentucky Resolutions of 1797, which asserted a state had the right to nullify laws that were not to its liking. With comparable ambivalence, Eastwood's characters insist on the right to life, liberty, and the pursuit of justice but are almost always reluctant to abandon law, no matter how flawed.

If there is one important difference in the historical visions of Eastwood and Jefferson, it's that Jefferson evinced an optimism, a sunny confidence in the perfectibility of human beings, which Eastwood lacked for
most of his career. Jefferson believed in the future, and the intensity of this
faith ultimately mattered more than the contradictions in his thinking.
Jefferson knew America would change, and he welcomed it. Although he
had his fears, fears that narrowed his vision amid the sectional tension
that clouded the end of his life, it's not hard to imagine him endorsing a
racially egalitarian society were he to be resurrected in the flesh. It's something Jefferson edged toward his own lifetime, and the depth of his enthusiasm was such that he enjoyed tremendous popular support even as
he remained every inch the Virginia aristocrat. Even when it has required
selective memory, his legacy has been repeatedly invoked in the Age of
Jackson, the Age of Roosevelt, and the Age of Reagan.

Unlike Jefferson, Eastwood came of age in a moment of doubt and
imperial failure. Ironically, though he usually came off as a more composed figure than John Wayne, he lacked the geopolitical confidence that
girded Wayne's image. As Garry Wills explained in *John Wayne's America*,
"Wayne did not normally have the contempt for his opponent that Dirty
Harry does. The Wayne hero could be calm, in a time of the empire's
dominance."[52] The empire isn't dominant in the age of Dirty Harry; he
works in the shadow of Vietnam. So, in a veiled way, does Josey Wales.
When he says, at the end of that movie, "I guess we all died a little in that
war," the audience knows it's not really (or only) the Civil War that's being
referred to. Eastwood could never have succeeded as a popular artist had
he embraced a version of American life rooted in unvarnished Jeffersonian optimism.

Yet in his brighter moments, Eastwood has offered his viewers a sense
of hope in the widening array of people who enter the arena of American
life. This is not something that happens as a result of the organized effort
of the state, and tragedy always lurks. Eastwood's people are *represented*,
not entitled, much less collectively organized. Respect is something that
must be earned but is available to all.

In his classic "regeneration through violence" trilogy of books on the
frontier, the great cultural historian Richard Slotkin distinguishes between the "progressive" and the "populist" strains in Western tradition.
The former he associates with Theodore Roosevelt; the latter with
Jefferson. "Progress in the populist style is measured by the degree to
which the present state of society facilitates a broad diffusion of property,
of the opportunity to 'rise in the world,' and of political power. Where the
progressive idealizes greater centralization and efficiency and sees these

as the basis for America's assumption of a Great Power role in world affairs, the populist values decentralization, idealizes the small farmer-artisan-financier, and either devalues (or opposes) the assumption of a Great Power role or asserts that the nation derives both moral and political power from its populist character."[53] What makes Eastwood distinctive is that, unlike many of his predecessors, he never took Jeffersonian virtue for granted. Josey Wales and Dirty Harry were skeptical populists. And that has made them very attractive ones in the country of our hearts.

Though we have all been collectively surprised by the depth of his impact, it is unlikely Clint Eastwood's work will prove as durable as that of Thomas Jefferson. Eastwood's corpus is not world-changing, and he came on the scene at the end of something rather than the beginning of something. But for now, he burns bright as someone who has given us a version of the United States that connects past and present in what might be termed a loose institutionalism. And one of redeemed promise. "The American Dream is, in fact, composed of many dreams—of which, surely, the dream of an old age rich in competency and usefulness is the last, largest and most difficult to achieve," Richard Schickel wrote of him in 2010.[54] Watching him do it, amid our doubts and his, is an American Dream come true.

CHAPTER 2

———

Shooting Star

Daniel Day-Lewis and the Persistent Significance of the Frontier in American History

Master narrative: U.S. history as the rise
and fall of rugged individualists

I was on my way to an engagement with Daniel Day-Lewis the other day when I ran into Frederick Jackson Turner. It had been a while; the last time I really spent time in Turner's company was a quarter century ago when introduced to him by a beloved mentor at a seminar during my first year of graduate school. The seminar was a workshop in intellectual portraiture; our job in the course was to choose a figure and paint our own, talking about, and thus informing, our classmates in the process. Our teacher started us off with a few examples, the first of whom was Turner.

Turner is to the historical profession what Sigmund Freud is to psychology: a towering giant of a century ago whose ideas are now consciously rejected by just about everybody in his profession—and unconsciously absorbed by just about everybody else. Turner's 1893 essay "The Significance of the Frontier in American History" is probably the single most important piece of historical scholarship ever published in the United States. Written at a time when the modern research university was emerging, it was an example of a literary genre—the analytic essay of the kind you're now reading—that was just coming into its own. Turner was a founder of the American Historical Association (AHA) and its journal, the *American Historical Review*, which remains at the apex of the discipline.

A Wisconsin native, Turner first delivered "Significance" on the evening of July 12, 1893, at an AHA meeting in Chicago, held amid the fabled World Columbian Exposition held in that city to celebrate the four-hundredth anniversary of Christopher Columbus's arrival in America. It seems almost comical to imagine the thirty-one-year old

53

Turner (then, as now, young for a historian) standing in the front of a room talking to about two hundred colleagues while thousands of his fellow Americans were taking amusement park rides, surveying the huge temporary stucco buildings of the so-called White City, and watching the "exotic" foreign exhibits—like the hootchy-kootchy dance of a Syrian performer named Little Egypt—at a site that was artificially lit thanks to the technological innovations of the Westinghouse Corporation. Many of those historians had also spent the day at the Exposition, some attending a special performance of Buffalo Bill Cody's Wild West Show. Turner's talk was the last of five addresses delivered that day; he followed one entitled "Early Lead Mining in Illinois and Wisconsin." According to a later account, the audience reacted to Turner with "the bored indifference usually shown a young instructor from a backwater college reading his first professional paper." But like Westinghouse lighting, the so-called Turner thesis unveiled in Chicago would prove to be more durable than any of these fleeting material realities, in large measure because it was so succinctly stated at the end of the first paragraph of his paper: "The existence of an area of free land, its continuous recession, and the advance of American settlement westward, explain American development."[1]

From the vantage point of more than a century later, it may be hard to appreciate just how edgy an assertion this really was. Turner had been trained back east at Johns Hopkins, under the tutelage of the legendary Herbert Baxter Adams. Adams was a proponent of the then-dominant "germ" theory, which argued that Western civilization owed its origins to the forests of Germany, out of which emerged a Teutonic seed that spread across western Europe, jumped to America, and now dominated the world. Like so much academic thought of the time, this approach to history was modeled on science, both in its new emphasis on empirical research and in its use of a biological model—more specifically a (Social) Darwinian model—to explain historical change.

Like his predecessors, Turner embraced a process-driven approach to history—colleagues and students remember him as an obsessive collector of data and maps—and invoked science as fact and metaphor. But his inclinations were decidedly on the environmental side of the Darwinian equation: he was fascinated by protean adaptability, not by fixed destiny. America was a place that *did* something to people, he said: it made them Americans. Which is to say it turned them into something new and unique in historical experience. And that's because they had lots of room to evolve through a renewable cycle of scouts giving way to traders, farmers, and capitalists in scattershot sequences that stretched from sea to shining sea.

Over the course of ensuing decades, the Turner thesis itself evolved from maverick idea to common sense, ratified by Turner's appointment at Harvard in 1910. By mid-century, it had a wide impact on subsequent historians. But in the second half of the century the thesis came under increasing attack on a variety of fronts. Some scholars questioned Turner's data, others its implications, particularly his assertion that the frontier was the engine of U.S. democracy. The most serious challenge came from those historians, notably Patricia Limerick, who rejected the assumptions underlying the very idea of the frontier and the implicit omissions involved in discussing "empty" land that was in fact inhabited by multicultural populations. To Limerick, Turnerism was little more than a racist fantasy; at one point she joked that for her and like-minded scholars the frontier had become "the f-word."[2]

Such people are surely right that Turner made some serious omissions in formulating his theory, omissions that reflect his limited perspective, and omissions that now make the theory impossible to accept at face value. But I'm less interested in whatever objective truth there may be in the thesis than in its cultural power: how Turner described the frontier, what it meant to him, and how his conception of it remains in the bloodstream of our national life.

The first point to be made in this context is something people don't often recognize about "Significance": it's a gorgeous piece of writing, deeply imbued with love—an emotion that's not supposed to surface in academic writing (which is lifeless without it). Take, for example, this stretch of prose, in which I hear Walt Whitman singing:

> The wilderness masters the colonist. It finds him a European in dress, industries, tools, modes of travel, and thought. It takes him from the railroad car and puts him in the birch canoe. It strips off the garments of civilization and arrays him in the hunting shirt and moccasin. It puts him in the log cabin of the Cherokee and Iroquois and runs an Indian palisade around him.

Turner's acute visual sensibility is also evident in an ecological analogy: "As successive terminal moraines result from successive glaciations, so each frontier leaves traces behind it." And a bibliographic one: "The United States lies like a huge page in the history of society. Line by line as we read this continental page from West to East we find the record of social evolution...Particularly in eastern states this page is a palimpsest.

What is now a manufacturing State was in an earlier decade an area of intensive farming."

Turner's frontier is a living thing: it "leaped" over the Allegheny Mountains, "skipped" over the Great Plains, "pushed" into Colorado, with "tongues of settlement" reaching into wilderness. Ever situated in specific locations, it is simultaneously a process moving ever forward, recreating itself in what Turner called "this perennial rebirth, this fluidity of American life." My favorite expression in this regard is Turner's evocation of the Mississippi River: "On the tide of the Father of Waters, North and South mingled into a nation."

Turner did not consider the frontier an unalloyed good. While he viewed it as a usefully nationalizing phenomenon and a wellspring of democracy, he also recognized that a frontier mentality tended to resist even benevolent forms of outside control and fostered a grasping materialism. It also led to a lax approach to government that abetted the creation of a spoils system. Moreover, Turner clearly understood, even if he didn't dwell on it, that the extension of the frontier was a matter of conquest for which he used the correct imperial term of "colonization."

But the biggest problem Turner has with the frontier in 1893 is that it's dead. He makes this clear in the first sentence of "Significance," which discusses recently updated information from the U.S. Census Bureau indicating the disappearance of an unbroken line in the American West, which he described as "the closing of a great historic moment." What the Mediterranean had been to the Greeks, the frontier had been to the Americans. "And now," he wrote in a closing sentence laced with melancholy, "four centuries from the discovery of America, at the end of a hundred years of life under the Constitution, the frontier has gone, and with its going has closed the first period of American history." The Turner thesis, in effect, was the frontier's obituary.

What would take its place? Turner did not say. Richard Hofstadter, himself a distinguished historian, would write seventy-five years later that the latent pessimism of the frontier thesis was in sharp contrast to the ebullient optimism Turner attributed to frontier communities.[3] But while Turner never offered an alternative—indeed, he had considerable trouble writing books and never quite realized the huge potential suggested by "Significance"—his politics were considered generally consonant with those of his friend and colleague Woodrow Wilson, who of course became the president of the United States and a leader of the Progressive movement. For such people, the frontier was less a living reality—as it had been for the previous generation of political reformers, the Populists— than a metaphor that denoted opportunity on a large scale in a new domain. That's why Turner called the closing of the frontier the end of the *first* period of American history.

The frontier remained fertile symbolic terrain for much of the twentieth century, nowhere more obvious than in the 1960 presidential campaign of John F. Kennedy, whose slogan was "the New Frontier." But its appeal went a good deal beyond politics, evident in the rhetoric of the space program as well as that of the Internet. Nowhere, however, was its power more evident than in U.S. cultural life. Turnerism is the bedrock of assumptions for the whole genre of the Western, for example, and the Western, in turn, is the seedbed of other cultural genres stretching from sci-fi to hip-hop. Along with the legacy of slavery, the frontier is what makes American culture American.

But if people of the twentieth century experienced the transformation of the frontier from reality into myth, those of the twenty-first are witnessing its transformation from myth into memory. Now belief in the frontier as a living symbol is *itself* receding in our imaginations. The proximate cause is our economic situation, which has cast doubt on the upward mobility that so many of us have considered our birthright so long, and that is so deeply intertwined with our sense of a frontier. This sense of doubt is not new. It has recurred periodically throughout American history, such as during the Great Depression and amid the political scandals and economic stagflation of the 1970s. The current narrative of geopolitical decline, however, is one of rare and growing depth.

But I am speaking in terms of elusive abstractions now. A notion of decline is surprisingly slippery, subject to multiple definitions and conflicting data. A gay man or a black woman, to cite two examples, might well see ascent where others see descent. Still, without insisting on accuracy or universality, I'm interested in what I consider a widely shared, if inchoate, perception of decline as a historical artifact. In recent years my apprehension of it has gradually taken shape through a set of six films about American history that have been released in the last twenty years. The thread that connects them is the British-born, adoptively Irish actor who as far as I know has never heard of, much less read, "The Significance of the Frontier in American History." But allow me to broker an introduction. Frederick Jackson Turner, meet Daniel Day-Lewis.

———

As a general proposition, there's nothing particularly surprising about foreigners explaining the United States to Americans. A long tradition stretches from the prose of expatriate Frenchman Hector St. John de

Crèvecoeur in the eighteenth century to the films of Taiwanese immi-
grant Ang Lee two centuries later. Like countless travelers to America,
Daniel Day-Lewis left his homeland. But his adopted country is not the
United States; it is Ireland, a nation of emigrants more than immigrants.

Day-Lewis was born in London on April 29, 1957, of distinguished
lineage. His father, Cecil Day-Lewis, was a leftist writer who went on to
become poet laureate of Great Britain. His mother, Jill Balcon, was a film
and radio actor and the daughter of Michael Balcon, a British-born Baltic
Jew who entered the nascent film industry at the turn of the twentieth
century and rose to become head of Ealing Studios, where he collaborated
with the likes of Alfred Hitchcock.

Day-Lewis spent the first years of his life in the upscale Greenwich sec-
tion of London, in a childhood that is described in multiple accounts as
"middle class."[4] Yet this is hard to believe. The mere fact that he was
raised with live-in nannies suggests some degree of affluence. So does the
string of literati that appear in accounts of his youth. So does the fact that
he attended elite boarding schools. The first of these, Sevenoaks, was traditional, and Day-Lewis hated it. He was later allowed to transfer to the
more progressive Bedales, where his thespian aspirations first took root.
As a child, he had a cameo appearance in the 1971 John Schlesinger thriller,
Sunday Bloody Sunday.

Over the course of the next decade, Day-Lewis embarked on the career
trajectory of a professional stage actor. He appeared in a series of school productions and upon his graduation from the prestigious Old Vic Drama
School endured the feast-or-famine existence that characterizes the life of
people struggling to make a living as artists. He appeared in high-profile
Royal Shakespeare Company and National Theatre productions and did
television work for BBC movies and television shows. There were also occasional cameo appearances in big-budget productions like the 1982 Academy Award–winning Best Picture, *Gandhi* (he played a racist South African),
and a supporting role in a 1984 remake of *Mutiny on the Bounty*.

Day-Lewis made a major step toward stardom in the mid-1980s as
a result of his wildly divergent performances in two films whose simul-
taneous release generated international attention. The first of these,
My Beautiful Laundrette, started out as a BBC television drama written
by Pakistani-British screenwriter Hanif Kureishi and helmed by veteran director Stephen Frears. A vivid document of Thatcherite Britain,
the film is a cross-class, interracial, gay love story between an upwardly
mobile Pakistani entrepreneur with strong family connections and a
London punk (Day-Lewis) reconsidering his thuggish ways. Shortly
after finishing his work on *My Beautiful Laundrette*, Day-Lewis landed

a role in another British film, this one an adaptation of the 1908 E. M. Forster novel *A Room with a View*. Interestingly, the part Day-Lewis sought and won was not the lead figure in a love triangle, but rather that of the arrogant Cecil Vyse, whose snobbery costs him an engagement to the young woman played by Helena Bonham Carter. Day-Lewis's ability to humanize this almost cartoonish character was a principal reason why he won a New York Film Critics Circle award for Best Supporting Actor.

While the two movies certainly raised Day-Lewis's profile internationally, they did not transform his career immediately. His next major film project was a starring role as Tomas, a doctor, in a 1988 screen version of Milan Kundera's 1984 novel, *The Unbearable Lightness of Being*, a love story set amid the Prague Spring of 1968. It was not a commercial success. Nor was *Stars and Bars* (1988), in which he plays Henderson Dores, a hapless London art dealer.

Ironically, the role that transformed his career was that of an unlikely real-life character: the handicapped Irish writer and poet Christy Brown (1932–81). Teaming up with the seasoned stage director but film neophyte Jim Sheridan, Day-Lewis gave a tour de force performance in *My Left Foot* (1989), which won him an Academy Award for Best Actor in 1990. It was in this role that Day-Lewis's growing penchant for staying in character for an entire production became a source of widespread comment (and, for the crew that had to treat this able-bodied man as if he were paralyzed, some irritation). But there seemed to be no arguing with the results. Day-Lewis would team up again with Sheridan for *In the Name of the Father* (1993), in which he played Gerry Conlon, an Irishman wrongly jailed with his father for terrorism, and *The Boxer* (1997), movies that capture the claustrophobic character of Ireland at the time of "the Troubles." The intensity of his identification with the country is suggested by his decision to reaffirm his connection with the land of his father's birth by becoming an Irish citizen in 1987.[5]

Yet he continued to make false steps. Following *My Left Foot*, Day-Lewis once made another offbeat foray, this time to Patagonia, where he played an itinerant Irish dentist working for an American charity in *Eversmile, New Jersey* (1989), a garbled British-Argentine production. He then embarked on a Royal National Theatre tour of *Hamlet*. This turned out to be a disaster, not so much in terms of reviews, which were mixed, but in the emotional strain the role seemed to impose. About three-quarters of the way through the production the actor suddenly froze onstage in October of 1989. He never returned to the show—or the stage.

It was at this point that Day-Lewis crossed paths with Michael Mann, a writer/director/producer who rose to fame on the strength of his work on the fashionable 1980s television series *Miami Vice*. Mann was leveraging his commercial Hollywood power to direct a surprising project: a big-budget version of James Fenimore Cooper's 1825 novel, *Last of the Mohicans*. Certain that Day-Lewis was perfect for the lead, Mann succeeded in recruiting him for it. It probably wasn't all that hard. Long a fan of American movies—and a devotee of Method-actor predecessors like Robert De Niro—Day-Lewis was fascinated by the United States. "I didn't know America," he said in 2007, explaining why he went to see *Taxi Driver* over and over again upon its release in 1976. "But that was a glimpse of what America might be, and I realized that, contrary to expectation, I wanted to tell American stories."[6]

We now need to break the chronology of this story. Day-Lewis made a string of movies about the United States between 1992 and 2012, ranging from the seventeenth-century world of the Puritans in *The Crucible* (1997) to the aftermath of the 1960s in *The Ballad of Jack & Rose* (2005). Though they were not made in that order, and though it's very unlikely there was much in the way of a conscious design, they nevertheless trace a thematically unified narrative arc. So we're going to follow them in the sequence of their settings, not their production, and begin, as well as end, in New England.

In the process of doing so, I hope to persuade you that Day-Lewis is a Turnerian: his characters are essentially frontiersmen, even if they happen to be a gang member or a lawyer on a New York City street. One of the things that means to him, as indeed it meant to Turner, is a core restlessness with formal institutions.

In this restlessness, Turner and Day-Lewis are inheritors of the Jeffersonian tradition. As I discussed in the preceding chapter on Clint Eastwood, Jefferson was also ambivalent about institutions. But Jefferson and Turner were at heart tinkerers professing optimism that Americans would continue to construct ad hoc arrangements in response to environmental conditions. By contrast, Day-Lewis, even more than Eastwood, is different in this regard: a powerful current of fatalism courses through his characters. They can't be contained in buildings, and they can't seem to survive outside them, either. For all the richness with which Day-Lewis brings them to life in their respective worlds, they are men out of time.

The fact that a Hollywood version of Arthur Miller's classic 1953 play *The Crucible* ever got made is surprising. It is, of course, a bright star in the firmament of American theater and a staple of high school English classes. It also single-handedly turned the Salem Witch Trials into a form of allegorical shorthand for McCarthyism in the 1950s. But the remote setting, depressing ending, and message about the defects of American society make *The Crucible* less than crowd-pleasing. While one might expect some form of independent film production to surface sooner or later, a major studio shoot on location in Massachusetts would be very unlikely under any circumstances.

Except for the fact that Robert Miller, the playwright's son, was friendly with Joe Roth, the head of 20th Century Fox in the 1990s. As it was, it took years to get the film in the production pipeline. And it could very plausibly have been abandoned when Roth left Fox for Disney. But the new management kept it on track.[7] There had been hopes that this prestige project—Arthur Miller himself adapted the screenplay, and the cast included highly regarded actors like Joan Allen and the legendary Paul Scofield, directed by Briton Nicholas Hytner—would generate Oscar, and thus box office, buzz. Neither materialized. This nevertheless remains a beautifully rendered, if austere, work of art.

The Crucible is a story that's typically read one of two ways. The first and perhaps primary one is what prompted Arthur Miller to write it: as a warning about the dangers of social conformity and letting irrational fears—in particular a fear of Communism that dominated American public life at the time of the play's premiere—govern everyday life. The second tends to see the story in terms more specific to its time and place: seventeenth-century New England. Such an angle of vision leads one to view it less as an indictment of American character generally and more as one of self-righteous Puritanism specifically.

Both of these views have cogency, of course. But I'm not particularly interested in tracing either. In part, that's because it's been done so often. In part, too, it's because I think the Puritans have gotten a bit of a bum rap, as if they were the only people who ever burned witches or showed intolerance. Or as if the people who finally stood up to the witch hunters, sometimes becoming martyrs in the process, were not themselves Puritans of the best kind. Instead, I'd like to look at *The Crucible* through a different lens, one that comes into focus through Day-Lewis's rendering of its protagonist, John Proctor. And that is to see the movie as a frontier story.

There are some good historical reasons to do so. Salem, Massachusetts, is not typically seen as a frontier town; after all, it was founded in 1626, even before Boston, and was sixty-six years old when the witch trials took place. Still, if Salem itself was not in fact a frontier, it was quite close to a bona fide one: the district of Maine, which would be part of Massachusetts until 1820. For most of the seventeenth century, the beaver trade and timber industry of northern New England were major sources of prosperity for Massachusetts.

The outbreak of King Philip's War in Rhode Island in 1676, which spread northward and lingered until later in the decade, broke a relatively long stretch of peaceable relations with the region's Indians. The outbreak of another war in 1689—popularly known as King William's War, but known in the region as the Second Indian War—destabilized the region still further. These wars destroyed lives, livelihoods, and homes and created a significant number of refugees, some of them ending up in Essex County, where Salem is located. The distinguished historian Mary Beth Norton has documented that a significant number of accused witches as well as their accusers had ties that can be traced to Maine in the 1670s and 1680s. Just how decisive a factor Indian war really was in triggering the witch trials is open to debate. Few events in U.S. history have been subject to more different explanations. But it is certainly plausible to see frontier-related stresses as a factor in what went wrong in Salem in 1692.[8]

As far as the makers of *The Crucible* were concerned, this is all inside baseball. In the original script for the play—and in the movie—Miller has the first of the accusers, Abigail Williams, pressure her confederate, Betty Parris, by saying, "I saw Indians smash my dear parents' heads on the pillow next to mine, and I have seen some reddish work done at night, and I can make you wish you had never seen the sun go down!"[9] This fictive context is important in establishing a basis for the core malignancy of Williams's character. But it's more in the spirit of background information than a proximate explanation for her behavior. The real Williams was a child in 1692; Miller makes her a young woman whose jealousy over her severed sexual relationship with John Proctor leads her to accuse his wife, Elizabeth, of witchcraft.

Moreover, Miller made a crucial decision at odds with the preponderance of historical opinion that has crucial racial implications. In fact and in the play, the first accused witch is a slave named Tituba. Although seventeenth-century New Englanders were often imprecise about racial identity, she is repeatedly referred to as an Indian—"Tituba Indian," "the Indyen Woman," and so on.[10] Miller, however, unambiguously makes her black. Such a move would appear to be more consonant with Miller's larger political aims, in that scapegoating an African American makes for more pointed commentary in a moment when the modern civil rights movement was bubbling up into mass consciousness. Tituba remains un-ambiguously black in the movie (ably played by Charlyane Woodard). If anything, of course, racial scapegoating had only become a topic of greater awareness in the decades since the play.

All this said, the adaption of the play into a movie forty-three years later resulted in a subtle shift in the story's frame of reference—one that moved it back toward the frontier. "In a sense, *The Crucible* is the first western, because the frontier was there and they were the first pioneers," director Nicholas Hytner explained in 1996.[11] It is perhaps inevitable that Miller, in adapting his work for a new medium, would open it up. For example, the opening and closing events of the story, namely the girls' participation in an occult ritual and the hanging of important characters, take place offstage. In the movie, they are shot on exterior locations.

The most important element in establishing a frontier dimension for the film version is the portrayal of Daniel Day-Lewis's John Proctor. To put it most simply, the film version of *The Crucible* underlines the degree to which Proctor was an outside man. This was true in fact: the real Proctor, who was about sixty in 1692, lived on the outskirts of Salem proper, where he operated a tavern. Proctor appears to have been a local icono-clast: he was among the first to ridicule the witchcraft proceedings; alleg-edly beat his servant, Mary Warren, who confessed to witchcraft and ac-cused others; and stood up for Elizabeth, who was his third wife. This may be why he was the first male to be accused of witchcraft, and why he was hanged for it.[12]

The film version of *The Crucible*, exploiting the possibilities of the medium, makes Proctor an outside man in a much more literal sense as well. Our first view of him, about ten minutes into the film, shows him threshing wheat in a field with his sons. The imagery seems to come straight from a Winslow Homer painting: big open spaces, water in the distance, brilliant blue sky. The camera pans from the inlet to the interior to reveal his wife, Elizabeth (a superb Joan Allen), summoning him. This establishing shot of a family idyll outdoors was not incidental. In describ-ing the search for locations in the audio commentary accompanying the DVD release of the film, director Hytner said, "It became clear to us that the real authentic landscape of the first Puritan settlers of America was integral, very, very important not just to the world of the story but the story itself." Noting that Salem was not the forbidding landscape of Maine or Nova Scotia, Hytner described the location on Hog Island, near Ips-wich, as "a land that promised everything," one that offered the Proctors "a hard-won life, but a life infinitely better, more rewarding than their ancestors would have been enjoying in England."

WILD, WILD EAST: Day-Lewis as John Proctor in *The Crucible* (1996). In some important respects, the Salem, Massachusetts, of 1692 was a frontier town. *(20th Century Fox)*

Over the course of the movie, a remarkable allegory unfolds: Proctor is pulled into ever-darker interiors. That first summons from Elizabeth begins his descent. Over the course of the next hour we see him in his house, where he is trying to repair his rocky relationship with his wife in the aftermath of his infidelity, and where it is clearly darker even as light still streams in. We also see him at various locations in town. At first, these interiors do not really diminish him. Although (unlike the real Proctor) he's not a large man, Day-Lewis nevertheless commands attention. In part, this is a matter of costume; he arrives in town for the first time dressed in a rugged coat and hat, looking like Davy Crockett's Yankee ancestor.

Significantly, his first two encounters with Abigail (played by Winona Rider, with whom Day-Lewis would also be paired in *The Age of Innocence*) take place outside. In the first, early in the movie, he runs into her outside a building on a cloudy day, and while the wild spirit that led to his transgression briefly resurfaces with a kiss, he wills himself back from the brink and informs her he'd sooner cut off his arm than have sex with her again, allusions to the Gospels of Matthew and Mark.[13] Their second meeting, in which Proctor warns Abigail to stop accusing Elizabeth of witchcraft, takes place in the woods. It's sunny, but the two characters are dappled in shadow. When they meet a final time, with Proctor in a claustrophobic prison cell, both characters are engulfed in darkness.

Institutional walls close in on Day-Lewis's Proctor in other ways as well. Seeking to protect her husband from an embarrassing exposure of his extramarital affair, Elizabeth lies on his behalf—and in a moment of irony suggesting how this world has been turned upside down, a shaft of light streams through a courtroom window as she does so. When a series of new accusations leads to pandemonium, Proctor storms outside, where a changeable New England downpour has suddenly cleared. In bright sunlight, standing in an inlet that evokes the baptism of the adult Christ, Proctor angrily declares that God is dead. He is tried, convicted, excommunicated, and sentenced to death.

Yet there remains a ray of hope. The also condemned Elizabeth Proctor is pregnant and so will not be executed while an innocent soul would also perish. Amid growing doubts about the trials, Proctor is offered a deal: a pardon in exchange for a confession. Elizabeth is summoned to convince her husband to accept the deal; she makes no promises but is allowed to confer with him on the freezing, windy coast.

This is the most moving scene in the movie, and one of the most moving scenes of mature marital love ever depicted in a Hollywood film. Two ravaged people, braving a bone-chilling wind, confess their weaknesses to each other. Elizabeth admits that her severity about her husband is rooted in doubt about her own worthiness as a plain woman; Day-Lewis's John fears that his refusal to satisfy his persecutors by confessing to witchcraft amounts to the sin of pride. John decides that for the sake of his wife and children, one as yet unborn, he will "confess." If anything, the town officials are even more relieved than the Proctors.

But Judge Thomas Danforth (the great Scofield), overplaying his hand, is not content to get Proctor's signed confession. He also demands that Proctor, in the parlance of the Communist witch hunts, name names. This is where Proctor digs in. The final scene of the movie shows Proctor and other recalcitrants who refused to admit to a crime they did not commit mounting the gallows for the outdoor execution scene. They recite the Lord's Prayer; the final image of the movie shows a rope against the sky, suggesting the thread of guilt and obligation that connects us to them.

In art and life, the Salem Witch Trials were a disaster wrought by Puritans, the most institutionally minded people in British North America. The deaths of nineteen people and the concomitant misery that resulted were a by-product of the social conformity implicit in the communitarian character of Puritanism. But one of the many paradoxes of Puritanism is that this communitarian impulse was accompanied by another, individualistic one that was at least as powerful. The Puritans had always placed great value on the primacy of the individual conscience; the belief that one's own relationship to God mattered more than what pope or king might say is precisely what brought them to America. And it's that independence of mind that led the John Proctors of New England to stand up to, and finally defeat, tyranny from within.

This libertarian strand of cultural DNA that had drifted across the ocean found a hospitable climate on these shores. As Frederick Jackson Turner would later write in "Significance," "the frontier is productive of individualism." Turner would often point to "antipathy to control" in contrasting the frontier mentality with that of the eastern establishment. As he well knew, however, the eastern establishment was *itself* a product of the frontier and never entirely transcended it. In an obvious and irrefutable sense, John Proctor is a tragic figure. But as embodied by Daniel Day-Lewis in this movie, he is a fierce and willful force whose intensity cannot be contained by his death. His children, literal and figurative, will conquer a continent—a topic that would be the focus of the next film in the Day-Lewis sequence of U.S. history.

In the almost two centuries since its publication in 1826, James Fenimore Cooper's *Last of the Mohicans* has been like the sheet music for a pop song: a loose set of characters and plot points in a standard that has been rearranged and embellished countless times. Like a lot of pop classics, Cooper's source material lay in the public domain, namely collective memory of the French and Indian War, which ended a quarter century before he was born. Cooper, who was raised in upstate New York—his father was a large, and controversial, landowner in the baseball Mecca we know as Cooperstown[14]—wrote about a time when the region was a frontier, and in so doing wrote what many scholars of the Western consider an early example of the genre.

Actually, *Mohicans* was part of a larger frontier saga, sometimes referred to as "the Leatherstocking Tales," five novels that can plausibly
be considered the Harry Potter books (or, given the out-of-sequence arrival of each installment, the *Star Wars*) of the nineteenth century. The
Leatherstocking in question was a protagonist who went by a series of
other names, including Natty Bumppo, Hawkeye, the Pathfinder, La
Longue Carabine, and "the trapper." Over the course of this multipart
story, Cooper's ever-restless protagonist, in good Turnerian fashion,
keeps pushing to find open horizons, beginning in the Northeast with
The Deerslayer (1841; what we might today call the prequel was published last) and ending, as an old man, on the Great Plains with *The
Prairie* (1827).

From a modern standpoint, Cooper's fiction is almost unreadable in its
stilted language and slack pacing. What *has* lasted in *Mohicans*—what
indeed has proven to be amazingly supple—is a set of characters and a
loose plot. The names sometimes get changed, and minor characters get
added or subtracted, but at heart the story involves the intersection of two
sets of people with a villain who brings them together. One set consists of
(the real-life) Lieutenant Colonel George Monro, who commands a fort
on the Hudson, and his two (apparently fictive) daughters, Cora and her
younger sister, Alice. The girls are on their way to a reunion with their
father, brought by Major Duncan Heyward, who is in love with Alice.
These travelers are accompanied through dangerous terrain by an evil
Huron Indian guide named Magua. Magua is believed to be an outcast
from his people, and thus a reliable ally. In fact, he is working for the
French army under the command of the Marquis Louis-Joseph de Montcalm. Magua seeks revenge against Monro for giving him the "firewater"
that precipitated his alcoholic disgrace.

The second set of characters includes the novel's protagonist, here
called "the scout" or La Longue Carabine, as well as his companions,
Uncas, and Uncas's father, Chingachgook, the surviving remnants of the
Mohican tribe.[15] These Mohicans unwittingly run into Magua at the very
moment he intends to realize his evil design, and they stop him, though
they fail to prevent his escape.

A series of chases and captures follows. In the climactic one, Cora and
Uncas die at the hand of Magua,[16] and Magua in turn is dispatched by the
scout. At the joint funerals of Uncas and Cora, whose low-key but poten-
tially problematic multiracial attraction has been fortunately prevented by
their deaths, Chingachgook sadly muses that he is the last of the Mohicans.

In the last hundred years, the principal medium through which this story
has been retold has been film—hardly surprising, given the proto-cinematic

quality of the story. The first movie version of the novel, short and silent, came out in 1911. A 1920 version, an impressively executed piece of work with lots of exterior shots, also silent and selected for the National Film Registry, generally follows the outline of the novel. A 1932 twelve-part serial version of the story—cheap, unintentionally comical, but surely thrilling to people like my father, who as a kid would have gone to see the weekly episodes as part of a full slate of Saturday matinee moviego- ing—ends with Chingachgook dead and Uncas as the last Mohican. The best-known version of the movie prior to 1992 was the 1936 version star- ring Randolph Scott, who went on to be a fixture of Westerns through the fifties.[17]

So by the time director Michael Mann and co-screenwriter Christo- pher Crowe tackled *Mohicans* in the early 1990s, they had a treasure trove of material to work with, which, in addition to the novel, included the famous nineteenth-century account of the French and Indian War by Francis Parkman, the diaries of the French comte de Bougainville, and more contemporary accounts.[18] That said, the most important precedent for the filmmakers of the 1992 movie was a long tradition of artistic li- cense. Once again names get tweaked (in a somewhat gratuitous homage to a pair of nineteenth-century writers, Hawkeye is renamed Nathaniel Poe) and characters get rearranged. This time, Heyward is in love with Cora, not Alice, while Alice pairs off with Uncas. The most crucial change in this version of *Mohicans* is the skillful way it sharpens the geopolitical dimension of what is typically treated as a frontier tale. The character of Montcalm is both appealing and ambiguous, and the elaborate rituals in- volving the surrender of Fort William Henry, depicted with great pomp, underline the way in which British and French imperial officers have far more in common with each other, even as adversaries, than with their colonial and/or Indian allies. Even better in this regard is the scene in which Nathaniel negotiates for the release of Cora and Alice with an Ottawa. The only way they can converse is in French, the lingua franca of the eighteenth-century world.

One of the more important renovations in *Mohicans* '92 is the way in which Mann & Co. effectively turn it into a movie about the coming of the American Revolution, a subject with a surprisingly benighted cinematic history.[19] Again, the DNA for this was always there, most obviously in 1936. But the filmmakers play up the tension between local colonial mili- tias, who are primarily concerned with protecting their homes, and the professional British military, which has its own strategic objectives. Their divergent interests become an issue when the militiamen seek to leave the fort to defend their hearths and are barred from doing so by Monro, even when Nathaniel informs him that Indian war parties are indeed ravaging local residents. Major Heyward, who has witnessed the destruction in the countryside, affirms Monro, the man he hopes will someday be his father-in-law. This decision backfires in that it completes Cora's tilt away from Heyward and toward Nathaniel—part of her larger Americanization, and one way in which the movie as a whole does more with its female characters than any previous version of the story.

Of course, the pivotal figure in this regard—the linchpin of the movie, and that of the point I'm trying to make in this chapter—is the character of Nathaniel, more specifically *the Nathaniel of Daniel Day-Lewis*. This is much more than a matter of which lines of the script he utters. To put it simply, the Day-Lewis incarnation of Cooper's frontiersman is a singularly magnificent figure. Though he lacks the muscularity of the typical movie-star hero, he is an impressive physical specimen: lanky but taut, strong but agile. But Nathaniel's presence is much more than physical. The Hawkeye of all too many *Mohicans*—nowhere more so than the original—is a hayseed who's not (quite) as dumb as he looks. Randolph Scott's Hawkeye is one of the better ones, because the geniality he gives the character doesn't undercut his sense of competence. But Day-Lewis blows his predecessors away with his sheer intensity. More than that: it is an intensity of self-assurance. "I liked the idea of a man who had not been touched by 20th-century neurosis," he explained later. "A life that isn't drawn inwards."[20]

As such, Day-Lewis's Nathaniel is the quintessential frontiersman. "You call yourself a patriot and loyal subject of the crown?" a sneering British officer asks at one point, wondering why Nathaniel shows no inclination to enlist in the militia. "I do not call myself subject to much at all," he replies dryly. When Nathaniel joins the war effort, which he does provisionally, it's for the sake of his budding romance with Cora, not king or country.

Mann underlines Hawkeye's—and, increasingly, Cora's—specifically American frontier identity in their love scene at the height of the siege of Fort William Henry, consummated with the musical theme from the soundtrack, which fuses a Scottish reel and a Native American beat. Day-Lewis's chemistry with co-star Madeleine Stowe had a demographic appeal that cut across gender lines and ensured the film's commercial success. But it's also crucial to Nathaniel's central place in Day-Lewis's gallery of American character portraits. Nathaniel's relationship with Cora faces all kinds of logistical complications—"Stay alive!" he shouts with furious rage on the eve of her capture by Magua, "I will find you!"—yet the strength of that love, its uncomplicated purity, is unquestionable.

NATIVE SON: Day-Lewis in *Last of the Mohicans* (1992). By far the most compelling of the many embodiments of James Fenimore Cooper's protagonist, the role also represented the apogee of strength and hope in Day-Lewis's gallery of frontier figures. *(Tri-Star)*

Never again would Day-Lewis play a person so straightforwardly in love, so unconflicted internally, whatever the chaos around him.

This romantic clarity is of a piece with the larger sense of integration that marks Nathaniel's character as a whole. He is a perfect Turnerian specimen, as at ease in a pickup game of lacrosse as he is dining at the cabin of his friends, teasing Uncas about his prospects of finding a Delaware bride in Kentucky—"Kentuckeeee!" he says gleefully, a man truly at home even as a visitor.

The fact that Nathaniel is *not* the entirely restless loner of Cooper's saga, that there's a place in his life for a woman who by the end of the film will stand by his side wherever he may go, is very much a part of the film's larger design. The movie eschews the traditional funeral scenes of most *Mohicans* by having Chingachgook spread the ashes of Uncas over the western mountains amid a setting sun. He observes, as most versions of the story do, that he's now the last of the Mohicans. As sorry as we feel for

Chingachgook, this version of the movie—as I will discuss, there are in fact two 1992 versions, with subtly, but significantly, different endings—has a hopeful feel. That's because we feel so strongly that, the tragedy of Uncas notwithstanding, Nathaniel really is Chingachgook's son (we moderns consider race and even parenthood a social construction, after all), and that in his presumed merger with Cora—whose name takes on a new significance—the seed of a new national identity will be planted. As a hybrid, it will be resilient. And it will have plenty of room to grow. In this, the first film Day-Lewis made about American history, he embodies the frontier in its brightest phase and at its greatest height.

One of the more notable—and, given the circumstances of its unveiling in Chicago, ironic—limits of Frederick Jackson Turner's vision involved his difficulty incorporating cities into his vision of U.S. history. As the esteemed environmental historian William Cronon has observed, "Turner consistently chose to see the frontier as a rural place, the very isolation of which created its special role in the history of American democracy. Toward the end of his career, he looked with some misgiving on the likelihood that there would be an 'urban reinterpretation' of American history that might 'minimize the frontier theme'—as if frontier history had little or nothing to do with cities."[21]

And yet as Richard Hofstadter, himself also a critic of Turner, admitted, "the great merit of Turnerism, for all its elliptical and exasperating vagueness, was to be open-ended. The frontier idea, though dissected at one point and minimized at another, keeps popping up in new forms, posing new questions."[22] It is in this spirit that a frontier perspective can help us understand the role of Daniel Day-Lewis in the next installment of his cinematic history, *Gangs of New York*.

New York, it should be said, is not typically viewed as frontier territory any more than Salem, Massachusetts, is. For one thing, it's an island, not a continent. For another, it was effectively urban from the moment of its Dutch inception as New Amsterdam. And yet one can plausibly view Manhattan as a frontier in two senses. First, like the rest of North America, New York was a geographic space that was settled along an irregular line of development over a long period of time, albeit from south to north rather than from east to west. And second, the frontier was a process of demographic transformation, as immigrants of one kind or another gradually gave way to other ethnic and racial groups, often in the process of gentrification. Only by the end of the twentieth century did the entire island essentially become an enclave of affluence. These twin processes were captured in the prose of Luc Sante, whose now-classic study *Low Life* was an important influence on the filmmakers, Day-Lewis in particular. "The conquest of Manhattan was a microcosm of that of the whole of America, with its spaces so vast it was assumed that they could be squandered and there would still be so much left over that errors could be overlooked," Sante wrote. "In New York the natural wilderness was much more concisely and thoroughly swept away, so that a human wilderness could take its place."[23] This notion of a *human* wilderness is important: whether at the OK Corral or on Broadway, it wasn't just the landscape that made the Wild West wild.

Like Michael Mann's *Last of the Mohicans*, the 2002 Martin Scorsese film has a twisty history. If *Mohicans* began as a novel rooted in historical events, *Gangs* began as a history laced with fiction. The core source material was *The Gangs of New York*, a 1928 book by journalist and crime writer Herbert Asbury. As Russell Shorto points out in his foreword to the 2008 edition, Asbury "was working with material that would be hard to verify even if you were getting it as events unfolded. His sources are themselves tellers of tall tales."[24]

Nevertheless, the broad parameters of the world Asbury described have long been accepted as true. Since New York lacked a recognized and effective police force well into the nineteenth century, an active gang culture flourished in the city's poorer neighborhoods, like the Bowery and the Five Points, typified by the presence of informal clans with colorful names like the Plug Uglies, the Shirt Tails, and the Dead Rabbits (according to Asbury, *dead rabbit* was slang for a rowdy, athletic fellow).[25] The character Day-Lewis plays in the movie, Bill Cutting, a.k.a. Bill the Butcher, is modeled on the real-life figure Bill Poole, a butcher who was shot to death amid a series of gang vendettas and whose dying words, after lingering for fourteen days, were reputedly "Goodbye boys, I die a true American."[26]

Martin Scorsese first encountered *The Gangs of New York* in 1970 and almost immediately hoped to make a movie of it. His friend the critic and screenwriter Jay Cocks discovered the book independently around the same time and began working on a screenplay. Scorsese and Cocks knew at the outset that the project would be difficult to realize, because it couldn't be shot in New York—the world of the movie had utterly disappeared—and would thus require the recreation of lower Manhattan on a massive scale. After a flurry of initial activity in the late seventies, the project lapsed into turnaround.[27]

The rise of independent cinema in the 1990s, and in particular the success of Miramax under brothers Bob and Harvey Weinstein, fostered films that broke the box office formulas that had dominated major-studio moviemaking since the 1980s. Scorsese was thus able to revive the project with the backing of the Weinsteins. By no means was it smooth sailing from here; power struggles and delays dogged the picture, whose shoot ran long and whose release was postponed multiple times.[28]

One of the bigger challenges Scorsese & Co. faced was casting. Some Hollywood firepower for the movie was provided by Cameron Diaz, cast as the main love interest in the story. The lead role—or what in theory was the lead role, anyway—went to Leonardo DiCaprio. DiCaprio plays Amsterdam Vallon, son of the Irish-born gang leader Priest Vallon (Liam Neeson), who experiences Hamlet-like ambivalence in trying to avenge Priest's death at the hands of Bill the Butcher. The young heartthrob, whose critical cachet in the nineties was vastly augmented by his success as a leading man in the hugely successful *Titanic* (1997), brought to the project not only tremendous box office potential but also a bankroll: he, like Scorsese, agreed to be partially liable for cost overruns.[29]

The keystone of the project was nevertheless Day-Lewis. As is often the case, getting him on board took some persuading. There were anecdotal reports at the time of the film's release that Scorsese had coaxed him out of retirement in Italy, where Day-Lewis had reputedly become a shoemaker. Once on board, Day-Lewis got ready for *Gangs* with his customarily intense physical and psychic preparation. He exercised with venom-filled Eminem music every morning and inhabited the rage of Bill the Butcher whether or not the cameras were rolling.[30] In 2007, Day-Lewis observed that "in America, the articulate use of language is often regarded with suspicion."[31] But the remarkable thing about his Bill the Butcher is the spellbinding way in which his savage intelligence is expressed with a unique patois that fuses profanity and poetry. One such moment occurs late in the movie when Boss Tweed (Jim Broadbent) comes to see the Butcher to remonstrate with him after the killing of Monk McGinn (Brendan Gleeson). The Butcher, slicing up a piece of sizzling meat, addresses Tweed in biblically apocalyptic language:

I know your works. You are neither hot nor cold. So because you are lukewarm, and are neither cold nor hot, I will spew you out of my mouth. [He's quoting Revelation 3:16.] You can build your filthy world without me. I took the father. Now I'll take the son. You tell young Vallon I'm goin' to paint Paradise Square with his blood. Two coats. I'll festoon my bedchamber with his guts. As for you, Mr. Tammany

fucking Hall, come down to the Points again and you'll be dispatched
by mine own hand.

This is great dialogue, and it's animated by great delivery. Day-Lewis
accompanies "two coats" with a sign of the cross, made with a knife in his
hand. And "festoon" is delivered with lusty aggression: "I'll festoooon
my bedchamber with his guts." Ironically, there's something downright
Catholic about the way this militant Protestant uses a biblical idiom in
secular context. But there's also something appropriate about this, in that
the Butcher considers the papist Priest Vallon the last worthy adversary
he's ever had. In any case, the effect is utterly riveting, and an illustration
of why Day-Lewis utterly dominates the movie.

Indeed, he almost overwhelms it. Nominally, the plot of *Gangs of New
York* concerns Amsterdam Vallon's loss of his father in a gang fight in
1846 and his return, after sixteen years of reform school, to kill the Butcher,
only to fall under his sway and become a virtual son. This patricidal
struggle takes place against the backdrop of a fratricidal one: the Civil
War, which engulfs New York in the form of the Draft Riots of 1863, a
five-day episode of urban anarchy that would be quelled only by the arrival
of troops returning from Gettysburg.

It quickly becomes clear, however, that the movie belongs to Day-Lewis's Bill the Butcher. We first see him about five minutes into the film;
Scorsese's camera starts on the ground, where the Butcher stamps the
snow from his shoes. As the camera pans up his flowing coat and red/
white/blue sash of combat, we see a figure that, like his character in *Last
of the Mohicans*, does not have the kind of gangling physical presence
we've come to expect from our movie stars. But his internal power is so
tightly coiled, his murderous rage, as evident as it is, held (temporarily) in
check, that it's impossible not to be awed.

It's appropriately ironic that the Butcher's gang goes by the name of the
Native Americans. The historically accurate term denotes what was at the
time a growing number of U.S. citizens who were increasingly hostile to
the rising tide of immigrants, especially Irish immigrants. This tide would
crest with the power of the American, a.k.a. Know-Nothing, Party in the
1850s, part of a nativist movement that proved to be a temporary but powerful force in nineteenth-century U.S. politics. Of course in our day the
phrase *Native American* is a synonym for Indian. Though the Butcher is a
passionate racist who considers only white Anglo-Saxon Protestants real
Americans, his situation in *Gangs of New York* resembles no one's more
aptly than that of a Delaware sachem confronted with growing numbers
of outside interlopers and deciding to take a stand against them.

NATIVE AMERICAN: Bill the Butcher goes into battle at the start of *Gangs of New York* (2002). Even on a New York street, Day-Lewis's characters are frontiersmen. *(Miramax)*

In that opening scene in the winter of 1846, the mighty Priest Vallon and his Celtic horde are vanquished by the Butcher-led Natives, who prevail despite their enemy's greater numbers. Yet the Butcher has only bought time. He can manage, even absorb, the steady stream of new arrivals for an interval. Indeed, it's one of the paradoxes of the Butcher's character that he can employ his former enemies, and even tease them affectionately about their ethnic foibles. But like a hydra-headed monster, Vallon's legacy returns in the form of the son with the ironically Teutonic name—"Amsterdam"—who will ultimately challenge the Butcher for supremacy. In the meantime, however, the unwitting chief takes a shine to the kid and nurtures him in the ways of tribal power. As such, he's like a triumphant Indian warrior who incorporates the kin of vanquished foes into his own clan.

Over the course of the almost three-hour movie, Amsterdam struggles to reassert his true patrimony. But the truly overwhelming forces that Bill Cutting faces do not come from knives, or even guns, but from the mortal threat of votes and the overwhelming force they can ultimately impose on behalf of those who control them. The first person to realize this, naturally, is Boss Tweed. He starts out as an eager collaborator with the Butcher but comes to see him as an obstacle to consolidating his power. Instead, Tweed turns his attention to the new arrivals that will be the shock troops of a renovated Democratic Party. "There's the building of our country right there, Bill, Americans aborning," Tweed says down at the docks as Irish immigrants arrive. The Butcher's reply: "I don't see Americans. I see trespassers."

TWEED: You're a great one for fighting, Bill, I know. But you can't fight forever.

BUTCHER: I can go down doing it.

TWEED: And you will.

BUTCHER (*who was walking away but now turns around*): What did you say?

TWEED: I said you're turning your back on the future.

BUTCHER (*waving a pointed finger*): Not our future.

Yet another irony: the Butcher puts his hand on young Vallon's shoulder as they depart from the scene. A piece of tour de force filmmaking follows, as the camera tracks from immigrants disembarking from one ship to newly recruited Union soldiers embarking on another, as coffins are lifted from that vessel to join the immigrants on the dock. Though it's highly unlikely anything like this actually ever happened, there's an allegorical truth here about the way immigrants were raw material to be consumed in a not-so-virtuous cycle of death and rebirth.

When, about two-thirds of the way through the movie, the Butcher learns the true identity of his protégé, he turns on him with ferocity. In a scene more shocking than any gang fight, he murders Vallon's Irish mentor, Monk, who has been elected sheriff on a Tammany ticket, in broad daylight. "See if his ashes burn green," he says to the horrified onlookers after throwing a knife into the conciliatory Monk's back—a move reminiscent of a tomahawk throw—and bashing his head in with the very club Monk used to use in his own gangbanging days. But this is only a prelude of the bloodbath to come.

By the time Vallon and Bill the Butcher have their climactic confrontation, however, their blood feud is beside the point. For it is taking place against the backdrop of a much larger one: the Civil War. At the very moment of their fight, the city is engulfed by the Draft Riots, a mass protest against conscription by the working class against the power of the state, to which the state responded with a massive show of federal force in the form of the Union Army. Seemingly irrelevant for so long, the government finally becomes the real enemy of the gangs of New York.

The Civil War is traditionally represented as the triumph of federal government over a feudal plantation elite. But in *Gangs of New York*, it's not only slaveholding southerners who are steamrolled by the power of the national state; so is a local urban subculture as well. In "The Significance of the Frontier in American History," Turner depicts the power of the state as an implacable, but largely benign, force that stitches the nation

ON THE WARPATH: Bill the Butcher murders Monk McGinn (an unseen Brendan Gleeson) in *Gangs of New York*. In resisting the rising tide of foreign occupation, his character is not unlike a Native American sachem fighting to hold his ground. *(Miramax)*

together. Here, it's a terrible swift sword that slices away existing growth to make room for a new society.

Scorsese underlines the real-life imposition of martial law with an embellishment that did not in fact happen by bringing Union naval batteries to New York Harbor, whose guns pulverize the paving stones of Paradise Square. The Butcher and Vallon can barely find each other amid the rubble, and the former is mortally wounded by a large piece of shrapnel that lodges in his gut. So we see something resembling grateful affection when the dying Butcher has a final moment with Vallon, both men on their knees, because he knows that Vallon will deliver the final blow. "Thank God: I die a true American," the Butcher says, the line reputedly delivered by the real Bill Poole. Vallon then delivers the coup de grace by plunging a knife into him, an act of vengeance and compassion.

Gangs of New York represents a transposition of roles for Daniel Day-Lewis: in *Last of the Mohicans*, he was Hawkeye; this time he's effectively Chingachgook. Like generations of dime novel readers and fans of Westerns, we admire him in his savagery, which has a kind of nobility even as it is unacceptable as a basis for contemporary society. Like Indians of the frontier, Bill the Butcher must die so that we, a non-WASP multiracial majority, might live. It's Leonardo DiCaprio's Vallon who represents the synthesis of cultures that will survive as a hearty hybrid and make a modern America.

And yet we remain haunted by the specter of the natives.

———————

At one point early on in his 1993 movie *The Age of Innocence*, Martin Scorsese briefly shows us the Fifth Avenue mansion of widow Catherine Mingott, the maverick matriarch whose granddaughter May Welland (Winona Ryder) is engaged to marry Newland Archer (Day-Lewis). The voice-over narration informs us that Mrs. Mingott lives "in an inaccessible wilderness near the Central Park." This literary joke in Edith Wharton's novel cues Scorsese's cinematic one: far from an "inaccessible wilderness," Fifth Avenue near Central Park has long been some of the most crowded and valuable real estate on the planet. In the mid-1870s setting of this story, however, we see a single house in a remote urban outpost. Referring to *the* Central Park is another signal this is not yet territory that has been incorporated into the linguistic fabric of New York life. While the elite leisure class lives safely north of the Five Points that would have been dominated by Bill the Butcher when Newland Archer was a boy, Mrs. Mingott lives beyond the pale of settlement. But her power is great enough that the people of her milieu, prospective grandson-in-law among them, will respond to a summons uptown. *Way* uptown.

For Archer himself, however, the primary point of orientation is neither north nor west. It is east. This is not simply a matter of him getting his suits from England or listening to his operas in Italian. For Archer inhabits an *aesthetic* frontier, importing the latest books from Europe and taking in the latest gallery exhibitions from contemporary painters at home and abroad. That's why the unexpected return of his fiancée's cousin, the expatriate Countess Olenska (Michelle Pfeiffer), proves so unsettling. The countess, fleeing an unhappy marriage to a Polish nobleman, is finding readjustment to the world of her childhood difficult, not only because her of status—which will only become more problematic if she proceeds with her intention to divorce the count—but also because she is impatient with the Old World pretenses of New World poseurs. "It seems stupid to have discovered America only to make it a copy of another country," she observes to Archer at a ball early on in the movie.

The Age of Innocence both is and isn't Martin Scorsese territory. It is, of course, set on his home ground of Manhattan, the locale of a number of contemporary Scorsese films like *Mean Streets* (1973) and *Taxi Driver* (1976), as well as historical dramas like *New York, New York* (1977), which was set in the forties. Scorsese has always been fascinated by tribal ritual and the often unspoken codes that shape the behavior of local subcultures, especially violent behavior (there's no bloodshed here, but a casual brutality lurks beneath a veneer of civility). And the set of visual signifiers in this movie, from place settings on a dinner table to flowers—an extended, and often misleading, metaphor—provided a feast for his imagination.

In another sense, however, *The Age of Innocence* takes place on an entirely different planet than that of the ethnic working class that is Scorsese's metier. Based—very closely, including a good deal of voice-over narration by Joanne Woodward taken verbatim—on Wharton's 1920 novel, *Innocence* is a sharply observed portrait of Wharton's youth, the elite New York of the *Social Register*, a community of old-money Vanderbilts, Roosevelts, and Astors. So it is that the reigning social arbiters of the movie, the van der Luydens, have Dutch names.

Also in sharp contrast to Scorsese, Wharton approached her art from a distinctly female point of view. To some extent, her work can be described in terms of the dilemma of strong women in an inescapably male world. Interestingly, many of Wharton's most memorable characters—like Lawrence Selden in *The House of Mirth* (1905) or the title character of *Ethan Frome* (1911)—are men. Yet her most sympathetic male characters also tend to be ineffectual, lacking the will to act decisively before it's too late. (Scorsese's characters, by contrast, are impulsive figures played by the likes of Harvey Keitel and Joe Pesci, who do great harm by acting instinctively.) *The Age of Innocence* is told from Newland Archer's point of view, but early on Wharton's narrative adopts an ironic tone toward him. Archer is described "as at heart a dilettante" who thought himself more enlightened than he really was when it came to women, particularly the woman who was to become his wife. "He meant her (thanks to his enlightening companionship) to develop a social tact and readiness of wit enabling her to hold her own with the most popular women of the 'younger set.'" But, the narrator notes, "how this miracle of fire and ice was to be created, and to sustain itself in a harsh world, he had never taken the time to think out."[32]

Archer does not remain cluelessly complacent. In essence, the novel is a story of growing awareness—a loss of innocence about others' lack of innocence. This remains the narrative core of the movie. But the vein of sarcasm that salts Wharton's prose is removed from the Newland Archer of Martin Scorsese/Daniel Day-Lewis. Unlike in his other roles, Day-Lewis looks every inch the aristocrat. As with every other American he's played, however, his character is *in* a world but not quite *of* it—and has the strength to stand apart comfortably. From the beginning of *Innocence*,

Newland Archer has little patience for the superficiality of the men or the pettiness of the women around him. He shows proto-feminist indignation at the way that divorce is simply not considered a feasible option for the Countess Olenska, even as anyone familiar with her situation concedes her husband's behavior has been outrageous. And he's as open with his opinions on the matter with his mother and sister as he is with the senior partner at the law firm where he works.

Archer is nevertheless afflicted by an ambivalence that ensnares him. His independence and curiosity draw him to the countess, even as he tries to counteract his attraction by seeking to accelerate his engagement. Paradoxically, as the family's attorney, he's urged to entangle himself in her legal affairs. Even more paradoxical is that Archer's desire to resolve his turmoil by marrying sooner is also thwarted by his fiancée and her family. At one point, he asks her in exasperation, "Can't you and I just strike out for ourselves, May?"

Archer's plaintive query—"Can't we strike out for ourselves?"—is the Turnerian pivot in Day-Lewis's American history. Previous Day-Lewis characters lit out for the territory or staked a claim, but Newland Archer finds himself at the mercy of events beyond his control—and, as he will come to realize, beyond his understanding. May's family will give him what he says he wants at precisely the moment he no longer wishes to get married. And yet he sees himself as having no real alternative to going ahead with the wedding. This act fails to resolve his ambivalence; the countess remains in the picture, and his desire for her intensifies, leading him to take risks that endanger his standing in his family and his community. Yet when Archer finally decides to force the question he finds he has been totally outflanked, not only by his wife but by a set of confederates who, with the assent of the countess, maneuver him into submission.

The scene in which this happens is exquisitely painful. The Archers have just hosted a dinner party for the departing countess, who will be returning to Europe (it's at this meal that he realizes that everyone, including his wife, has long assumed he's been having an affair that has not only never been consummated, but which he believed was a secret). During the dinner, Archer talked of travel—once again, he was looking east—but somehow the conversation never attained a degree of seriousness. Now, alone with May in his library, he attempts to take up the subject, speaking of plans for going to India or Japan. "I'm afraid you can't do that, dear," she says, rising in her chair to tower over her husband before then curling up with her head in his lap. She's having a baby, she explains without ever saying so directly, and therefore the two must remain together. There will be no frontier for the ironically named Newland Archer.

This scene sparks a memory of another actor, one Day-Lewis is said to admire: Jimmy Stewart. Interestingly, in citing his admiration for this giant of classic Hollywood, Day-Lewis expressed a preference not for the Stewart who starred in a series of psychologically sophisticated Westerns under the direction of Anthony Mann in the 1950s but rather for the Stewart of Frank Capra movies.[33] The most famous of these, of course, is *It's a Wonderful Life* (1946), in which Stewart plays George Bailey, the would-be adventurer who is repeatedly prevented from leaving his hometown of Bedford Falls and ultimately becomes a pillar of his community. As a number of observers (myself among them) have noted, Bailey's life at the end of the story is less wonderful than Frank Capra would have us believe.[34] Yet for that very reason, the things he trades his freedom for become all the more precious.

In one respect, Archer has an advantage over George Bailey: he finally does make it to Europe. In the film's closing sequence, Scorsese cuts— actually, it's more like a seamless transition—from that last scene between Archer and May in his library to the same room decades later, where he reluctantly assents to making the trip with his son, Ted. When they get to Paris, Ted suggests, with studied offhandedness, that they visit Dad's former flame. Archer is shocked his son knows about the countess. Ted explains that on her deathbed May told him he was in good hands because "once, when she asked you to, you gave up the thing you wanted most." Archer replies (twice) that "she never asked me." But the point, perhaps, is precisely that the request could be unspoken. "It seemed to take an iron band from his heart to know that, after all, someone had guessed and pitied. And that it should have been his wife moved him inexpressibly," the narrator informs us. Perhaps this is why Archer finally refuses to join Ted when they stand on the threshold of the countess's Parisian apartment. "What will I tell her?" he asks his father incredulously. "Just tell her I'm old-fashioned," Archer concludes in what is the final line in the movie. He will not cross that frontier.

———

At first glance, the next figure in Daniel Day-Lewis's American gallery marks a return to the fierce intensity of John Proctor, Nathaniel Poe, and Bill the Butcher. He is, moreover, a bona fide westerner—about as western you can get: a Californian (the genuine frontier article, which is to say a transplant). We meet him in 1898, five years after Turner delivered his famous "Significance of the Frontier" address, and almost a decade after the frontier was declared closed. But starting out in the rocky desert of the

Golden State, he is a pathfinder nonetheless, the prophet of a new frontier who connects a promised land to the Pacific. His name has a remorseless clarity: Daniel Plainview. His rise and—significantly—his fall are charted in the 2007 film *There Will Be Blood*.

Like most Day-Lewis projects, this one is grounded, albeit loosely, on an old literary source, *Oil!*, the 1927 Upton Sinclair novel. Sinclair first came to fame on the strength of his 1906 muckraking novel *The Jungle*, which detailed the appalling state of the meatpacking industry and led a reluctant President Theodore Roosevelt, who preferred to lead rather than follow when it came to social reform, to sign the Pure Food and Drug Act the same year. Sinclair had a very long and commercially successful career that stretched well into the 1950s, but *The Jungle* is really the only novel for which he is remembered today. ("I aimed at the public's heart and by accident hit it in the stomach" is his famous line on the book.) While Sinclair could write prose of riveting social realism, he tended to undercut it with a didactic impulse that veered into propaganda. That's what happened in *The Jungle*, which ends as a virtual Socialist tract. Sinclair ran unsuccessfully for governor of California as a Democrat in 1934, with a platform to End Poverty in California (EPIC), and his populist tendencies are evident in *Oil!* as well. The novel tells the story of James Arnold Ross, a fictionalized character based on oil tycoon Edward Doheny, through the eyes of his son, Ross Jr., nicknamed Bunny. We meet Ross and his son in 1912 as he gets his start in petroleum drilling. Over the course of the next fifteen years he becomes a major operator, reluctantly drawn into a cartel whose illegal activities culminate in the Teapot Dome Scandal, in which naval oil reserves in Wyoming were leased to private operators in exchange for a bribe.[35] The scandal did much to tarnish the administration of President Warren Harding, whose reputation waned rapidly after his unexpected death in 1923.

Oil! had been culturally dormant for decades when it was discovered by Eric Schlosser, a modern-day muckraker whose exposé *Fast Food Nation* garnered a good deal of attention when it was published in 2001.[36] Not surprisingly, Schlosser was asked a lot about Sinclair, whom he knew chiefly from *The Jungle*. Schlosser was nevertheless curious about his polemical godfather and dipped into Sinclair's vast body of work. He was particularly intrigued by *Oil!*, which he thought could make a good movie. So he optioned the rights from the Sinclair estate. At the same moment, it turned out there was someone else interested in the novel: the screenwriter/director Paul Thomas Anderson. The two agreed to collaborate.[37]

When Anderson began working on the project circa 2004, he was still only in his early thirties. He had made four relatively small movies that were nevertheless hailed for their striking originality, among them *Boogie Nights* (1997), a surprisingly loving portrait of a group of pornographic filmmakers, and *Magnolia* (1999), a sprawling family saga with seemingly disparate characters whose lives converge. The screenplay that Anderson eventually produced, renamed *There Will Be Blood* (for reasons I've never been able to ascertain), would only use a sliver of Sinclair's novel, principally the father-son relationship in the oil business and a clutch of incidents.

But the differences between novel and screenplay are about more than plot details. *Oil!* is at heart a story of labor. The main narrative line is that of Bunny's gradual radicalization and the need to break free of his father's loving but misguided hopes for him. Ross Sr. is certainly an arch capitalist, albeit one whose unstinting affection for his son leads him to make allowances and tolerate people far different from the plutocratic allies to whom he defers. The protagonist of Anderson's screenplay, however, is a ruthless independent operator who proves as hostile to bigger operators as he does to smaller ones. Yet his primary adversary in the movie is not workers, or even fellow oil titans, but instead an evangelical preacher named Eli Sunday (Paul Dano), a minor figure in the novel clearly patterned on dubious preachers of the twenties like Aimee Semple McPherson (whose extramarital affair and less than credible claims of being kidnapped made her a national joke). This is, in my view, a mistake, and perhaps an illustration of the way that neoconservative politics and economics have impoverished our imagination about class conflict, which was much more vivid and urgent then than it is now. Philosophically pure plutocrats have always been a bigger problem than hypocritical preachers, and Anderson's elevation of Eli Sunday to a major character says more about the politics of the Bush era than of the Harding era.[38]

Certainly the Daniel Plainview of Daniel Day-Lewis would have been as capable of staring down a labor leader as anybody else. Mindful of his intensity, Anderson wrote the screenplay with Day-Lewis in mind. Day-Lewis, for his part, had seen and liked Anderson's 2002 film *Punch Drunk Love*, an unusual love story starring the unlikely figure of *Saturday Night Live* alumnus Adam Sandler. Day-Lewis signed on to the project even before the screenplay was finished. As was true with his previous characters, he made this one wholly his own—and indeed won his second Academy Award for it.

Plainview, like his Day-Lewis predecessors, performs the paradox of projecting self-containment. But more than any of his predecessors, he moves deliberatively toward the fixed objective of mastering an independent domain, seizing opportunities and exploiting them with an element of calm deliberation that makes him seem less reactive than John Proctor, Hawkeye, Bill Cutting, or Newland Archer, all of whom are responding to events rather than consciously shaping them. Day-Lewis is able to convey this sense of methodical purpose without uttering a word; indeed, in a splendidly audacious piece of filmmaking, the first eighteen minutes of *There Will Be Blood* are silent, evoking the early days of film, but in full color with brilliant desert landscapes and the unnerving soundtrack of Radiohead's Jonny Greenwood. In a calm yet nevertheless fast-paced sequence that moves from 1898 to 1912, we watch Plainview evolve from wildcatter to small businessman. When one of his workers accidently gets killed after equipment falls down a well, Plainview adopts the man's child, H. W., as his own. We quickly realize that whatever his personal motives may have been, such a move is a shrewd investment, because it allows him to depict himself as a family man when he seeks leases from individual Californians to drill on their property.

But Plainview's virtue is beside the point: it's his power that compels our attention—and, perhaps, our reluctant admiration. Yet at the very moment of his triumph we begin to see him unravel. Some corporate types offer to buy Plainview out; they're seeking to capitalize on his hard work while willing to make him a millionaire in the process. Plainview will have none of it: what would I do with myself, he asks rhetorically. I don't know, one of the men tells him; you could spend more time with your boy. This is an innocuous remark made twice in an offhand, small-talk kind of way. Plainview's reaction the second time is utterly irrational. "Did you just tell me how to run my family?" he asks in his voice of quiet rage. "One night I'm going to come into your house, wherever you're sleeping, and cut your throat." His counterpart is stunned. "Have you gone crazy, Daniel?"

Not entirely, but he's on his way. With a mania driven by spite, Plainview not only refuses to sell but builds a pipeline to the Pacific so that he can retain control over the flow of his oil. He still cares about his family, but does so in a dysfunctional way, sending H. W. away to a special school against the boy's will. When a man shows up claiming to be his long-lost brother, Henry, Plainview accepts him into the fold. One night he confides to Henry, "I have a competition in me. I want no one else to succeed. I hate most people." He takes comfort in Henry's company. But when he figures out that Henry is not in fact his brother, Plainview's reaction is utterly cold-blooded.

Plainview's emotional and material avarice warps him into madness and self-destruction. In the last half hour of the film, which is principally set at the Plainview estate in 1927 (shot in the actual Doheny mansion), we watch the now-alcoholic Plainview alienate H. W. for good by revealing that his son is not in fact his child in a cruelly calculating manner. We also see a blackly comical showdown with the slick but desperate Eli Sunday, in which Plainview reveals he's sucked wealth right out from under the preacher (the screenplay dialogue "I drink your milkshake!" is adapted from actual testimony in the Teapot Dome Scandal.)[39] The movie culminates in a final scene of grisly violence that shows Plainview is beyond redemption. He refuses to accept affiliation—commercial or familial—of any kind. But the resulting isolation is inexorably self-destructive.

The message of *Blood* is clear: that the acquisitive imperatives at the heart of the frontier mentality, unmoored from any broader social, cultural, or affective ties, devour those who embrace them. The frontier, which more than anything else was a state of mind, here becomes an addictive end in its own right, and mindless nihilism is the result. Bill the Butcher died for something; Hawkeye and Newland Archer lived for something. But Daniel Plainview lost his way extracting wealth from the land in the name of nothing but himself. *That* frontier, a frontier that settled into the recognizably modern contours of corporate capitalism in the twenties, has been our lot ever since. There are people who keep insisting it's wide open, and the only place to live. But it's never seemed more desolate.

<hr>

To date, Daniel Day-Lewis has not made a movie about the 1960s (or a movie about the United States in the 1960s, anyway; in his 2009 film *Nine*, he plays an Italian film director modeled on Federico Fellini). But the legacy of the counterculture shadows the final character in his gallery, Jack Slavin, in his 2005 movie *The Ballad of Jack & Rose*, which is set in 1986. It's not a pretty picture, in large measure because it shows us a frontier that is not only closed but barren.

As with *The Crucible*, this was a family enterprise. *The Ballad of Jack & Rose* was written and directed by Rebecca Miller, Arthur's daughter, whom Day-Lewis met while working on *The Crucible* and married shortly thereafter. He was first offered the part before he met Miller, and turned it down.[40] As a career move, I would say that changing his mind was a mistake: this is not a very good movie (perhaps not coincidentally, it's also the only one of Day-Lewis's American sextet that isn't based on a preexisting source like a play or novel). But it is nevertheless a revealing one when juxtaposed against the rest of his work.

One reason why is a piece of subtitled information we get at the start of the movie as to its setting: "an island off the east coast of the United States." (The film was shot on Prince Edward Island.) Like Bill the Butcher fighting off interlopers on his island, Jack Slavin is also resisting the encroachments of the outside world—in this case, a real estate developer played by Beau Bridges. But the house in which Slavin has virtually barricaded himself is essentially the opposite of a frontier: it's a collapsing preserve. And it's collapsing around its protagonist, who's afflicted with a vague illness that we understand is not yet crippling but will be fatal.

Slavin is the quintessential environmentalist who loves trees and hates people. A Scottish immigrant who came to the United States and became a citizen—"I fell in love with this country, or what I thought it was going to become," he explains at one point—he used a family inheritance to buy a compound that was once a countercultural haven. But now, in the aftermath of his wife's death, the homestead is inhabited only by himself and his teenaged daughter, Rose (Camilla Belle), with whom he has a borderline incestuous relationship.

In apparent recognition of this unhealthy situation, Slavin invites a girlfriend from the mainland and her two sons to come live with them. This proves to be a poor arrangement, because Rose resents her and seeks revenge by throwing herself at the boys, one apparently gay, the other (Paul Dano, who would go on to work with Day-Lewis in *There Will Be Blood*) an exploitative lout. Slavin is progressively more enraged by him, which Rose uses as a lever to convince her father to dump his girlfriend. "I wish it could be just us like it was before," she tells him after running away and hiding in one of the developer's houses. "The happiest man in the whole world."

The very imbalance of this sentiment suggests the instability of their relationship: Rose repeatedly says that she plans to commit suicide once he dies. In the end, Slavin dies a relatively tidy death, and Rose—to whom this story really belongs—turns their home into a funeral pyre. (First he was Hawkeye, and then he was Chingachgook; now a Day-Lewis character is effectively Uncas.) We see Rose in an epilogue two years later on a Vermont collective. In effect we've come full circle, back to the edge—the far eastern edge—of Puritan New England. The frontier has become a garden. It's a much smaller world.

———

About halfway through this chapter, I mentioned that there were two different versions of the 1992 *Last of the Mohicans*. The first—the one shown in theaters and in the VHS release of the movie on home video—concludes the way most versions of the story typically do, with Chingachgook sprinkling the ashes of Uncas, declaring that he is the last of the Mohicans. It's at that point that the music swells, the camera pulls back, and the credits roll.

The second version of *Mohicans*, the "Director's Expanded Edition" DVD, was released in 1999. It includes extra battle footage at Fort William Henry, which is of some interest to military enthusiasts and cineastes wondering about how the scene was staged. But the real difference comes at the end. Cora, whom we have seen standing apart from Nathaniel and Chingachgook during the funeral rites, comes over and embraces Nathaniel. Then Chingachgook launches into a brief final monologue:

CHINGACHGOOK: The frontier moves with the sun and pushes the red men of the forests in front of it. Until one day there will be nowhere left. Then our race will be no more, or be not us.
NATHANIEL: That is my father's sadness talking.
CHINGACHGOOK: No. it is true. The frontier place is for people like my white son and his women and their children. One day there will be no more frontier. And men like you will go, too. Like the Mohicans. And new people will come. Work. Struggle. Some will make their life. But once, we were here.

Frederick Jackson Turner's "The Significance of the Frontier in American History" was a lament wrapped in hope. Turner dealt with the current of existential dread that runs through his realization that the frontier had closed by writing sunny prose and by arming himself with a Progressive faith that new frontiers would come along in the twentieth century to replace the old one. "In place of old frontiers of wilderness, there are new frontiers of unwon science, fruitful for the needs of the new race; there are frontiers of better social domains yet unexplored," he wrote ebulliently in 1914, two decades after "Significance." I can't help but be moved by the old man's lyricism: "Let us hold to our attitude of faith and courage, and creative zeal. Let us dream as our fathers dreamt and make our dreams come true."[41]

So we beat on, boats against the current. Here in the twenty-first century, the most obvious truth about the frontier myth is that mythologies themselves are finite resources. They get consumed and recycled no less than land. If there is a saving grace—or, at any rate, a rough justice—in the racist brutality that has threaded this myth, it is that the people who made it are themselves compost.

These days, I can barely order a burger at a McDonald's or watch a cable news broadcast without an Iroquois warrior (Onondaga? Oswego?) looking over my shoulder. When I'm making my bed or checking my e-mail I hear Bill the Butcher threaten Mr. Tammany fucking Hall, and Hawkeye making a joke about Uncas having many children in Kentuckeee. And from time to time, I hear the splashing water of Frederick Jackson Turner performing his ablutions on the morning of his talk on the frontier.

Go get 'em, kid. We'll wait here.

CHAPTER 3

———

Equal Work

The Mystique of Meryl Streep

Master narrative: U.S. history as a journey
for women from private to public

> This determined, abiding fascination is what she thinks of as
> her soul (an embarrassing, sentimental word, but what else to
> call it?).
>
> —Michael Cunningham, in an interior monologue
> of Virginia Woolf, *The Hours* (1998)

I can't say she didn't warn me. "The progression of roles you take strings together a portrait of an actor," Meryl Streep conceded in a 1998 profile with *Interview* magazine. "But it's a completely random process. In other words, which role was available which year has more to do with who was running a studio or who was bankrolling a particular project or who the costar was. The people who write about films always attempt to find a through line to a career. There is a through line to a life based on the choices you make, and so you can discern some things about an actor. But not necessarily a lot."[1]

The choices you make: that's the premise of this book. And that there may be more to them than you (or she) might think. Actually, there are "through lines" to Streep's life that are reasonably discernible. Like this one: she's a feminist, in the general sense of feminism as a belief in the political, economic, and social equality of the sexes.[2] Streep is legendary for the diverse array of characters she has played: not just wives, mothers, daughters, and sisters but also clerks, journalists, teachers, and politicians. All of them are strong characters who assert themselves in their respective environments. So does Streep herself, who has been active in any number of environmental or political causes over the years, particularly those related to food. In 2012, she revealed that she donated her $1 million acting fee for *The Iron Lady* (2011) as part of a larger effort on behalf of founding a National Museum of Women's History on the Mall in Washington, D.C., for which she serves as national spokesperson.[3]

Of course, to call Streep a feminist is not really to say all that much. Notwithstanding the difficulties some women, particularly younger ones, have with the term, the affirmation of gender parity is not an especially rare or unconventional proposition in U.S. society, at least as a matter of genteel public opinion. More specifically, Streep is a liberal feminist, which is to say that her version of feminism focuses more on notions of equality, as opposed to assertions of female power that rest more on ac-centuating gender difference (consider the contrast between Hillary Clin-ton and, say, Madonna in this regard).[4] Though Streep's versatility as an artist has always been widely noted, her persona, particularly in recent years, has had a distinctly bourgeois cast that appears to be the natural home of liberal feminism.[5]

As you may have noticed, there's a motif in this book that pairs the subjects of each of my chapters with real-life historical figures. I do not mean to suggest close biographical, or even conscious, ties between these people, but rather a congruence in their thinking that cuts across time, place, and profession. I've already suggested such an affinity between Clint Eastwood and Thomas Jefferson and their small-scale communi-tarianism, as well as the frontier mythology embraced by Daniel Day-Lewis and Frederick Jackson Turner. Subsequent chapters will link Denzel Washington with Malcolm X, and Tom Hanks with Abraham Lincoln. (Jodie Foster, as we'll see, is something of a special case.) For Meryl Streep, the pivotal figure is Betty Friedan (1921–2006).

In some ways, Friedan and Streep are an unlikely couple. Though she is widely remembered as the prototypical suburban housewife, Friedan's background was Jewish, midwestern, and grounded in leftist politics before she embarked on a career as a public intellectual and activist.[6] Streep, by contrast, has a largely northeastern and WASP background and has relatively few political affiliations comparable to the National Or-ganization for Women (NOW), of which Friedan was a founder in 1966. Yet both were products of elite Seven Sisters educations: Friedan at Smith; Streep at Vassar (though Vassar went co-ed while she was there). And Streep explicitly and implicitly embraces many of Friedan's positions, from pay equity to surrogate motherhood (they sided with the rights of birth mothers).[7]

Streep was fourteen years old when Friedan published *The Feminine Mystique* in 1963. Decrying the nominally celebratory, but in fact demean-ing, embrace of traditional womanhood, the book is widely considered the opening salvo of second-wave feminism.[8] Streep was part of the first generation of women whose entry into the paid labor force was given the imprimatur of both political statement and common sense in *The Feminine Mystique.* If she and her cohort faced challenges that demonstrated their struggles were far from over, they faced these obstacles confident that history was on their side.

Friedan's stock is relatively low in contemporary feminist historiography, and indeed she was a controversial figure within the women's movement even in her lifetime. In part, this reflects the ideological as well as tactical disputes endemic to social movements generally, and feminism in particular. In part, too, it reflects Friedan's feisty (or, less charitably, prickly) personality. But the principal objection raised about her work— one that retains its cogency a half century later—is its liberal provincialism. For Friedan, work was typically a matter of a career, not a job. "Hers was a thoroughly middle-class perspective," writes Christine Stansell, a leading scholar of women's history. Stansell notes that Friedan suggested housewives liberate themselves from the drudgery of housework by hiring a cleaning woman—"as if a cleaning woman did not count as an oppressed woman." (Given who cleaning women have traditionally been, Friedan's remark had a racial subtext as well.) For Friedan, Stansell observed, "there was one remedy and only one. Women had to get back to work."[9]

Streep, of course, lacks the credentials, temperament, and inclination for feminist polemics. But in the enormous variety of roles she has played in the past four decades, she has represented a diverse world of women in ways that have both brought the feminine mystique into focus and dramatized the ways they can move beyond it. But—and this is a key way in which she can be seen as truly "Friedanian"—Streep's work also follows the trajectory of Friedan's later thought, one in which she rejected the more radical elements in feminist theory by continuing to value motherhood and other aspects of domesticity *alongside* engagement in public institutional life. In her 1981 book, *The Second Stage,* Friedan warned women not to let their struggle to break the feminine mystique cause them to fall into the femin*ist* mystique and reject a truly integrated approach to gender.[10] The remarkably deft way in which Streep has illustrated this principle, a deftness that encompasses sidestepping some of the more problematic aspects of Friedan's thought (such as what some see as a homophobic current running through it) while affirming its most pragmatic and attractive dimensions, has made her an even more powerful vehicle for sustaining Friedanian thought than Friedan herself.

Streep's metanarrative of liberal feminism unfolds in three distinct stages. The first, which runs roughly through the first decade of her career, is marked by characters whose self-assertion is typically played out in their private lives, particularly as wives and mothers. Then, for a brief period in the late 1980s and early 1990s, she took a series of parts that satirically comment on gender roles, part of a broader move away from drama toward comedy. Streep's feminism shifted again at the turn of the century, this time focusing on women whose power is played out in public, institutional settings. These phases are not completely segmented, and one of the most distinctive aspects of Streep's career is the way in which she has blended her roles. Indeed, one might say that Streep's signal achievement as a feminist has taken the form of dramatizing the ways a woman can experience a full, if never easy, life with any number of public and private permutations—as well as the cost of not allowing this to happen. I nevertheless believe that these phases are reasonably distinct and usefully traced as such. The "through line" may not be entirely straight, and blurs at times. But it is one worth tracing if it allows us to see a bit more clearly how women have, and have not, changed.

———

Meryl Streep is a child of suburbia. Suburbia has had its thoughtful critics, but for her it appears to have functioned the way it has been most fondly imagined: as a kid-friendly place where an intact nuclear family, relative prosperity, and access to the metropolis nurture a garden where success and happiness twine. It is surely no accident that Streep and her husband, sculptor Don Gummer, chose to spend the majority of the time they were raising their own four children in small-town Connecticut. If the set of characters that comprise this study shows nothing else, it is that there are multiple roads to artistic achievement.

Mary Louise Streep was born on June 22, 1949, in Summit, New Jersey, the eldest of three children. Her ancestry is mostly German; one branch of her family line goes back to William Penn.[11] At the insistence of her father, a marketing executive at Merck pharmaceuticals, she was named after her mother, who after her christening (as a Presbyterian) rued the decision and started calling her Meryl. The family spent much of her childhood in Basking Ridge and Bernardstown, two towns in central New Jersey, on the western rim of metropolitan New York.[12]

The elder Mary Streep had been a commercial artist before having children and continued to work as a freelance illustrator after they were born. But motherhood was her vocation, and one that, notwithstanding the professional aspirations she nurtured for her daughter, made a deep impression on that child. Streep has referred to her mother's example frequently in her work, both in gratitude and as a source of inspiration for specific characters, whether they happen to be mothers or not.[13]

Both Streep's parents were musical—Dad played piano, Mom was a singer—and Streep had ambitions of becoming a singer herself (her younger brother Harry became a dancer and choreographer).[14] She has a beautiful singing voice that she has deployed to good effect in a number of films, among them *Postcards from the Edge, A Prairie Home Companion*, and *Mamma Mia!*

Streep's voice lessons were part of a larger cultural education that included frequent trips to the theater, musicals in particular. Still, an early love of the performing arts was only one element in the mix of a classic postwar childhood. Her 1967 high school yearbook portrait shows her to be an attractive, if somewhat unusual-looking, blonde, and the accompanying list of activities includes being named Homecoming Queen as well as membership in the National Honor Society. Interestingly, acting in school musicals is not on the list, despite the fact that she appeared in enough to engender envy among her rivals (a problem that would become familiar in the years that followed).[15]

When Streep entered Vassar in 1967, same-sex education was still the rule among elite undergraduate institutions. But that was rapidly changing; indeed, Streep was a junior when the school went co-ed in 1969. She did not like it. In particular, she objected to the way men took over leadership positions in student activities and dominated political discourse. "Everybody was a miniature Abbie Hoffman in front of a swarm of adoring girls," she remembered. "I just thought it was bullshit."[16]

Fortunately, by that point, she had carved out a domain of her own as a dramatic actor, where her talents awed her teachers. She got her first work as a professional actor with the Green Mountain Guild, a Vermont troupe, supplementing her income by working as a waitress. Streep decided within months that if she were to have a future in the business she would need graduate training, so she applied to the three-year master of fine arts program at Yale Drama School; she was accepted and awarded a scholarship. Streep's Yale years were the crucible of her career. The training she received there was the theatrical equivalent of a boot camp, fostering a range and intensity that would make much of what followed seem downright easy by comparison.[17]

But not everything. Shortly after Streep's graduation from Yale in 1975, she made the transition to the New York stage, performing with the New York Shakespeare Festival (where she met fellow actor and future fiancé John Cazale) and the Public Theater under the direction of Joseph Papp. These, too, were grueling proving grounds. By this point, however,

Streep's career was on a steep upward trajectory, earning rapturous reviews in a string of shows. She received a Tony Award nomination for
Best Actress in a 1976 production of Tennessee Williams's *27 Wagons Full
of Cotton* and was poised for stardom.

Ironically, it was television, a medium in which Streep has done relatively little work, that made her a household name. After landing a small
part in the 1977 NBC movie *The Deadliest Season*, as the wife of a hockey
player, Streep was cast in a leading role in *Holocaust*, a 1978 ABC miniseries that followed in the wake of the hugely successful *Roots* (1976). She
played Inga Helms Weiss, the gentile wife of a Jewish artist (James
Woods), whose prosperous family is sucked into the Nazi vortex. *Holocaust* was not as successful as *Roots* in terms of its reception or subsequent
reputation, but it premiered during the golden age of television as a mass
medium and was viewed by some 120 million people, roughly half of the
U.S. population.[18] Streep, who won an Emmy for her work in the multipart series, nevertheless correctly described her role in *Holocaust* as "unre-
lentingly noble" and says she took it largely for the money, as her fiancé,
Cazale, was terminally ill with cancer. Upon her return from shooting the
series in Austria, Streep nursed him until his death.[19] (She began dating,
and married, Don Gummer later the same year.) Streep returned to television in 1997 as the mother of an epileptic child in *First Do No Harm*, for
which she was also nominated for an Emmy. She won her second Emmy
for her work in the 2003 HBO miniseries *Angels in America*, in a tour de
force clutch of parts that included Ethel Rosenberg, an angel, and, most
amusingly, an almost unrecognizable elderly male rabbi.

It was in movies, however, that Streep made her stand. Her first film
role was small but significant: a snarky friend of playwright Lillian Hellman in the 1977 film *Julia*, which starred Vanessa Redgrave in the title
role and Jane Fonda as Hellman, both of whom won Oscars. Though
generically related to the "woman's film" or "weepie" that was a staple of
moviemaking in the mid-twentieth century, *Julia* was packaged and perceived as a sign of the new power and prestige of women in the movie
business in a feminist age. While this would prove to be a false dawn,
Streep's association with the project positioned her as A-level talent.
Fonda, twelve years Streep's senior and a feminist trailblazer in the movie
business, conferred her blessing: "This one will go far," she told director
Fred Zinnemann.[20]

Fonda was right. But Streep has always had her critics, and they have
come in a variety of forms. Some criticism has been the result of her early
uneasiness with her peers, a problem that dogged her throughout her
high school, college, and graduate education.[21] Streep has also had critics

who have been less than enchanted by her style of acting. She can hardly be faulted on her technique, and her mastery of voices and accents—she learned Polish as part of her work in her Oscar-winning performance in *Sophie's Choice*, used a Danish accent for *Out of Africa*, and has spoken the queen's English in roles that range from the Victorian servant of *The French Lieutenant's Woman* in 1981 to *The Iron Lady* thirty years later— has been dazzling. But to some that's precisely the problem: her acting calls attention to itself. Katharine Hepburn told her biographer Scott Berg that she considered Streep among her least favorite contemporary actresses, dismissing her with this bitchy appraisal: "click, click, click."[22]

The best known, and most damaging, of Streep's critics was Pauline Kael (who, as you may recall, was not particularly fond of Clint East- wood, either, though for the opposite reason: she didn't think he was an actor at all). Over the course of her first decade or so in movies, Kael as- serted that Streep acted "only from the neck up," speculating that "in her zeal to be an honest actress, she allows nothing to escape her conception of a performance." Kael, too, could be bitchy, describing Streep as "our lady of the accents." In 1994, three years after Kael's retirement, Streep offered her reaction to such criticism: "It's so awful that someone you admire hates what you do." Later, she was less diplomatic. "You know what I think?" she asked in 2008, seven years after Kael's death. "That Pauline was a poor Jewish girl at Berkeley with all these rich Pasadena WASPs with long blonde hair, and their heartlessness got to her; then, years later, she saw me." *New York Times* reviewer Elvis Mitchell came to his former colleague's defense: "Kael being quite dead, she can't address Streep's psy- choanalysis, but one might also think she wouldn't have gotten far as a critic if she relentlessly avenged these theorized college slights with unde- served digs against everyone on screen with long blonde hair, a not un- common feature for an actress. One might think it's possible to simply not like Streep's acting style." Hepburn and Kael weren't the only ones who could be bitchy.[23]

Still, on balance, it's hard not to be impressed by her overall equanimity, particularly in the context of far more crude dismissals. In a 2008 interview with *Entertainment Weekly*, Streep claimed that during her audition for a leading role in *King Kong* (1976), a part that ultimately went to Jessica Lange, producer Dino De Laurentiis asked his son in Italian, with Streep in the room, "Why did you send me this pig? This woman is so ugly!" Streep responded in Italian, "I'm very sorry that I disappoint you."[24]

Even in the case of a high-prestige project like *Out of Africa*, and an enlightened director like the late Sydney Pollack, Streep felt forced to contend with traditional ideas of femininity. In a documentary on the making of the film, she described Pollack as believing she was not sexy enough to play the part of Isak Dinesen and said she wrangled a meeting with him to further discuss the part. "I went, pathetically, to that meeting in a very low-cut blouse with a push-up bra," she recalled. "I'm really ashamed to say that I did, and it worked. That's the really sad part." Streep related the story lightheartedly, but her tone never entirely undercut the words. Subsequently, when James Lipton interviewed Streep for *Inside the Actors Studio*, he noted that he had recently interviewed Pollack, who reported no such recollection. "I knoooow," she replied to laughter. "He probably doesn't remember. You know, he probably doesn't remember that was the thing. But"—she pauses for comic effect—"that *was* the thing."[25]

Of course, she could afford to be magnanimous. Streep has had about as charmed a professional life as a woman could have had in the American Century, which is a way of saying that it's been charmed indeed, and yet faintly damning those who have smudged the quality of that life. Streep has noted that she does not have a production company the way many male movie stars, among them Eastwood and Hanks, do. "I don't have anybody directing my career, it just depends on what scripts come," she said in 2010. "If I like them I do them."[26] Now in her sixties, she has been phenomenally productive, with dozens of films to her credit, among them four movies in 2007 alone.

In an important sense, Streep's entire career has been a matter of using her talent and power to give voice to women. That career began at a propitious time; she had more opportunities than her predecessors did. But it also began in a culturally conservative one that decisively shaped Streep's feminism. The product of an anti-institutional moment, her statements on behalf of women took, if not an *anti*-institutional tone, then a largely *non*-institutional one: the political was personal. Generally speaking, early Streep characters dwell in a private sphere, not a public one. Even exceptions to this rule, like her role as a politico in the largely forgettable 1979 film *The Seduction of Joe Tynan*, foreground romantic concerns while relegating her professional work to the margins. Over time, her characters have become more forceful, public, and powerful people. Yet she has managed to bridge the divide between both spheres, endowing her characters with a wholeness and dignity rarely seen in public discourse. It's *this* mystique that has made Streep's body of work miraculous.

Though, as I've indicated, Meryl Streep underwent a long and rigorous apprenticeship, and did some relatively high-profile television and film work in the late seventies, the movie that turned her into an "overnight sensation" in 1978 was *The Deer Hunter*. In part, that's because the film, which won an Academy Award for Best Picture, was a sensation in its own right and became a Hollywood legend for a whole host of reasons. One was that its success led United Artists to give director Michael Cimino broad license for his next film, *Heaven's Gate* (1980), whose colossal cost overruns helped plunge the studio into bankruptcy. Another was that it was among the first major Hollywood films to deal with the Vietnam War and included a notorious plotline involving Russian roulette as a betting game among the Vietnamese. A third was its extraordinarily gifted cast—which included Robert De Niro, Christopher Walken, and Streep's fiancé, John Cazale, in the final appearance of his brief but brilliant career—that showcased a new generation of actors.

Streep's character, a supermarket checkout girl named Linda, provides crucial ballast for this male-dominated cast. We first see her on the morning of a friend's wedding, in a gaudy pink bridesmaid's dress, making breakfast for her alcoholic father. When she brings it to him, he assaults her. But Linda is not a passive victim. When we next see her, it's at the bungalow that her boyfriend, Nick (Walken), shares with his buddy Michael (De Niro), making a plan with Nick to stay in their place while the two are in the army. She may look willowy, but she's got a spine.

Linda's mettle threads the movie. De Niro's Michael has a soft spot for her, but he's not going to steal his buddy's girlfriend. Linda, however, shows interest in taking up with him. At one point, she takes the sexual initiative with Michael, managing to maintain both her poise and her feeling for him despite his inability to overtly return affection. In her scenes with De Niro, Streep deploys a tactic that would become a standard part of her thespian repertoire: looking directly at her acting partner, then turning her head away, her eyes cast down, sometimes rolling her eyes as she does so in moments of levity or irony (we viewers are ever-so-briefly in on the joke). What's quite striking about this technique is that it manages to convey shyness and assertiveness simultaneously—feminine feminism, as it were. This delicate balance goes to the heart of her performance in *The Deer Hunter*, in which her character is largely at the mercy of events beyond her control, but still manages to quietly express herself in ways that are both moving and life-affirming.

In her next two movies, *Manhattan* and *The Seduction of Joe Tynan* (both 1979), Streep played professional women, a writer and a politico respectively. As such, these characters are prototypes for a post-feminine-mystique order. Significantly, however, they are women whose careers are secondary to their sexual relationships with men. *Manhattan* is a fabled work in Woody Allen's writing/directing career, but one whose May-December romance with the high school student played by Mariel Hemingway would never fly in terms of contemporary mores, even without the later controversy surrounding Allen's relationship with his adoptive stepdaughter. Streep plays his ex-wife, Jill, who now has a lesbian lover and is writing a tell-all about her marriage with Allen's character, Isaac Davis. A walking stereotype of the feminist as castrating bitch, Jill's character as written is so over-the-top as to amount to misogyny. But Streep endows her with a confidence and intensity that makes her almost appealing. Still, there's only so far that can go. Jill only has two scenes in the movie and is defined in terms of being a foil for Allen's persona, right down to her literary career, which consists of turning her personal life into commerce in the form of a book with the title *Marriage, Love and Divorce.* ("Look at you, you're so threatened," she says amusedly to Isaac, even as we know he is right to be.)

Far more important was her third film of 1979, *Kramer vs. Kramer*, for which she won an Academy Award as Best Supporting Actress. Streep plays Joanna Kramer, an emotionally distraught woman who leaves her husband and son to find herself. Far more than any other character in the Streep canon, Kramer is a vivid embodiment of what Friedan called "the problem with no name," which she described in terms of "the growing despair of women who have forfeited their own existence, although by so doing they may also have evaded that lonely, frightened feeling that always comes with freedom."[27] The movie shows her claiming that freedom and the price it exacts from her as well as from her husband and son.

Ideologically, Joanna Kramer is a tough sell. In part, the rhetorical deck is stacked against her in the source material for the movie, Avery Corman's 1977 novel, which, for all its good intentions, has a distinctly male point of view. ("Feminists will applaud me," his Joanna declares when she leaves her husband at their New York apartment, in stilted dialogue that characterizes the book.)[28] It's also because Streep's co-star, Dustin Hoffman, was a strong-minded actor with figurative weight he wasn't afraid to throw around. Streep, who was married and had her first child by 1979, took the part as a matter of conviction, determined to make a case for Joanna as a woman who loved her child but who was in too much personal anguish to continue without respite. "I think that if there's anything that runs through all my work, all my characters, it's that I have a relationship with them where I feel I have to defend them," she said.[29]

UNEASY EMBRACE: Streep as Joanna Kramer, reuniting with her son even as she looks back at her ex-husband (Dustin Hoffman), in *Kramer vs. Kramer* (1979). "If there's anything that runs through all my work, all my characters, it's that I have a relationship with them where I feel I have to defend them," she said of her feelings for the character. *(Columbia Pictures)*

Streep made her case for Joanna Kramer by arguing for changes in the script, successfully persuading director Robert Benton to rewrite her courtroom testimony for custody of the couple's son toward the end of the film. In particular, she added a key line responding to assertions that Ted Kramer had been the primary parent for the couple's child for eighteen months by noting that Joanna had been so for five and a half years. "We listened," Benton later explained. "And she became the real Mrs. Kramer."[30]

But that Mrs. Kramer remains first and foremost a mother. In the book, her career aspirations, which turn out to involve working as a clerk for Hertz, become a source of bitter humor: "She left her family, her child, to go to California to rent cars," Joanna's own mother notes incredulously to Ted.[31] In the movie, Joanna testifies that she's a sportswear designer. While Ted's career in advertising is central to the course of the movie, this passing mention is all we hear about Joanna's. Any work outside the home is incidental.

Streep continued to play strong-minded women in all of her film roles of the 1980s, but the power her characters wield is generally in the shadows cast by male characters. She landed a high-profile double role in the 1981 film *The French Lieutenant's Woman*, based on the 1969 novel of the same name by John Fowles. It would not appear to be particularly promising movie material, except that it was skillfully adapted by playwright and fellow Briton Harold Pinter, who created a parallel movie-within-a-movie plot involving late-twentieth-century actors making a romantic drama set in the Victorian era. Interestingly, the film also grapples with some of the same issues as *The Feminine Mystique*. "It is my thesis that as the Victorian culture did not permit women to accept or gratify their basic sexual needs, our culture does not permit women to accept or gratify their basic need to grow and fulfill their potentialities as human beings, a need which is not solely defined by their sexual role," Friedan wrote.[32]

As such the film suggests both the possibilities and limits of feminist vision. The two pairs of main characters in *The French Lieutenant's Woman*, played by Jeremy Irons and Streep, are both in love. Their fates appear to hinge on their different historical circumstances. In one case Streep is an abandoned woman, left desolate by the unseen French lieutenant of the title, who insists on lingering as a social outcast in a seaside town until she becomes a source of growing fascination for the affianced gentleman played by Irons. In the other, her character is a privileged professional actor in metropolitan London, empowered to conduct an extramarital affair and largely dictate its conditions to the (also married) Irons. But as with the novel, the point of the movie is very much that things are not what they seem. The French lieutenant's woman has more resources, principal among them the power to beguile, than her pursuer realizes. And while the professional woman is, in the parlance of the time, "liberated," the problems she is seen grappling with are primarily romantic. (It might have been interesting, for example, to have a scene with her arguing with her director about the portrayal of her character.) I don't want to go overboard in emphasizing how the bottle is half empty here: women are central to both plotlines. But in retrospect their compass of action seems limited, precisely because the overt tenor of the discourse is emancipatory.

The same might be said for *Still of the Night* (1982), in which Streep is a blue-blooded antique dealer named Brooke Reynolds, who may or may not have anything to do with the murder of a man who was undergoing psychoanalysis at the time of his death. Nor is Streep any more compelling as a housewife in *Falling in Love* (1984), much ballyhooed at the time of its release for her reunion with De Niro. This time the two play married Westchester suburbanites who reluctantly fall in love courtesy of the Metro North commuter railroad. For all the variety of these characters—ingénue, femme fatale, housewife—they still seem circumscribed in gender archetypes, however much Streep stretches them.

Even a movie that seems a world away—1985 Best Picture *Out of Africa*, set in colonial Kenya—turns out to be pretty much the same old story. *Africa* is, from a visual standpoint, simply gorgeous. But its racial politics amount to little more than a postcard for imperialism, and its gender politics are also finally retrograde. For once of many times, Streep plays a real person, Danish writer Karen Blixen, later known to the world by her pen name, Isak Dinesen (1885–1962). From the start, we see her as a maverick figure. During a frigid European hunting expedition, she proposes a marriage of convenience with a friend, Baron von Blixen-Finecke (an amiable Klaus Maria Brandauer), whereby the two will start a dairy farm in Kenya, which turns out to be a coffee plantation because he changes his mind without telling her. Mrs. Blixen arrives in Kenya and blithely walks into a men's-only private club, causing a stir. (Naturally, they'll collectively stand her a drink by the time the movie is over.) She also takes a strong hand in running the plantation, not only because her husband would rather go hunting, but also because that's the kind of woman she is—a woman who, when she receives a message from her husband asking her to send supplies to him and British soldiers fighting the Germans in East Africa in the First World War, insists on trekking across dangerous terrain and delivering them in person (with a retinue, of course). But none of this, or even a Blixen writing career we know about chiefly through the flashback voice-over device that frames the film, can compete with the romantic charms of Robert Redford, who plays her British lover Denys Finch Hatton with an incongruous American accent. Redford is admittedly a powerful draw, but their relationship—she pining away while he repeatedly takes off—puts the film in *very* familiar grooves.

By contrast, *Heartburn* (1986) suggests progress. Streep again plays a real person, in this case the journalist, later turned writer/director, Nora Ephron. ("It's a little depressing to know that if you go to an audition to play yourself, you would lose to Meryl," Ephron later joked.[33]) The film, directed by Mike Nichols, is based on the 1983 roman à clef of the same name, both of which chronicle the rise and fall of Ephron's marriage to *Washington Post* writer Carl Bernstein, played by Jack Nicholson. It's refreshing to note that we *do* see Streep's character in workplace settings, unlike her husband, known to the world for his role in breaking the Watergate story. Not surprisingly, her working style is more fluid—the personal and professional aspects of her life are apparent both in her showing up for meetings pregnant and in her warm relationship with her younger boss, played by Jeff Daniels, who appears wistfully attracted to her. Moreover, the movie ends with its protagonist leaving Bernstein because of his infidelity without another man waiting in the wings, an overt break with the normal logic of romantic storytelling. Such an approach makes real demands of an audience, even a predominately female audience, and the pitch for its sympathy for the protagonist is further strained by the obvious elite status of a woman who can afford to be divorced, even with children. No doubt about it: this is a feminist movie, of the kind Friedan would approve. But it is decisively feminism of the private sector.

There were some Streep projects of the 1980s in which the nongendered aspects of her character's life were truly important. In *Plenty* (1985), based on the David Hare play, she is Susan Traherne, a British woman whose small but dramatic role in the French Resistance during World War II, depicted in the opening sequence, makes everything that happens in her life subsequently pale by comparison. We see her in a number of jobs, among them a cushy one in advertising, whose mindlessness infuriates her. Traherne has a tryst with another operative (Sam Neill) early in her life, from which she never recovers, subsequently marrying a diplomat (Charles Dance) whom she treats with indifference that sometimes crosses the line into cruelty. The same can be said of a prior relationship with a young working-class man (Sting) with whom she seeks to father a child without attachments. In the context of her career, *Plenty* is a fascinating experiment for Streep: she plays a stunningly unpleasant character.

Streep did make a couple of movies in which her synthesis of public and private feminism was far more successful from both an ideological and an artistic standpoint. The best example is *Silkwood* (1983). Streep is the title character, a real-life metallurgy worker at a nuclear power plant in Oklahoma. Divorced, with children who live with their father, Silkwood shares a house with two co-workers, her lover (Kurt Russell) and a lesbian friend (Cher). The rhythms of their everyday life, both in terms of casual humor and domestic tensions, seem more authentic and contemporary than those of *The Deer Hunter*. "That's the thing I'm most proud of in this movie," she said in 1983. "It accurately depicts the work force and how people keep their sense of humor no matter how bad things get."[34]

Streep plays Silkwood with a low-key antiauthoritarian attitude, rendering her as an appealingly profane, pot-smoking good ol' girl who at one point flashes her breast on the job as a riposte to some heckling men. That antiauthoritarian disposition hardens as she gradually realizes that inadequate safety measures endanger workers at the plant, danger that ultimately engulfs Silkwood herself. Her growing labor activism attracts attention in Washington, but at the cost of multiple personal relationships, with men and women alike, among them Russell, who nevertheless still loves her. The real Karen Silkwood died in murky circumstances in a 1974 car accident, just as revelations at the plant where she worked were about to go public (they would ultimately force its closure). Some critics disliked the ambiguity of the film's ending, which was aesthetically as well as politically unsatisfying.[35] But Streep's Silkwood herself belongs in the pantheon of her characters for the fully integrated quality of her life, a truly three-dimensional feminism of family, friendship, and work of the kind one rarely sees in movies.

Another noteworthy example of such three-dimensionality is Streep's turn as Helen Archer, a fictional character in the 1987 film *Ironweed*, based on William Kennedy's Pulitzer Prize–winning novel. This may seem like an odd statement, in that the movie is about homeless alcoholics in the Depression-era Albany of 1938. (Streep is paired again with Nicholson, an impressive piece of teamwork when one considers they played a Washington, D.C., power couple the previous year in *Heartburn*.) Helen, cut off from her family, is jobless and nearly hopeless. But we learn she was once a singer in concerts and on the radio. At one point she, Nicholson, and a friend (Tom Waits) wander into a local nightclub and chat up the bartender (Fred Gwynne), a former singer and recovering alcoholic himself. When Helen ingenuously gushes about his singing and mentions that she too once performed, he insists she take the stage and sing a tune. Helen tentatively begins a version of "He's Me Pal," a pop standard circa 1900, which she dedicates to Nicholson. But her performance gains in intensity—Streep's singing talents are put to very good use here—and the room takes on a remarkable glow, even if her teeth are blackened and her clothes tattered. Helen finishes to rousing applause. "My God, Helen, this is as good as it gets. You were born to be a star," Nicholson tells her. "You think so?" she replies, tentative pleasure in her voice, and the two kiss, protected from view by their hats, the iconic image that became the movie's poster.

As we've been suspecting, though, it's all been a fantasy. The camera cuts to Helen finishing her song, much less impressively than imagined, to a crowd that's less impressive, and less impressed, than imagined. (Her man is still waiting for her, though, and the kind bartender, ironically, buys her a drink.) It's a beautifully heartbreaking moment in a vivid but painful movie. It also represents a rare moment of fusion in a woman's life, where she is doing something she loves in a public setting for a man she loves, and that man is there to support and savor labors that generate positive attention from the crowd, even if not as much as we wish for her. Helen is a tragic figure precisely because her vision of a career was not a mere illusion, just as Nicholson's love for her is both real and destructive.

I've been applying a specific litmus test to Streep's work here, measuring the degree to which her characters stretch beyond the confines of the feminine mystique in a (Reagan) era when the Equal Rights Amendment failed to come to fruition and an antifeminist backlash took root.[36] But even as she made some efforts to stretch boundaries, Streep was no ideologue. It's notable, then, that two of Streep's greatest performances were a matter of embodying women whose gender identities—particularly the gender identity of mother—are avowedly at the center of who they understand themselves to be.

The first is what for a long time was Streep's signature role, that of Polish émigré Sophie Zawistowski in *Sophie's Choice* (1982), for which she won her second Oscar, this time for Best Actress. The movie, based on the semiautobiographical 1979 novel by William Styron, is presented from the point of view of an aspiring novelist named Stingo, who moves to Brooklyn in 1947 after finishing his education in the South. He rents a room in a large house whose residents include a vivacious couple, a dashing Jew named Nathan (Kevin Kline) and Streep's mysterious and alluring Sophie, a Polish-Catholic refugee who fled Nazi Germany. The three enjoy each other's company, but it becomes increasingly apparent to Stingo that Nathan, who presents himself as a high-powered chemist, is a fraud as well as a schizophrenic prone to jealous rage.

Though Nathan is demonstrably insane, he is right in one respect: Stingo is falling in love with Sophie. She, too, is not who she appears to be: she claims her father was an anti-Nazi professor, though we later learn he was an anti-Semitic apologist for the regime. Sophie had a lover in the resistance movement in occupied Poland, who was caught and executed. Sophie herself was caught smuggling a ham for her dying mother and sent to Auschwitz with her two children. With almost unimaginable cruelty, a camp official tells her she must choose which of her children should live. She chooses her son, who is sent to a concentration camp (we don't learn anything beyond that), while her daughter goes to a crematorium. It is a scene as wrenching as any in modern cinema.

Streep's performance is awe-inspiring on many levels, most obviously in the way she reverse-engineered her way to English as a second language by learning Polish. As with *The French Lieutenant's Woman*, she compels attention by managing to hold something in reserve that you can sense without ever being told. In his analysis of her performance, film scholar James Naremore notes that "unlike the typical nineteenth-century performers, who tended to arrange their faces in a picture to indicate 'grief,' Streep tries to register a repressed emotion, so that her look communicates something more like 'grief held in check by an attempt to remain calm.' "[37] Such techniques telegraph a tragic outcome, even as Stingo desperately flees Nathan's murderous rage with her. But Sophie simply cannot relinquish the horror of the past. Indeed, one suspects her decision to cast her lot with Nathan after the war, a man who abuses her and with whom she can never finally be happy, is an act of self-sabotage.

One might superficially compare Sophie with other mysterious Streep characters like the French lieutenant's woman. Even without her Holocaust backstory, though, there's a gravity to Sophie that suggests a knowledge and experience beyond her role as Nathan's housewife. In a 1983 interview, Streep responded to a journalist's question about whether Sophie worked while living in New York by saying, "Yeah. Not that we ever saw. But yeah, she worked. Still, that wasn't what that movie was about."[38] Instead, what it's about is a mother's grief. Sophie indulges Stingo with a night of fantasy, but returns to Nathan, with whom she commits suicide. The tragedy of her death is a life defined in terms of others.

Sophie's Choice was a showcase for Streep's talents. But her acting in *A Cry in the Dark* (1988) is all the more powerful for its understated quality. Here she's another true-life character, Australian Lindy Chamberlain, who became ensnared in a media maelstrom in 1980 after she was accused of murdering her infant daughter despite her insistence that the child had been killed by a dingo, a wild dog indigenous to Australia, during a camping trip. Streep mastered yet another accent for this role, but it's the helmeted quality of Chamberlain's expression, the puritanical mien of a committed Seventh-Day Adventist, that she captures in her performance. *A Cry in the Dark* performed poorly at the U.S. box office, probably because American viewers were not widely familiar with the scandal, and because the material is so difficult. Streep nevertheless earned yet another Oscar nomination for the role.

By the end of the 1980s, then, Streep was not simply a movie star but a cinematic brand—a virtuoso known for high-wire characterizations in artistically challenging dramas. Asked by a film professor at the University of Kansas in 1988 whether she still took a secret delight in jumping into a movie with a new face on, Streep said yes with a laugh. "It's part of what I get criticized for," she noted. "But that's what the joy of it is for me."[39]

In the years that followed, Streep began seeking out somewhat different joys.

In 1989, Meryl Streep turned forty. By that point, she had crossed into "woman of a certain age" territory, and as such had entered rocky shoals. It has long been the conventional wisdom that female stars fade fast in Hollywood. While there have always been exceptions that have ranged from Katharine Hepburn to Susan Sarandon, illustrations of premature commercial fades—Meg Ryan, Michelle Pfeiffer, and Melanie Griffith, all a decade *younger* than Streep—are not hard to generate. Though she has never gone more than three years without appearing in a movie, and has appeared in two or more movies in the same year a dozen times, there is a general perception that Streep's star power dimmed in the 1990s. Partly this was a matter of choice; these were years when she was actively raising children, and logistical considerations, like the locale of a shoot, have often been factors for her. Undeniably, though, the quality of the roles she took was sometimes weaker, principally when the women she played were so saintly as to lack the edgy interest of a Joanna Kramer or Karen Silkwood. Still, Streep was never a passive recipient of parts, and while it's clear that she acted on instinct, there's notable consistency in batches of choices that she made in the second decade of her career.

The first such batch of choices involved a set of roles that satirically deconstructed the idea of womanhood itself. The conventional wisdom is that after ten years of appearing in serious drama, Streep made a leap into comedy. This was indeed a shift, and while critical and commercial reception was initially mixed, it proved to be a durable one: Streep has been a reliable cinematic source of laughter ever since. It's those first few movies, especially a quartet of films she made between 1989 and 1992, that I want to focus on here. Though they were not highly regarded, they're strikingly coherent in the way they play with notions of gender.

The first and perhaps most obvious example is *She-Devil* (1989). In what was widely regarded at the time as an odd piece of casting, Streep's co-star was Roseanne Barr, a stand-up comedian approaching the peak of her status as a working-class icon of feminism on the strength of her hit TV series, *Roseanne* (1988–97). The dramatic contrast between the aristocratic-looking Streep and dumpy-looking Barr, which was played to the hilt, is essentially the core premise of the movie. *She-Devil*, based on British writer Fay Weldon's 1983 novel, *The Life and Loves of a She-Devil*, had been made into a four-part BBC television series in 1986. The main storyline of all iterations involves a housewife and mother named Ruth Patchett, whose accountant husband leaves her for a famous romance novelist named Mary Fisher. Patchett systematically responds to this betrayal by dismantling the public and private pillars of her husband's and Mary's life. In its explosive garishness—at one point Ruth blows up her house so that she can dump her kids with her husband and Mary—the film version of *She-Devil* makes the BBC series seem downright prim by comparison. Barr goes out of her way to accentuate ugliness as Ruth (as in ruth*less*), though she'll undergo a transformation before it's all over.

But it's Streep's performance that endows the movie with a comic zing by giving us a Mary Fisher who's both sharply observed and almost impossibly over-the-top at the same time. The funniest scene in the movie is a *Lifestyles of the Rich and Famous* profile by the real-life host of the series, Robin Leach. "They find ways to make the man feel important and comfortable," the aptly named Fisher says of her novels, her blond tresses framed by a pink dress, pink nails, and poodle with pink ribbons. Mary later condescendingly marvels about "all the little families, mommies and daddies and dear little children tucked away for the night. How lucky they all are." She will of course get her comeuppance, and Streep is as at least as game in playing her descent, already under way when she snappishly evades being caught in a lie about her age.

Ruth, for her part, begins her revival by entering the workforce, something she does in the service of retribution, but which results in an entrepreneurial venture that empowers her employees. These strongly feminist accents are undercut a bit, in that the story ends with Ruth's husband rejoining the family after his release from prison for embezzlement, which she helped expose: why would she want the lout back? Mary ultimately recovers from a tepidly received final novel—she's seen painfully ignored at a mall book-signing—to reinvent herself with a memoir, *Trust and Betrayal: A Docu-novel of Love, Money and Skepticism* (our last view of her is at a bookstore signing flirting with a charming Frenchman). Revenge may be sweet, but it need not be complete. Besides, the Other Woman was never the primary problem anyway; the feckless man was.

Streep followed up *She-Devil* with the more upscale comedy *Postcards from the Edge* (1990), based on Carrie Fisher's 1987 autobiographical novel about recovery from addiction set among the Hollywood elite. Though it's less pointed in its gender politics than *She-Devil*, the Mike Nichols–directed *Postcards* is nevertheless a departure for Streep. For the first time—and surprisingly late at that—she is a daughter rather than a mother, as the struggling adult child of a major star, presumably Fisher's famous mother, Debbie Reynolds, played by Shirley MacLaine.

There's a pleasant postmodern fizz to *Postcards*, in that it calls attention to its own artifice. The film opens with a dramatic sequence about a drug cartel that turns out to be a movie-within-a-movie, though the narcotics angle is real enough: Streep's character, actor Suzanne Vale, is fired for taking a snort in her trailer. At other points in the movie, we learn that what we think is a city street is really a movie set, and Streep spends a long stretch of the film ironically wearing a police officer's costume.

Though much of the plot turns on her relationship with a wayward playboy producer (Dennis Quaid), her character's struggle is typical of that facing the boy seeking to become a man: What will I do with my life? How do I emerge from the shadow of a powerful parent and gain my own public identity? How will romance fit into, as opposed to define, this picture? The script, also written by Fisher, concludes by suggesting that Suzanne has begun to resolve these questions.

Postcards, then, had some serious currents running through it, notwithstanding its comic tone. By contrast, Streep's next movie, *Defending Your Life* (1991), proceeds from a presumably grave question—what happens after we die?—but is so light it almost floats off the screen. Writer/director Albert Brooks plays Daniel Miller, a morose Los Angeles advertising executive who drives his brand-new luxury car into an oncoming bus and dies. He awakens in "Judgment City," a kind of purgatory where the events of his life are reviewed through a judicial hearing that will decide whether he will graduate to a higher form of consciousness or be forced to repeat human life in what amounts to Southern California Hinduism. Fortunately, Judgment City is a pleasant place to pass the time; you can eat all you want for free and never gain an ounce. While there, Daniel meets his dream girl, Julia (Streep), who is charmed by his jokes. There are lots of comic bits about Julia's higher standard of living in Judgment City, owing to the fact that she was a nicer person than Daniel was. Despite their divergent verdicts, true love conquers all, even in heaven.

Streep agreed to act in *Defending Your Life* because she was charmed when Brooks pitched it to her, poolside, while she was filming *Postcards from the Edge*. But her motives in taking the role seem to have been in part a matter of playful experimentation with gender expectations. "I know Albert feels he's written a whole woman, a completely full-blown person," she said in a 1991 *New York Times* profile. "I didn't know how to break it to him, he's really not done that. He's written an idea of a woman. And I did my best to fill those silver slippers. But it was also fun. I thought, 'Ah, the hell with it. You're dead. You can do whatever you want.'"[40]

Streep's next movie, *Death Becomes Her* (1992), was a black comedy on the order of *She-Devil*. Like *She-Devil*, this is a story of romantic rivalry, but its main theme is a veritable American obsession: aging, a subject especially vexing for women. (It's also one that engaged Friedan, who wrote a 1993 book, *The Fountain of Age*, on the subject.) Streep's character is an actress who steals and marries the plastic surgeon boyfriend (Bruce Willis) of her frenemy (Goldie Hawn). Hawn's character, plunged into despair and obesity, ends up in a psychiatric ward but, like Ruth Patchett, gets rejuvenated by the prospect of revenge. Her antagonist, meanwhile, has also aged and gained weight, while the alcoholic plastic surgeon is reduced to working as a mortician. Unbeknownst to the other, each of the women imbibes a magic potion that reverses the effect of aging. The film moves into slapstick overdrive as the women commit grotesque acts of violence against each other, none of which is fatal. (*Death Becomes Her* won an Academy Award for its special effects.)[41] Ironically, though the two women reconcile, they find themselves dependent on the plastic surgeon to spruce up their brittle, if immortal, bodies, until, even more ironically, they find themselves dependent on each other. The movie thus ends on a comic, though not particularly satisfying, be-careful-what-you-wish-for note. *Death Becomes Her*, like other Streep films of the period, nevertheless makes an important point: that the feminine mystique attacked by Friedan was hardly a relic of the past three decades later, even among people who might have thought of themselves as beyond it.

Streep's relaxed, often comic, approach to aging would be ongoing. In the short term, her interests in the mid-nineties involved deepening her gender inquiry on another front by making a foray into a typically male enclave: the action-adventure film. Her next movie, *The River Wild* (1994), is set on the Salmon River in Idaho, where a Boston-based couple with marital problems (Streep and the always excellent David Strathairn) take their tween son on a whitewater rafting trip. By coincidence, they depart at the same time as violent criminals who are fleeing a robbery. Streep's character, Gail, is an expert oarswoman with experience navigating dangerous rapids. Kevin Bacon's well-played villain, Wade, wants her help but bides his time with a friendly demeanor that fools her and her son but not her husband. In a carefully calibrated exercise in equality feminism, the family is saved by both Gail's bravery and her expertise, along with crucial contributions from her husband. Gail, though, is the central player in the drama, the one who pulls the trigger for its resolution. Though predictable and forced, *The River Wild* represents an interesting experiment with genre in the context of Streep's career.

It was an experiment all the more notable because by mid-decade there were signs Streep's career was losing steam, not only commercially but artistically as well. One critic described her box office appeal as "waning," though Streep attributed this perception to a shift in moviegoing attitudes, in that most of her (female) audience was seeing her films on video.[42] In terms of aesthetics, the problem was not Streep's performances but that the material she was choosing seemed thinner, at least in gender terms.

Her 1993 movie *House of the Spirits*, based on the 1982 multigenerational saga by Chilean writer Isabel Allende, was unusual in a number of respects, among them its Latin American setting, the narrative's magical realism, and a stellar cast that included Jeremy Irons, Winona Ryder, and Antonio Banderas. Disappointingly, Streep plays a bland, saintly matriarch. The same problem afflicts *Before and After* (1996), in which she is a New England wife, mother, and doctor whose life is plunged into turmoil when her adolescent son is accused of murder. Though her husband (Liam Neeson) has all kinds of ideas about how to protect him, and a sharp lawyer (Alfred Molina) has a clever strategy for getting an acquittal, Mother Knows Best that Honesty is the Best Policy.

More interesting is Streep's performance as Francesca Johnson, the expatriate midwestern housewife and mother who savors a brief interlude of infidelity in *The Bridges of Madison County* (1995). Directed by Clint Eastwood, this is one of those movies—*The Devil Wears Prada*, to be described below, is another—that is vastly better than the treacly (1992) book on which it is based. A major reason is Streep's minutely observed performance, bolstered by her good chemistry with Eastwood. The core point of the film—spouses and mothers are far more complicated than many people, particularly their children, imagine—is worthwhile. It should give anyone, male or female, pause before describing someone as "just" a housewife.

This point is made in a somewhat different form in *One True Thing* (1998), based on the Anna Quindlen novel, in which Streep plays Kate Gulden, a Martha Stewartesque housewife whose conventionality and fidelity to her inconstant professor husband (William Hurt) appall her ambitious journalist daughter (Renée Zellweger), particularly after Kate is diagnosed with terminal cancer. But it's Kate who's appalled by her daughter's suggestion that she turn her domestic pursuits into commercial opportunities, and she must ultimately explain to her that the work of nurturing people, whether among friends and family or through volunteering in her community, is more than a career: it's a vocation. Again, a point well taken. But you find yourself wishing Kate was less spotless than her kitchen; it might have been nice, for example, if she were obsessed with a slovenly next-door neighbor, had a spat with a close friend, or maybe just ran over the family cat in a moment of agitation. Her perfection ultimately compromises the power of the message.

One character who's certainly not spotless is Lee, the aspiring Ohio cosmetologist of *Marvin's Room* (1996), based on the 1990 play by Scott McPherson. Lee is the mother of two sons, the eldest of whom is a troubled youth (Leonardo DiCaprio) who burns down their house. Lee is also the sister of Bessie (Diane Keaton), who has remained home in Florida for many years to care for her ailing father. The problem now is that Bessie has cancer. Perhaps Lee or her sons are a match for a bone-marrow transplant; perhaps Lee will have to take care of her family and aging aunt now that Bessie is sick (like hell she will, Lee says). *Marvin's Room* is a nicely acted ensemble piece—Robert De Niro plays Bessie's doctor—and it is ongoing testimony to Streep's willingness both to play complicated people and to give us women with multiple identities, even if her working-class persona isn't fully persuasive.

Perhaps the most interesting thing about *Marvin's Room* is the (independent) studio that released it: Miramax. Though it was acquired by Disney in 1993, founders Bob and Harvey Weinstein continued to exercise considerable artistic independence within the Disney empire and used it to make smaller-scale but artistically ambitious movies. This approach to filmmaking comported well with Streep's, and she would make a series of films with Miramax over the next decade, as well as with other small independents. They would provide her with a haven as the big studios became increasingly obsessed with big-budget extravaganzas built around comic book characters, sequels, or both.

By decade's end, then, Streep's career was in flux: active, varied, but lower profile. She had drifted away from the private feminism that dominated her work from the late seventies to the late eighties, and the gender critiques/experiments of the early nineties. With the coming of a new century, Streep's work took another turn, one that in some respects would fulfill Betty Friedan's fondest dreams. The line would thus bend, but remain traceable back to a critique of the feminine mystique.

———

Teachers. The next twist in Meryl Streep's career—the point when she began offering fully realized visions of a feminist life in which public pursuits matter as much as private ones—arrived with her portrayal of a pair of teachers. In a way, that's not remarkable: teaching has long been considered a job for women, in part because it's work women have long done at home. So it was an apt fulcrum for her to tip away from women whose lives were defined more by their gender identities and toward ones whose professions were central to their conception of themselves.

It's a bit ironic, though, how this point was first illustrated: in the 1998 movie *Dancing at Lughnasa*. That's because the film is set in the culturally hidebound rural Ireland of 1936. This is one of those small-scale, actor-driven ensemble pieces that characterized Streep's work at the turn of this century. *Lughnasa* is a coming-of-age story, told from the point of view of a child who recounts a memorable summer on the family farm when his errant father returns to the family from a long sojourn, as does his missionary uncle, who is only intermittently lucid. Streep plays Kate, an aging spinster who rules over her four unmarried sisters and elder brother with an iron hand. She strongly disapproves of the boy's father, her brother's candor, and any other deviation from Catholic orthodoxy. Streep's pursed lips capture Kate's pinched, anxious persona.

But this is not her whole story. For Kate is also a teacher at a local parochial school—or is until the priest who runs it tells her she is likely to be redundant come fall. This represents a serious potential economic setback for the family. It's also a personal disaster for Kate, not only because her job is clearly close to the center of her identity, but also because it is the source of the authority that allows her to boss her siblings around. Without it, she will be a husk of herself. Such knowledge tempers our distaste for Kate and shows how the lack of a career can be a tragedy for women, even for women we may not particularly like.

Conversely, having a career can right a life that is otherwise going off the rails. This is the story of *Music of the Heart*, the 1999 Miramax feature about the real-life Roberta Guaspari, a violin teacher who won national acclaim (and some criticism from the back-to-basics crowd in school reform wars) for her work at a public school in East Harlem. We meet a despairing Guaspari when she has returned home to New York with her two sons after her husband has left her, needing a job. A genial former classmate (Aidan Quinn) directs her to a principal-friend (Angela Bassett), who hires her as a music teacher on a fill-in basis. *Music of the Heart*, a rare foray outside the horror genre for director Wes Craven, fits squarely in the charismatic-teacher-changes-lives tradition that has long been a Hollywood staple, but it's better than most in that there are sustained scenes of Streep's character in the classroom, interacting with students. Moreover, the movie avoids the cliché that a good teacher can somehow transcend any other factor in a child's life. It also avoids unduly idealizing its star teacher with infallible pedagogic instincts. Streep's Roberta can sound unexpectedly harsh with her students, criticizing one for sounding worse than anyone else and demanding to know why, only to learn that the student's grandmother was mugged and killed. To be sure, the movie is stuffed with its fair share of feel-good moments, culminating in the big fund-raising concert at Carnegie Hall. That concert comes about because Quinn's character refuses to commit to a long-term relationship, and Boyfriend No. 2 helps catalyze it with his connections. But in *Music of the Heart*, men are secondary to the imperatives of a working woman and mother whose life makes a palpable difference in the lives of those for whom she labors.

Though *Dancing at Lughnasa* and *Music of the Heart* represent important statements in the evolution of Streep's cinematic feminism, both were small independent films with minuscule grosses compared with big-budget behemoths of the time like *Armageddon* (1998) or *The Matrix* (1999).[43] Moreover, *Music of the Heart* was followed by the longest interregnum in Streep's career: it would be three full years before she appeared in a starring role. Her youngest children were nine and thirteen in 2000, which may have played a part in this slowed output. They probably also played a part in her subsequent decisions to appear in the small role of the comically hapless Aunt Josephine in *Lemony Snicket's A Series of Unfortunate Events* (2004) and to provide the imperious voice of the Ant Queen in the animated children's movie *The Ant Bully* (2006). She also had a very funny uncredited cameo as herself—as a not very good actress—in the sublimely silly Farrelly Brothers film *Stuck on You* (2003).

What might be termed the Meryl Streep renaissance began at the end of 2002 with her appearance in two movies involving the portrayal of literary figures. The first of these, *Adaptation*, is a singular work in Streep's canon. *Adaptation* represented a collaboration between two of the most inventive figures in modern Hollywood: screenwriter Charlie Kaufman and director Spike Jonze. The two teamed up in 1999 for the weirdly brilliant *Being John Malkovich*, in which a series of characters manage to enter a portal in the famed actor's brain and experience reality through his eyes. *Adaptation*, which is about Kauffman's difficulty in trying to adapt *New Yorker* writer Susan Orlean's 1998 nonfiction book *The Orchid Thief* for the big screen, begins with scenes on the set of *Being John Malkovich*. Streep plays Orlean—or rather some facsimile of the actual person. It becomes increasingly clear as the story proceeds that Charlie Kaufman's (Nicholas Cage) obsession with Orlean makes the portrayal of her that we see onscreen increasingly suspect. For much of the movie, she's a consummate professional, an intimidatingly competent member of the New York literati. Which is entirely credible. Then Kaufman starts playing with her, incongruously scripting a sexual relationship with the repellent, if amusing, thief played by Chris Cooper. Indeed, her murderous behavior toward the end of the movie seems to come out of nowhere, its jarring character very much the point of the film's postmodern sensibility. The metatextual zaniness of *Adaptation*, the desire on a viewer's part to see just how this crazy story will play out, gives it a freshness that's quite rare in Hollywood moviemaking. And it's especially refreshing to see Streep, a blue-chip figure in the industry, lend her talents to such a project and take them to an entirely new level. In a more complex way than in *She-Devil*, her role deconstructs our notions of identity, gendered and otherwise.

The same month *Adaptation* appeared, Streep's other film of 2002, *The Hours,* was released. Though less so than *Adaptation*, *The Hours*, which screenwriter David Hare based on Michael Cunningham's 1998 novel, has an experimental literary air. Its tripartite structure depicts single days in the lives of three women, whose stories only converge at the end of the movie. One narrative involves Virginia Woolf (Nicole Kidman, wearing a now legendary prosthetic nose), struggling with depression as she begins to conceive her 1925 masterpiece, *Mrs. Dalloway*, originally titled *The Hours*, also the story of a day in a life. Another involves Laura Brown (Julianne Moore), a 1950s housewife and mother of a young son in Los Angeles who is fighting off suicidal impulses, in part by reading *Mrs. Dalloway.* The third involves Streep's Clarissa Vaughan, a bisexual New York book editor in 2001 nursing a beloved old gay poet/novelist friend (Ed Harris) through the ravages of AIDS on the day on which she plans to throw him a party—plot elements that allude to *Mrs. Dalloway*, which is his nickname for Clarissa. He's written a famous novel that features a thinly fictionalized version of his friend. By coincidence, early in the novel Clarissa walks by a movie production that stars none other than Meryl Streep, whom she tries, but fails, to glimpse emerging from her trailer.[44]

Streep's Clarissa Vaughan is among her most fully realized creations. She's a devoted friend of Harris's character, lover of a woman played by Allison Janney, mother of a college-age daughter played by Claire Danes, and a literary professional who midwifes writing into publication. This last role is more hinted at by devices like manuscripts on her desk than actually depicted. But love and work, art and life, are so thoroughly fused that it seems misguided to insist on isolating the strands.

Which is not to say that Clarissa is a flawless person. She tends to live in the past, haunted by a romance with the poet/novelist that withered on the vine of their youth. This is more than mere foible; it leads her to neglect her relationship with the character played by Janney (with whom Streep does some marvelously nuanced acting).

Clarissa is the only major character of *The Hours* who can be said to achieve anything resembling a happy ending, though it takes a suicide, one of two in the movie, for her to finally come to her senses, signaled by the great tenderness with which Streep gazes into Janney's eyes at the end of the story. In large measure, that happiness can be viewed as a matter of historical circumstance: as a woman of the twenty-first century, Clarissa has the capacity to achieve an integrated life of the kind that

Virginia Woolf and Laura Brown can only dream of (albeit as very privileged people). Having such a capacity is not synonymous with achieving it, however, and for Clarissa it's a near thing. Michael Cunningham and David Hare created this character; Stephen Daldry, most of whose prior work was for the stage, directed it. But Meryl Streep is the one who brings this Clarissa to life, with a voice and gestures that are experienced as a gift.

Streep offers a gift of a decidedly different kind in her next role as U.S. Senator Eleanor Prentiss Shaw in *The Manchurian Candidate* (2004), the first of a string of politicians she would play. This remake of the 1962 John Frankenheimer classic, directed by Jonathan Demme, was updated in a number of ways, among them tweaking the role originated by Angela Lansbury as the manipulative wife of a buffoonish, McCarthyesque U.S. senator. Streep's version, in which *she* is the U.S. senator, is a dazzling embodiment of evil incarnate. She makes a stem-winding speech on behalf of her son's reluctant candidacy for the vice presidency to a group of party insiders that alternates charm, sarcasm, and motivational brimstone. The studied polish of Streep's delivery subtly calls attention to itself, cueing the viewer that she is truly dangerous. Her character is no sane person's idea of a role model, female or otherwise; the raw power she demonstrates in public and private inspires awe nonetheless.

Streep offered an even richer portrait of a powerful, unpleasant woman in what will surely go down as one of her signature roles: Miranda Priestly, the boss-from-hell magazine editor of *The Devil Wears Prada* (2006). *Devil* is based on the 2003 novel by Lauren Weisberger. A roman à clef about her days working for the legendarily impossible Anna Wintour of *Vogue*, Weisberger's book chronicles the way Baby Boomers, in particular female professional Baby Boomers, oppress their successors. We certainly see plenty of situations in which Streep's Miranda exercises a casual brutality, evident in a rapid-fire sequence of her repeatedly tossing her fur coat on the desk of her assistant Andrea (Anne Hathaway). Her icily delivered signature phrase, "That's all," which comes directly from the novel, becomes a signature line of the movie.

The film version differs crucially from the novel in the locus of its generational sympathy. To a great degree, this is the result of the screenplay, which renders a much more three-dimensional portrait of Miranda, including glimpses of a marriage where she certainly does not rule the roost, and a power struggle over control of the magazine that almost forces her into premature retirement. "I thought it was written out of anger," Streep said of the novel, "and from a point of view that seemed to me very apparent."[45] Thus there's a memorable moment when Andrea cannot stifle a

POWER SURGE: Meryl Streep as Anne Hathaway's boss from hell in *The Devil Wears Prada* (2006). In the twenty-first century, Streep has repeatedly played difficult people who nevertheless elicit admiration—just as difficult men have always done. (*20th Century Fox*)

giggle over the seeming inanity of deciding between belts in two shades of blue to go with a sweater, whereupon Miranda delivers an impromptu lecture demonstrating the way the leaders of a multibillion-dollar industry make decisions about such colors—"cerulean," she clarifies—and thus shape the behavior of her clueless assistant.

Streep herself adds a lot to this role. Her expertly modulated voice—which, unlike the Miranda of the novel, she never raises—is key. There's also a fine scene where she appears without makeup in a hotel room, her vulnerability as apparent as her defiance. We find ourselves rooting for Miranda despite her obvious excesses. Which makes the movie a feminist triumph, in that we recognize, as we've always done in the case of men, that a leader need not be perfect or fair to nevertheless attract respect and even admiration.

Not all of Streep's career women of the early twenty-first century are so fraught. She offers one of the more amusing fusions of public and private personas in *Prime* (2005), in which she plays a Jewish psychotherapist in Manhattan who confidently treats a younger woman (Uma Thurman), until she realizes that this shiksa is dating her even younger son (Bryan

Greenberg). In *A Prairie Home Companion* (2006), based on the beloved Garrison Keillor radio show, she's a faded, nostalgic, but likable singer who performs, and reminisces, with her sister (Lily Tomlin) and daughter (Lindsay Lohan). In *Mamma Mia!* (2008), the film version of the buoyant ABBA musical, she's a hotel owner on a Greek island whose daughter is getting married and secretly invites three of her mother's former lovers, one of whom she's guessing is her father, to the wedding. This is among Streep's most lighthearted performances—she sings, dances, and at one point the pushing-sixty actress performs an impressive split while jumping on a bed—in a movie that became a global phenomenon (it grossed more than half a billion dollars).[46] *Mamma Mia!* offers a deeply attractive vision of what a late-middle-age American womanhood could look like. The same can be said of the comparably successful *It's Complicated* (2009), in which she plays a divorced bakery owner and mother of three adult children who's surprised to find herself trying to decide between two lovers, one of them her ex (Alec Baldwin) and the other a self-effacing architect (Steve Martin). Most of these movies amount to liberal feminist fantasies, in that the women in question have remunerative, prestigious, and emotionally rewarding careers. This is also true of *Julie & Julia* (2009), which projects such a vision back in time, depicting the happily married Julia Child's successful quest to find a professional calling (and grief over her inability to bear a child).

It's in this context of material striving that Streep's performance as Sister Aloysius Beauvier, the authoritarian nun of *Doubt* (2008), is so important. It suggests a feminist vision that is finally more capacious than that of Betty Friedan, whose work has a secular cast.[47] John Patrick Shanley wrote and directed this adaptation of his 2004 play about a 1960s priest (Philip Seymour Hoffman) who may or may not be a pedophile, the principal of the parochial school (Streep) who's convinced that he is, and the young nun (Amy Adams, who appeared with Streep in *Julie & Julia*) who's unsure. Shanley's exquisitely calibrated screenplay is constructed in such a way that it's impossible to say with any certainty whether Sister Aloysius's conduct in her pursuit of the priest, both intense and ethically ambiguous, is justified. For our purposes, what matters is that we're dealing with a working-class woman—something we know solely on the basis of her thick Bronx accent—who holds an important job that's not merely a career but a vocation. She wields real power, and does so through a series of techniques that include intimidation, passive-aggressive behavior, and a supple command of bureaucratic machinery. Sister Aloysius is thus a walking illustration of the maxim that it's women, not men, who really run the Roman Catholic Church.

DAMNED NUN: Streep as Sister Aloysius Beauvier in *Doubt* (2008). The triumph amid the tragedy of this film is a feminist vision finally more capacious than anything Betty Friedan prophesied. *(Miramax)*

Run, but not rule. As she herself states early in the movie, the priest she suspects is her boss. She regards *his* boss as incompetent at best and believes his former one is covering for him. To make matters worse, the mother (Viola Davis) of the African American child that Sister Aloysius fears is a victim of the priest believes that even if the allegations are true, this sexual abuse is less bad than the physical abuse her son endures at the hands of his father, at a school that represents real opportunity for the boy's future. So Sister Aloysius resorts to cunning by fabricating a conversation with another nun, using it to blackmail the priest into resigning. (Naturally, he's kicked upstairs.)

It is possible to finish watching *Doubt* and conclude that in overstepping her occupational boundaries, ignoring the wishes of a mother who believes she is acting in her child's best interest, and committing what she herself considers a mortal sin, Sister Aloysius is guilty of creating a deeply tragic outcome, if not downright evil. This is all the more so given that for most of the movie, the evidence for her suspicions against the priest amounts to little more than an observation that he fails to trim his fingernails. But it's not credibly possible to finish watching *Doubt* and fail to see that Sister Aloysius is a deeply committed woman who is willing to make grave personal sacrifices in order to do what she believes is right. Nor, given the recent history of the Church, is it possible not to see real prescience on the part of a woman who tried to prevent a great crime that was perpetrated by generations of men who failed to exercise their unchecked authority in a responsible matter. Meryl Streep's vision of feminism is bigger than that of affluent women who want a well-appointed home, regular orgasms, and glamorous careers. It's one in which fallible people often seek power, sometimes gain it, and occasionally use it for something larger than themselves.

It's also a vision that's now shaded with intimations of mortality. In 2012 Streep won her third Academy Award for playing Margaret Thatcher in *The Iron Lady*, directed by Phyllida Lloyd (who had also directed *Mamma Mia!*). While Streep's performance was widely hailed, many critics expressed impatience with the film's unwillingness to really engage with the major events of Thatcher's tenure as prime minister or to take a clear position on her politics. While I believe these complaints have merit, it's clear that the real focus of the film, most of which takes place with Thatcher as a widow on the cusp of senility, is the transience of power for women no less than men: Thatcher's only unconquerable enemy is time. Streep cannot have failed to consider that her own vast artistic powers are no less perishable. So it is that she, and we, must cherish them while we have them.

The great paradox of actors is that by pretending to be fake people they enliven our appreciation of real ones. In her 1998 appearance on the TV program *Inside the Actors Studio*, Streep groped her way toward expressing this idea in a way that bears quoting at some length:

> I was thinking about applying to law school and thinking that acting is a stupid way to make a living, that it doesn't do any good in the world. But I think it does, I think it does, there's a great worth in it. And the worth is in listening to people who maybe don't even exist or who are voices in your past and through you come through the work and you give them to other people. I think that giving voice to characters who have no other voice is the great worth of what we do. So much of acting is vanity. I mean, this [appearing on the show] feels so great to come here and sit here and have everybody clap. But the *real* thing that makes me feel so good is when I know I've said something for a soul, when I've presented a soul.[48]

Meryl Streep is a progressive feminist. I say progressive because the arc of her work, the not straight but clear line that runs through it, is one in which the lives of women have gradually improved. They win more control over the terms of their lives, power that begins at home but eventually moves outside the home. That power has precedents in the past in those who illuminated the way, but most of it is something whose emergence she charts in the history of our time. To a great degree, this realized dream is a substantively American one, grounded in aspirations that finally transcend gender. But realized dreams are also surprisingly complicated ones, with unexpected consequences, ambiguities, and unfinished work. Especially for women.

As her comments also suggest, Streep's progressive feminism has a powerful moral component, a belief in a living connection across time and space that binds individuals she describes as "souls," people who are more than the sum of their bodies. Sister Aloysius would probably not approve this use of the term. But Streep blessed her anyway. Sisterhood is powerful, indeed.

CHAPTER 4

Rising Sons

Denzel Washington, Affirmative Actor

Master narrative: U.S. history as an
intergenerational family drama

Roger Ebert didn't much like the 1998 movie *Fallen*. Nothing unusual about that; as the reigning dean of professional movie reviewers—an endangered species in an age of disappearing newspapers and proliferating blogs—Ebert routinely expresses disappointment with films. Somewhat more surprising was Ebert's disappointment with Denzel Washington. Ebert was among the first to recognize Washington's tremendous breakout potential. Back in 1989, he praised Washington's performance in the now obscure movie *The Mighty Quinn* as "one of those roles that creates a movie star overnight." He would render similar praise many times in subsequent years, on two occasions stating that Washington movies had brought him to tears (and on one of those occasions emphasizing how rarely this happens).[1]

But Ebert was not moved by *Fallen*, a supernatural serial killer movie in which Washington plays a character named Detective John Hobbes (that's Hobbes as in Thomas Hobbes, the seventeenth-century English philosopher who argued that life was "nasty, brutish, and short"). In this cross between the thriller and horror genres, Hobbes pursues a satanic soul escaped from the body of an executed serial killer, which now moves from person to person by physical contact. Washington, Ebert wrote, "is convincing as a cop, but perhaps not the best choice for the role of Hobbes, which requires more of a noir personality. There's something essentially hopeful and sunny about Washington, and the best noir heroes encounter grim news as if they were expecting it." Ebert felt "Washington plays Hobbes more like a conventional hero, and doesn't internalize the evil."

No one was more aware of this sunny perception of the actor than Washington himself, who took active steps to change it. His work as a rogue cop in the 2001 movie *Training Day* won him an Academy Award as Best Actor, no doubt in part because Academy voters were aware of what an artistic stretch it was. In 2007, he gave a performance of decided moral ambiguity in *American Gangster*, embodying the role of the real-life Frank Lucas, who ran a hugely successful business as a Harlem heroin importer before turning police informant. Ebert was not enchanted by either of them. He thought Washington's role in *Training Day* in particular was so over-the-top in its villainy as to strain credulity. (Washington waded into this territory again in 2012 with his role as a rogue CIA agent in *Safe House*.)

Making allowances for Washington's genuine achievements in such roles, I still believe Ebert's characterization of "something essentially hopeful and sunny about Washington" rings true. Even when he plays tortured souls, like the fierce Malcolm X or the defiant boxer Rubin "Hurricane" Carter, an undeniable glow of charisma flickers close to the surface.

And it's this core disposition, much like Katharine Hepburn's irrepressible intelligence, or Humphrey Bogart's hard-boiled virtue, that can explain much of Washington's durable appeal as a Hollywood icon. Which is incontestable: In the annual Harris Poll for America's Favorite Movie Star, Washington placed in the top ten every year in the first decade of this century (including three years in a row at No. 1 between 2006 and 2008).[2] Washington has appeared in more than three dozen movies in the thirty years since his debut in *Carbon Copy* in 1981, to say nothing of television appearances or celebrated stage roles like leads in Shakespeare's *Julius Caesar* in 2005 or August Wilson's *Fences* in 2010. To watch him be interviewed by Charlie Rose, which the generally reclusive star has been a number of times, is to be struck by a tremendous magnetism that draws its paradoxical appeal from its very unpretentiousness.

There is the small matter that Washington happens to be a black man. A long—and troubling—history of American love affairs with a certain kind of genial black actor, like Bill "Mr. Bojangles" Robinson or Hattie McDaniel, haunts anyone aware of it. The last great archetypal figure in this regard was Sidney Poitier, who struggled with ambivalence about being a white person's notion of an acceptable black person for much of his career. In some respects, Washington is a direct cinematic heir of Poitier's; indeed, it was Washington who presented Poitier with a lifetime achievement award at the 2002 Oscar ceremonies, the very night Washington himself took home a statuette for *Training Day*. "Forty years I've been chasing Sidney, they finally give it to me, what'd they do? They give it to him the same night!" Washington joked in his acceptance speech. "I'll always be chasing you, Sidney. I'll always be following in your footsteps. There's nothing I would rather do, sir."[3]

And yet, as everyone understands, much of Washington's success is understood in terms of the ways he's *not* Poitier, the way he *doesn't* have to shoulder the burden of the race. Poitier was a *black* actor; Washington is a black *actor*. Early on in his career, the young Washington won a small part in the 1986 Sidney Lumet film *Power* that had originally been written for a middle-aged white man.[4] Ever since, he has repeatedly taken roles that were either changed or not racially marked in the first place. Such choices have been important not only to him but to a white America whose collective self-esteem rests on a notion of racial progress.

At the same time, Washington also enjoys high regard among African Americans on their own terms. The very term "Denzel" connotes a black masculine brand. "My man is smooth like Barry, and his voice got bass/ A body like Arnold with a Denzel face," goes the lyric of the 1993 hit song "Whatta Man" by the female hip-hop trio Salt-n-Pepa. (The "Barry" is soul singer Barry White; the "Arnold" is Arnold Schwarzenegger.) In the 2010 book *The Denzel Principle: Why Black Women Can't Find Good Black Men,* author jimi izrael laments the challenges of living up to a daunting archetype. And Washington's appearance in four Spike Lee movies, most prominently *Malcolm X* (1992), gives him a kind of street cred he's managed to maintain alongside his mass appeal.

But to return to Ebert's original point: the core of Washington's appeal is his essential moderation. Actually, I'll go a step further and say that to a great degree he is a conservative star for a conservative age. Certainly there have been alternatives; Washington's fame has coincided with that of impressive peers like Don Cheadle and Delroy Lindo, whose appeal lies in their intimidating presence (and the ability for audiences to regard it at a safe distance on a screen).

It's striking to consider, for example, that Washington has never had an interracial romance with a white woman in any of his movies, a taboo that has been surprisingly durable into the twenty-first century, but certainly one a star of his stature could have shattered. As *New York Times* writer Nicholas Kristof asked rhetorically in a 2005 column, "When will Hollywood dare release a major movie in which Denzel Washington and Reese Witherspoon fall passionately in love?"[5] A Washington character did have an interracial affair—one featuring a steamy sex scene—with an Indian expatriate from Uganda in the 1992 film *Mississippi Masala*, directed by Mira Nair. But such a romance was written out of the 1993 film *The Pelican Brief*, based on a John Grisham novel in which the character was both white and sexually involved with the woman played by Julia Roberts. "Of course I wanted to kiss Denzel," Roberts later said. "It was his idea to take the damn scenes out." Washington has expressed unease about such roles, not wanting to do them for the sake of doing so (he's not fond of lovemaking scenes generally). Such considerations appear to have been a factor in his decision to drop out of the 1992 film *Love Field* with Michelle Pfeiffer.[6] (The role went to Dennis Haysbert.)

This sense of diffidence extends to racial issues offscreen as well. After Washington made the wry observation that as a result of Hollywood sexism, "men get older while women get younger," interviewer Charlie Rose pressed him about whether he thought race was a casting problem, too. "It depends," he said, deflecting the question toward whether race mattered in the makeup of specific characters rather than who plays them. Washington does not deny the reality of racism even in his own life; in 1995 he told the *Today* show he can still get in an elevator and have a woman grab her purse more tightly. "I want to take out my wallet and just tap her on the head and say, 'Honey, don't worry about it. I think I've got a couple more dollars than you,'" he joked.[7] But such statements are newsworthy because they're rare. It would not exactly be surprising to have Spike Lee, for example, say as much.

At one point early in the process of researching this chapter, I was going to title it (as opposed to subtitle it) "Affirmative Actor." The idea was to capture Washington's place in African American cultural history as a post-civil-rights figure, as well as his appealingly upbeat persona. As I got deeper into his body of work, however, I concluded that, conceptually speaking, "Affirmative Actor" isn't quite sufficient. In part, that's because it misses this conservative strain I'm talking about, a conservatism that's more social than political, and one that's not specifically racial. Washington is certainly a man of his time, but there's something distinctly old-fashioned about him, something rooted in, but not solely defined by, his African American identity—no, make that African American *heritage*.

And a big part of this persona, in turn, derives from the fact that in art and life Washington is a family man. (In marked contrast to many of his Hollywood peers, he's been married to the same woman for decades and has raised four children.) More specifically, many of Washington's roles circle around the relationship between fathers and sons, literal and figurative. History—African American history particularly, and U.S. history as well—is fundamentally a matter of generations and their relationship with each other. This generational vision informs Washington's notion of progress, measured in terms of personal achievement. It also shapes his notion of how social change is the result of honoring a bond of reciprocal responsibility between youth and elders. Finally, and perhaps most decisively, Washington's notion of fathers and sons has a powerful religious element grounded in a subtle but discernible spiritual life.

These strands—of race, family, and faith—coalesce in Washington's signature performance as Malcolm X. As anyone even vaguely familiar with
the life of that fiery civil rights leader knows, Malcolm X was a protean
figure. But Washington molded him into a highly disciplined family man
with a powerful faith in the redemptive power of organizations, faith that
survives disappointment or frustration with particular ones (whether the
U.S. government or the Nation of Islam). This fusion of right-leaning cultural values and left-leaning politics was the key to Malcolm X's appeal as a
social activist in the 1960s, as well to his symbolic revival in the late 1980s as
embraced by figures like the hip-hop group Public Enemy, which adopted
the iconography of Malcolm X. Though Washington would show more
confidence in the federal government than Malcolm X did (by portraying a
slave in the emancipatory Union Army, for example), his institutional commitment, though more pronounced than that of Clint Eastwood and Daniel
Day-Lewis, still skews small in the traditional liberal imagination.

But what Washington affirms is pretty big—bigger than a meritocrati-
cally defined political program, bigger than politics or even government.
It is, finally, an affirmation of fatherhood in the life of a people.

Two facts about Denzel Washington seem worth mentioning at the outset:
he's the son of a preacher, and his father was absent for much of his adolescence. It's possible to make too much of these facts, but his career trajectory suggests they count for something.

Washington was born on December 28, 1954, the second of three children.[8] His mother, Lennis, a onetime gospel singer, hailed from Georgia
but was raised in Harlem. His father, Denzel Sr., a Virginia native, was
named after the obstetrician who delivered him, a Dr. Denzel.[9]

Denzel Jr. was born, and spent his childhood, in Mount Vernon, New
York. A small city in Westchester County situated between the meaner
streets of the Bronx and the leafier lanes of Bronxville, Mount Vernon is a
liminal space in metropolitan New York. Washington's father worked for
the city water department and at a local retail store; his status as a Pente-
costal minister while living in Mount Vernon was apparently more an
aspiration than a career (his son remembers listening to congregations
consisting of no more than a handful of people). Washington's parents
divorced when he was fourteen, and his father returned to Virginia, continuing his ministerial work until his death in 1991.

The pivotal figure in Washington's life was his mother. A beautician
who owned and operated a series of shops, she passed her extroverted

personality and entrepreneurial pluck on to her son. In a brief auto-biographical sketch published in 2006, Washington described the job his mother got for him at a local barbershop when he was eleven or twelve:

> The place was run by a man named Jack Coleman, who took me on as a kindness to my mother. At least that's how I always look back on it. I thought it was the best job in the world. I had all kinds of hustles back then. You walked into the shop and I could tell right away how much money you had. I'd check out your shoes and I'd just know. I'd have people bringing me their dry cleaning and I'd take it out and deliver it back to their house. I'd run all kinds of errands. They'd step out of Mr. Coleman's chair and I'd be on them with a whisk broom, brushing off their collars saying, "Man, how you doin' today?" Or "Man, you look good." There was money to be made all day long, especially if you were respectful and solicitous.[10]

Sounds like something out of the Booker T. Washington school of entre-preneurial self-help.

Lennis Washington believed her divorce had a destabilizing effect on her son. Though he had never been a particularly good student, she managed to get him admitted to Oakland Academy, a school for largely afflu-ent and white students in upstate New York. His grades there were not strong enough to gain him admission to Yale or an adequate scholarship to attend Boston University, two schools he hoped to attend. Instead, he enrolled at Fordham in 1972. He began in pre-med, but his academic performance was so weak that he dropped out. Working at a post office and as a sanitation worker led him to return. He refocused his academic career by double-majoring in journalism and, rekindling a childhood thespian phase, in drama. Landing lead roles in university productions of Eugene O'Neill's *The Emperor Jones* and Shakespeare's *Othello* proved pivotal. It led him, while still an undergraduate, to a part in *Wilma*, a made-for-TV movie in which he portrayed the boyfriend of legendary track star Wilma Rudolph (played by Cicely Tyson). It was in making the movie that he met Pauletta Pearson, the woman who became his wife.

Following his graduation from Fordham, Washington won a scholar-ship for graduate work at the American Conservatory Theater (ACT) in San Francisco, but left the program in its second year to strike out on his own. His first film, *Carbon Copy* (1981), bombed. So he returned to New York and sought stage roles. In what proved to be a fruitful success, he portrayed Malcolm X in *When the Chickens Came Home to Roost*, a 1981 off-Broadway production that caught the attention of many critics, as well as the aspiring Spike Lee, who had nursed a lifelong ambition of making a biopic about the civil rights leader. Another role that would lead to a movie part was Washington's appearance in the original 1981 production of Charles Fuller's *A Soldier's Play*, which he would reprise in the 1984 Norman Jewison film *A Soldier's Story*.

It was in television, however, that Washington would win the fame and financial security that he would leverage, like Clint Eastwood and Daniel Day-Lewis, into a movie career. As Dr. Philip Chandler in the long-running NBC series *St. Elsewhere* (1982–88), he established a paradigmatic identity as an intelligent, accomplished, and imperfect professional.

Washington was able to use time off from the show to squeeze in a few movies. In the 1984 TV production *License to Kill*, he played the supporting role of a young prosecutor who needs all his wits in parrying a defense lawyer representing a drunk driver. In addition to Jewison's (low-budget) film version of *A Soldier's Story*, Washington also won a small but juicy role as a corrupt politico in Sidney Lumet's *Power* (1986). That movie proved to be a commercial and critical disappointment. So was *Cry Freedom*, a 1987 Richard Attenborough film about white South African journalist Donald Woods (Kevin Kline) and his relationship with antiapartheid activist Stephen Biko (Washington). Though the movie was much criticized for its lopsided focus on Woods rather than the more important Biko, Washington was repeatedly singled out for praise in a performance notable for his mastery of a South African accent.

But if Washington had made it as an actor by the end of the eighties, he had not yet broken through as a movie star. The turning point came in 1989 with his work in yet another ensemble project, the Edward Zwick Civil War film *Glory*, based on the real-life exploits of the African American Massachusetts 54th Regiment. For his performance as Trip, a misanthropic runaway slave, Washington received an Academy Award as Best Supporting Actor. From that point on, he would be a headliner.

But not an especially prominent one. While Washington would continue to generate critical praise with ambitious performances in movies like *Mo' Better Blues* (1990) and *Mississippi Masala* (1992), these were still relatively small-scale productions. Conversely, his big-budget projects of the time, *Heart Condition* (1990) and *Ricochet* (1991), were widely considered critical and commercial flops. He did receive an Oscar nomination as Best Actor for *Malcolm X* (1992), a movie with real artistic (and, to a lesser degree, box office) heft. But reviews were mixed for his next turn as Don

Pedro in the Kenneth Branagh production of Shakespeare's *Much Ado About Nothing* (1993).

Beginning in 1993, however, Washington appeared in a string of projects that did lift him to stardom. Some, like *Philadelphia* (1993), were hailed as great films. Others, like *Crimson Tide* (1995), were slickly made popcorn movies that sold buckets of tickets. Still others, like *The Siege* (1998), were controversial (in this case, for its portrayal of Muslims). And a few, like *Devil in a Blue Dress* (1995), were expensive box office duds.[11] But Washington gained the marquee status of people at the very top of his profession, a stratosphere inhabited by stars like Julia Roberts and Tom Cruise.

Of course, the primary point here is not to establish Washington's place in the Hollywood pecking order. As with all my subjects, his success is primarily important in the way it has allowed him a relatively high degree of control over his artistic choices, and what those choices reveal about him. One thing they clearly reveal is that the boy in the barbershop never disappeared: over the course of the last thirty years Washington has demonstrated a remarkable work ethic as one of the most tireless actors in Hollywood, and one with a large appetite for making money (though that has never been an overriding concern). What they also show is the unique degree to which Washington has embodied the material hopes, fears, and values of a rising black middle class in the wake of the civil rights movement—and the family tropes that govern his vision of history and politics.

———

Cinematically speaking, the first look we get at Denzel Washington is also the closest look we get at anything resembling a counterculture figure. In the 1981 movie *Carbon Copy*, he plays Roger Porter,[12] a late adolescent who shows up at the Southern California corporate office of a wealthy white corporate executive named Walter Whitney (George Segal). Whitney—a name orthographically close to "Whitey"—is saddened to learn that the boy's mother, with whom he had an interracial relationship, is now dead. But he's repelled by Porter, who arrives wearing dark glasses and a T-shirt bearing an image of the African continent with a heart in the middle. The boy sits with his feet up at Whitney's desk, making an ominous declaration: "Here I was thinking I was just another poor black orphan boy going to freeze in the cold white world." Whitney asks about the boy's father and is told, "You know how it is with us colored folks. We ain't much for marryin'." When Whitney objects to Porter talking about his own mother this way, Porter responds, "Of course not being married didn't make my mother less of a woman. It just made my father less of a man." Of course it turns out that man is Whitney himself.

A good white liberal, Whitney tries to make room for his previously unknown son, and this becomes the comic premise of a now dated movie. Whitney is trapped in a loveless marriage, his career dependent on his domineering father-in-law. As a result of his downward spiral, he and Porter end up in a ghetto apartment, and when the police mistakenly believe Porter is involved in a robbery, Whitney hides him and tries to run away, getting arrested himself. Porter visits his father in jail, revealing his behavior to be a ruse. "I didn't want anything from you," he explains, saying the point was never to extract money or a trust fund. "I didn't want you to like me because I was your son. I wanted you to respect me because I was Mom's son. But I looked in your eyes and you didn't see Mom. You saw black." Roger is in fact a scholarship student at Northwestern, Whitney's own alma mater. In the end the two ride off into the sunset, headed back to Chicago.

One of the things that makes *Carbon Copy* a weak movie is Washington's performance. His well-scrubbed cheer compromises the credibility of his ghetto masquerade, and while this is arguably the point—a father who can't really see his son for who he is—his acting can't quite escape the tinny quality of the movie around him. He is, for all his evident promise, miscast.

This is surely one reason why in seventeen of his next twenty feature film roles, Washington plays some variety of a middle-class professional—police chief, journalist, naval officer, political operative. There are exceptions (I'll be getting to them momentarily), but such roles will be the general rule for the rest of his career. This is, to put it mildly, not a representative sample of U.S. society. That might not mean much in the case of a white actor. But in the case of a black one it amounts to a political statement about the arrival of African Americans in mainstream society—the "talented tenth" W.E.B. DuBois invoked a century ago.[13] The difference is that Washington's characters are less black technocrats than black Horatio Algers.

Washington's message of integration is a multivalent one. In some cases, like *Power*, the black character's presence is meant to be taken for granted. In others, it's meant to send an overt message that times have changed. At one point in Alan J. Pakula's *The Pelican Brief*, Washington, who plays a reporter, meets his boss (Donald Sutherland) at Mount Vernon (as in that other Washington). Sutherland's character is annoyed that Washington has been impossible to reach. "I thought of dropping you into the ranks of the unemployed," he says wryly, "but I know damn well you'd slap me with a discrimination suit." In still other cases, like *Cry Freedom*, Washington is an activist engaging in direct advocacy on explicitly racial terms. Yet for all the diversity of these integrationist arguments, they're conducted in a context of Washington portraying people with social and financial capital, whether measured in professional skills, patterns of consumption, peer status, or family values. This is true even when a character's hold on such status is precarious, as it is for the small-business owner of *Mississippi Masala*, or when the character in question is a criminal, as in *American Gangster.*

Though it may sound odd, I consider Washington's portrayal of Malcolm X as one of those seventeen middle-class roles. In an important sense, of course, that's ridiculous: the fiery civil rights leader began his life as a small-time crook and became a convert to a religion specifically predicated on a rejection of many core tenets of American society. But Washington's Malcolm is a surprisingly chaste figure. To be sure, he is portrayed as having a flamboyant youth, but Washington—who played an important role in developing the character with Spike Lee—pulls punches in depicting the level of criminality that Malcolm himself claimed in his autobiography, though his most recent biographer, Manning Marable, believes the book exaggerated it for dramatic effect.[14] Yes, the Washington/Lee Malcolm takes drugs, but he isn't seen dealing them, the way he did in real life. Nor is he seen as the pimp he claimed to be. His vices are in any case less important than his eventual conversion to Islamic piety, a journey he takes with a sense of discipline and intellectual rigor that would warm the heart of a Puritan. And while his political activities inevitably meant the real-life Malcolm was absent from home much of the time, the Malcolm of the movie is positively Eisenhowerian in the domestic settings in which we repeatedly see him. As one of the mysterious agents (Lee's fellow director John Sayles) observes to another on a tapped phone line while Malcolm chats with his wife from a hotel room, "This guy makes [Martin Luther] King look like a monk."

Again, some facts of Malcolm's life suggest otherwise. Marable believed that his domestic life was quite strained—he virtually fled home after the birth of his children, and there is strong reason to believe that infidelity marked both sides of the marriage. Marable also suggested that as a young man Malcolm was bisexual.[15] Still, for all this, I don't regard the Washington/Lee portrait of Malcolm X—or, for that matter, the autobiography—as fundamentally untrue. For all the plasticity and nuance that Marable and others attribute to him, the postconversion Malcolm had an ascetic core that gained the admiration of many who rejected his precepts no less than those who embraced them.

Of the other three characters in Washington's early career that cannot really be considered bourgeois, two are rank-and-file soldiers: the runaway slave Trip of *Glory* and Private Pete Peterson of *A Soldier's Story*. As Washington made clear at the time of *Glory*'s release, he had repeatedly rejected roles of slaves, mindful of what that would project to audiences.[16] But to a great extent *Glory* can be understood in terms of Trip's struggle to overcome his own resistance to his evident leadership ability, talent apparent even to the commanding white officer (Matthew Broderick) who has him whipped. Peterson's (black) commanding officer holds him in similarly high regard, even if it is not reciprocated.

The third exception to the pattern I'm describing is *The Preacher's Wife* (1996): here Washington is an angel. Yet in an important sense Washington's angel is more professional than his predecessor. *The Preacher's Wife* is a remake of the 1948 film *The Bishop's Wife*. In that movie, Cary Grant plays the angel, one tempted by his attraction to the spouse of a man he's trying to help. "I'm tired of being a wanderer," he confesses at the end of the film. While Washington's angel is clearly drawn to her counterpart (Whitney Houston), he shows no such weakness.

Over the course of the past fifteen years, Washington's palette has widened somewhat. He played convicts again in Spike Lee's *He Got Game* (1998) and *The Hurricane* a year later, though in both cases the incarceration of the characters is questionable at best (in the former, it's the result of an accident; in the latter, it's a travesty, though, as with *Malcolm X,* the filmmakers of *The Hurricane* soft-pedal Rubin Carter's prior criminal record). In *John Q* (2002), Washington is a desperate laid-off factory worker who resorts to taking hostages at a hospital for the sake of his son's medical care. Easy Rawlins, another laid-off character in the Los Angeles of the 1940s, descends into the city's underworld as a private eye in *Devil in a Blue Dress*. In important respects, all these characters have stout middle-class values most often expressed in the form of a steady work ethic—in *Blue Dress,* Easy Rawlins takes a job as private eye largely to keep up with the mortgage payments on his cherished house. Even Frank Lucas, the ruthless criminal of *American Gangster*, runs his heroin business with a stone-cold sobriety in sharp contrast to his peers like Nicky Barnes (played by Cuba Gooding Jr.). In art as he was in life, Lucas is disgusted when Barnes becomes a cover story in the *New York Times Magazine*.[17] Like society ladies, self-respecting drug kingpins keep their names out of the newspaper.

The character of Lucas, whose behavior is in many respects monstrous, serves as an important reminder that sobriety is not the same thing as saintliness. Whatever their professional, personal, or material achievements, Washington characters are never paragons of virtue. His protagonists in *Heart Condition* (1990) and *Philadelphia* (1993) are slick attorneys. The military officer of *Courage Under Fire* (1996) and the CIA officer turned bodyguard of *Man on Fire* (2004) are alcoholics. The train dispatcher in the remake of the 1974 film *The Taking of Pelham 123* (2009) is a decent family man with a notably cool head in dealing with the terrorist played by John Travolta, but over the course of that movie we learn he was demoted for taking a bribe.

Still, at the end of the day—partial exceptions like *Training Day* notwithstanding—Denzel Washington characters are upwardly mobile (black) Americans with a stake in a system that generally has room for them, even when that room is on the margins, and even when that room is bounded by opposition. (His protagonist in *Training Day* is an evil cop, but again, one who polices his barony with brisk efficiency.) Yet another real-life Washington character, poet and activist Melvin Tolson of *The Great Debaters* (2007), is a college professor who secretly advises an interracial group of populist farmers seeking to resist the imprecations of greedy capitalists. And even when American society as we know it is gone, another Washington figure, the title character of *The Book of Eli* (2010), roams a postapocalyptic dystopia and battles petty autocrats like the one played by Gary Oldman, bringing a sacred book to a library and thus ensuring the survival of civilization. These are people who have fought long and hard to give their American Dreams a basis in reality. They're not going to give it up without a fight.

And they're not going to fight alone. Or for themselves alone.

"Let's start with a verse from Proverbs," Denzel Washington begins the closest thing he's written to an autobiography. "'Train up a child in the way he should go, and when he is old he will not depart from it.'" This from a volume whose epigraph comes from James Baldwin: "Children have never been very good at listening to their elders, but they have never failed to imitate them." The book, *A Hand to Guide Me*, is a commemorative anthology marking the centennial of the Boys and Girls Clubs of America, a mentoring organization for which Washington is a national spokesman. The Boys and Girls Clubs played a pivotal role in Washington's own life. Even when his father was still in the picture (though preaching on the road), the organization was an important source of role models. To this day, the actor reports, his signature derives from his attempt to copy the style of a childhood mentor. Washington's philanthropic work testifies to the depth of this experience for him. So does the way he describes his understanding of child development: "Show me a successful individual and I'll show you someone who didn't want for positive influences in his or her life."[18]

In surveying Washington's body of work, it's truly striking how many of his films involve such mentoring relationships. At first, unsurprisingly, Washington plays sons of one kind or another. Later, he transitions to father. There are lots of permutations on the theme; in recent years, he has been a paternal figure to females who range in age from child to adult. Whatever the variety, this mentoring role is a central trope of his career.

It's also a central trope in his vision of U.S. history. Washington has played a number of real-life figures, and a number of fictional ones in historical settings. Whatever the case, Washington's history is always to some degree personal—a father or child who inherits or transmits a legacy to others. The historical canvas, whether the Civil War or the civil rights movement, can be panoramic. Yet one way or another, his stories are typically family affairs.

In a small but important minority of cases (like *Carbon Copy*), the patrimony is literal. In *Mississippi Masala*, Washington's character runs a family business with his brother; he's close to his widower father, who is supportive but not particularly prepossessing. Actually, the more forceful presence in Washington's son roles is mothers. By 1990, when he was thirty-five and old enough be a father himself, he appeared in *Mo' Better Blues* as a selfish—but, thanks to the stringent discipline of his mother shown in flashback, hugely talented—leader of a jazz combo. The story is in large measure a tragedy, but it does end with Washington's character as a father himself, married to a woman with whom he imposes (slightly less) stringent discipline on that child.

The pivotal document of Washington's career-long fascination with fathers and sons is *Malcolm X*. The destiny of the Spike Lee/Denzel Washington Malcolm is cinematically foreshadowed by the fact that he is the child of Reverend Earl Little, a man portrayed far more positively than he is in the autobiography that is the primary source for the movie (and, for that matter, Manning Marable's biography).[19] *The Autobiography of Malcolm X* begins with a description of his father, but the movie version flashes back repeatedly to Malcolm's childhood, and the towering stance of defiance his father took in multiple family confrontations with the Ku Klux Klan before he was finally murdered. This defiance is resurrected by a son who also refuses to allow the prospect of a violent death to silence him.

The movie—again proportionally more than the book—is also at some pains to establish Malcolm the Nation of Islam convert as a devoted husband and father, even as his activism pulls him away from home. And for all his unshakable militancy—his lifelong insistence on white supremacy as the primary problem; his dismissal of "Uncle Tom Negro Preachers"; his contempt for laws enforced by those who have "traded in their white sheets for police uniforms"—Malcolm espoused the protection of black women and children in terms that just about any mid-twentieth-century middle-class white would find familiar. Hence Washington's rendition of a speech to an interracial audience at Columbia University:

> Mr. Muhammad is trying to get us on God's side, so that God will be on our side to help us fight our battles. When Negroes stop getting drunk, stop being addicted to drugs, stop fornicating and committing adultery, when we get off the welfare, then we'll be MEN. Earn what you need for your family, then your family respects you. They'll be proud to say, "That's my father." She's proud to say, "That's my husband." "Father" means you're taking care of those children. Just because you made them that don't mean you're a father. Anybody can make a baby, but anybody can't take care of them. Anyone can go get a woman, but anybody can't take care of a woman.[20]

Other Washington fathers are not quite so formidable. In *He Got Game*, Washington plays a convict given a furlough to convince his son, a high school basketball star, to accept a scholarship at the alma mater of a state governor. Though estranged, father nevertheless wants what's best for son, even if they disagree about what that means.

Most often, however, the father/son figures in Washington movies are surrogates. The plot of *A Soldier's Story* is a whodunit revolving around a repellent black sergeant who makes the lives of the soldiers around him miserable. When Washington's character, Peterson, challenges this behavior, the sergeant demands they settle their differences with a fight, which he wins by throwing sand in Peterson's face and knocking him out. Ironically, however, we later learn that he liked Peterson and indeed planned to promote him. ("Pete fought back," another character explains. "Sarge liked that.") But that relationship culminates in figurative parricide. As such, *A Soldier's Story* is an outlier on the Washingtonian spectrum, a cautionary tale to both fathers and sons about how *not* to serve each other, and thus how *not* to advance the race.

The other end of the spectrum is represented by a different soldier's story: *Glory*.[21] Once again, Washington plays a rebellious son in the character of Trip. The father this time is Sergeant Rawlins, played by Morgan Freeman. Trip oppresses those around him, calling one fellow private "snowflake" and a "nigger" who acts as "the white man's dog." Rawlins shows restraint amid these and other provocations, but finally intervenes like a parent scolding an errant child. "And what are you?" he asks Trip. "So full of hate you just want to go off and fight everybody 'cause you've been whipped and chased by hounds …You watch who you callin' a nigger. If there's any niggers around here, it's you. Smart-mouth, stupid-ass, swamp-runnin' nigger. You don't watch out, that's all you ever gonna be." The effect of this rebuke, while not immediate, is decisive. Trip will die bearing the regimental colors he had rejected earlier in the movie, as a prodigal son redeemed by a wise (and, we understand, loving) father.[22] One is also reminded here of John 15:13: "Greater love has no man than this, that a man lay down his life for his friends." In successfully achieving a relationship of mutual respect and affection with a man from a different generation, Trip is able to channel his rage and strike a blow for freedom on behalf of his people. In so doing, the son becomes a founding father of post-emancipation America, a young Moses for his people.

Washington's Malcolm X is at least as interested in surrogate father-son relationships as he is in biological ones. Indeed, one way to understand his story, particularly the movie, is Malcolm's search for a father to replace the one he lost in childhood.[23] He finds one in West Indian Archie in his hustling days, another in Baines while in prison, and finally in the Honorable Elijah Muhammad upon gaining his freedom. Each of these men ultimately proves to be a disappointment. Despite this, Malcolm takes his own responsibilities for surrogacy very seriously and is rewarded with deep loyalty and affection by a number of aides. Ironically, at one point in the movie this commitment leads him to send an associate away, because he believes the young man has an overriding obligation to Elijah Muhammad rather than to Malcolm himself. Though he loses his temper in the final moments of the movie, he recovers and apologizes, and it is this sense of disciplined integrity, which radiated outward to encompass a global vision of pan-African unity, that becomes his final legacy.

In *Malcolm X*, then, Washington is both a father and a son, and this is yet one more way in which the film is a fulcrum in his career. He would play a virtual son again in *Crimson Tide* (1995) as a naval officer forced to challenge an overly gung-ho superior (Gene Hackman). He is also a "good" son in *American Gangster*; to a great extent, the moral ambiguity of that film stems from Frank Lucas's devotion to his mother, which in part

PRODIGAL SON: Washington's Malcolm X finally meets the Honorable Elijah Muhammad in *Malcolm X* (1992). One way of understanding the film is as a man's search for a workable father. *(Warner Bros.)*

means serving as his brothers' keeper (a sense of family fidelity that, ironically, will prove to be his professional undoing). He is also positioned as the dutiful heir of Ellsworth Raymond "Bumpy" Johnson, who ran the Harlem underworld from the thirties into the sixties. But from here on out Washington is mostly the father.

Sometimes this role is indirect but nevertheless decisive. In the intentionally (and unintentionally) awkward buddy film *Heart Condition* (1990), Washington is a glib attorney who dies in a car crash, his heart transplanted into an ailing racist cop (Bob Hoskins). From that point on he's a ghost visible only to Hoskins, and the two bicker their way to Hoskins reuniting with his prostitute girlfriend, followed by marriage and a child. We viewers see Washington as a faded presence in a group photograph. The message: that love and family are solvents that dissolve racial barriers.

Very often Washington fathers are less men who act directly in this capacity than people for whom fatherhood becomes a catalyst for change in other aspects of their lives. The Joe Miller we meet at the beginning of *Philadelphia* is an ambulance-chasing lawyer with no interest in representing the AIDS-afflicted Andrew Beckett (Tom Hanks) in a wrongful termination suit. But the birth of his daughter seems to begin a process of softening his hard heart, perhaps because he comes to see Beckett as somebody's child (and perhaps because Beckett takes instant interest in the photo of the infant on Miller's desk and follows up on it when they run into each other later).

All this said, one of the great satisfactions in watching Washington's career unfold is the seemingly effortless combination of grace and gravitas by which he repeatedly becomes a father figure. In *Remember the Titans* (2000), he doubles as a literal and symbolic father in the role of the real-life Herman Boone, who presided over the racial integration of a suburban Virginia high school football team in 1971. In *John Q*, his fierce devotion to his seriously ill, and seriously underinsured, son leads him to take the inhabitants of a Chicago hospital's emergency room hostage. Ironically, they find themselves on his side (along the way, he straightens out a boorish and juvenile man on how to treat his girlfriend). Even when Washington is a downright evil surrogate father, as he is in *Training Day*, he's nevertheless mesmerizing, in part because you keep thinking that his evil acts may yet be part of some larger redemptive design for his young partner's (Ethan Hawke's) benefit.

The two films Washington has directed are both mentoring stories. *Antwone Fisher* (2002), based on the 2001 autobiography *Finding Fish*, tells the story of a sexually and emotionally abused child who struggles to overcome inner demons in the U.S. Navy on his way to finding love and an emotionally stable life.[24] Washington plays the composite character of a navy psychiatrist, Dr. Jerome Davenport. In the movie we see Davenport has his own (marital) struggles, and his relationship with Fisher is far from smooth. Nevertheless, Davenport is able to serve as father figure in a reciprocally positive relationship that allows Fisher to make the transition to adulthood.

For Washington, it's clear, *Antwone Fisher* represented a merger of artistic and personal interests. "I've always gotten a lot of joy out of seeing other people do well," he told Charlie Rose in 2002, who noted that Washington had made the project using largely unknown actors and an untested screenwriter. Washington also cast his decision to make the film, amid the inevitable uncertainties of the movie business, in terms of honoring a commitment to the real-life Fisher, who worked as a security guard on the lot of Sony Pictures before selling his screenplay. "I promised Antwone that I would take care of him," he explained. "He's been through enough in his life, and I said, 'I won't mess you up.'"

The second film Washington directed, *The Great Debaters*, is even more saturated in fatherhood of various kinds. Once again, he plays a real-life figure, this time the poet/professor/activist Melvin B. Tolson (1898–1966), who built and ran a highly successful debating team from the 1920s into the 1940s at Wiley College, an African Methodist Episcopal institution in

Marshall, Texas. The movie focuses on Tolson's relationship with three star pupils, among them child prodigy James L. Farmer Jr.; the elder Farmer was a professor at Wiley in the 1930s. The Farmers are played by the esteemed actor/director Forest Whitaker and the adolescent Denzel Whitaker, named after Washington.

Though it is threaded with subplots, the core of *The Great Debaters* focuses on Tolson's efforts to overcome internal and external conflicts he and his charges face as they gradually build an interracial reputation that culminates in an invitation to debate at Harvard (the real team debated at the University of Southern California).[25] Tolson mentors each of these three in different ways that include gently guiding the two older students through their tempestuous romance. James Farmer Jr. has his own father, who is a formidable figure worthy of emulation. But it's one of the subtleties of the film that Tolson represents an alternative male role model, and that he and Farmer Sr. can maintain a relationship of mutual respect amid political disagreement.

The potency of this message of racial and gender solidarity is quite powerful when one considers who James L. Farmer Jr. became: a founder of the Congress of Racial Equality in 1942, and a guiding light of the Freedom Rides of the 1960s, one of the most courageous undertakings in American history. An unfortunate by-product of the momentous changes of the 1960s is that we sometimes overlook their origins in activism of the 1930s and 1940s. Washington's decision to make this picture—and, one might add, his $1 million gift to reinstitute Wiley's debate team[26]—is thus an important contribution to African American collective memory. The implicit message of *The Great Debaters* is clear: good fathers make great men. And great men make history.

So, of course, do great women. The overall tenor of Washington's approach to fatherhood has been in terms of sons, but there have also been biological daughters who figure in his pictures: an infant in *Philadelphia*, little girls in *Malcolm X*, *He Got Game*, and *Remember the Titans*, and grown daughters in *Unstoppable* (2010). One of the more interesting dimensions of Washington's trajectory as an actor in recent decades has been his role as a surrogate father to women. As we've seen, interracial sexual relationships have been taboo. But some of his most satisfying work has come out of relating to females in other ways.

The first important example of this, albeit indirect, is *Courage Under Fire*. Washington plays Lieutenant Colonel Nathaniel Serling, a tank battalion commander involved in a friendly-fire incident during the Persian Gulf War, which we see in the opening sequence of the film. To avoid embarrassment, the army covers up the incident, decorating Serling for his valor (real enough) but relegating him to a desk job back in Washington. He is assigned the task of investigating whether Army Captain Karen Emma Walden (Meg Ryan), who was killed in action, is eligible to be the first woman to win the Congressional Medal of Honor for valor in combat. Serling discovers fishy inconsistencies in the stories of Walden's peers, which are rendered in *Rashomon*-like flashbacks. For Serling, whose relationship with his wife and children has suffered since his return from Kuwait, the Walden case increasingly becomes part of a redemptive quest for truth about his own past. In setting her record straight, he can set himself free.

A much more direct example of surrogacy is provided by *Man on Fire*. A remake of a 1987 film shot in Italy, this one is set in Mexico amid the kidnappings of wealthy people for ransom, typifying director Tony Scott's stylized, violent approach to moviemaking. It's also racist; the clear implication in the movie is that it takes a Yanqui—in what might be meant as a form of progress, a black Yanqui—to exact justice Mexicans are unable to achieve themselves. This is a trope in cinematic history that goes back a long way, at least as far as *The Magnificent Seven* (1960) a half century ago. That said, Washington does some of the best acting of his career, a good chunk of it ad-libbed, with nine-year-old Dakota Fanning, who plays the child in a family for whom Washington, a washed-up, alcoholic CIA agent, has been hired to serve as bodyguard. In a narrative arc you can spot a mile away, Washington starts out as the stony hired gun whose heart gets melted by a little girl. Still, the chemistry between the two is undeniable.

(SURROGATE) DADDY'S LITTLE GIRL: Washington and Dakota Fanning in *Man on Fire* (2004). As Washington has become a father figure, he's also developed mentoring relations across race and gender lines. (*20th Century Fox*)

A similar example of Washington finding fatherly rapport with a female character in a subpar movie is *The Bone Collector* (1999). Here he plays Lincoln Rhyme, a forensics expert injured on the job and rendered paralyzed. Depressed to the point of suicide, he is asked to assist in the pursuit of a serial killer, which he does from the hospital bed in his New York apartment. Along the way, he develops a professional relationship with—and, increasingly, a personal investment in—a young police officer played by Angelina Jolie. Naturally, she's confronted by hostility from her colleagues and the danger posed by her quarry, and, naturally, she's able to overcome such hurdles with Washington's aid. And, naturally, she coaxes him back from an emotional cliff and sets him on the road to psychological healing.

A Washington character performs similar work in *The Book of Eli*, directed by the (African American) brother team of Albert and Allen Hughes. Eli arrives in a town run by a local warlord (Gary Oldman), who initially courts him by sending a young minion (Mila Kunis) to seduce him. Eli rejects her advances—and rejects her efforts to join him as he strives to complete his mission to deliver a Bible to a California community. But she wears him down, and the two form a durable bond that will outlast Eli's death.

As he moved into the twenty-first century, Washington's capacity and believability as a mentor to black males and white females began to extend to white men as well. One move in this direction was his performance as Major Bennett Marco, the superior officer of Raymond Prentiss Shaw (Liev Schreiber) in Jonathan Demme's 2004 remake of John Frankenheimer's 1962 political thriller, *The Manchurian Candidate*. The remake cleverly repositions a Cold War tale as one of corporate corruption, leaving in place its science-fiction elements of mind control and the juicy role of a castrating mother. For our purposes what matters here is the convincing bond between Washington's and Schreiber's characters in one of those cases where we're meant to, and can, see them in a color-blind fashion. One reason we can is that in 2004 Marco and Shaw are much more directly snared together in the conspiracy than Laurence Harvey and Frank Sinatra were in the original. Washington's character is more helpless and tormented than Sinatra's; even his love interest, played by Kimberly Elise, isn't who she appears to be. Indeed, while we're meant to take for granted that Janet Leigh would fall for Sinatra in the original, there's something suspect about Elise's interest in an older man from the start.

Which points toward an emerging reality: by the second decade of the century, Washington, now a middle-aged man, was no longer the obvious stuff of teenage fantasy he had been in the 1980s and 1990s. But his bodily heft was accompanied by an artistic one, which he could wear surprisingly lightly. So, for example, his many complex maneuvers in the 2006 Spike Lee movie *Inside Man* include serving as a casual mentor to a fellow detective even as he parries the machinations of a bank robber played by Clive Owen and a political fixer played by Jodie Foster. Though they don't immediately recognize it, these adversaries quickly come to appreciate his authority and make adjustments in deference to it.

Similarly, Washington inhabits the role of a train engineer in *Unstoppable* with a sense of unself-conscious security that might have once been difficult for him. Here he's the seasoned veteran to the rookie white conductor (Chris Pine), their gruff hostility sanded down into mutual respect amid their ordeal in grappling with a runaway train. At a time when "working-class" was often considered synonymous with "white," and in a moment marked by a surprising absence of black characters at the movies, Washington occupied an important place on the nation's cultural landscape as a father figure.[27]

He played a twist on that role in 2012 in *Safe House*, where we see him as a secret-agent bad guy who is placed in the custody of the green Ryan Reynolds, who quickly finds he's in over his head. But that's less because of Washington's character than because of a set of other villains who appear to have it in for the both of them. There are shades of *Training Day* here, but with more familiar accents in that Washington finds himself tutoring Reynolds in the wicked ways of an undercover world in a partnership of convenience that deepens over the course of the story. Insofar as Washington has a future as a box office draw, one suspects it will be as a series of variations on what is now this well-established theme.

In recent years, Washington has begun citing Clint Eastwood as a role model for where he wishes to go in his career,[28] and one can indeed see him acting and directing for a long time to come. There are two important differences between them, however. One is that Eastwood's surrogate families have a more jagged, self-consciously alternative quality to them than Washington's—Eastwood has always played more of an outsider than Washington, notwithstanding the racial marginalization endemic to American life. The other is that there has always been a more obvious and comfortable spiritual dimension suffusing Washington's work—another father who has loomed over his career.

———

One fact about Denzel Washington bears repeating as we head toward a conclusion: he's the son of a preacher. It's possible to make too much of this, but his career trajectory suggests it counts for something. To my knowledge, Denzel Washington has never discussed his religious views in any great detail publicly, though one interviewer has reported him as describing his childhood as "family-oriented and religious."[29] Such a fact would be irrelevant at best for most Hollywood actors, but not Washington.

As noted, Washington's breakthrough role was *Glory*. As also noted, there is a powerfully moral and redemptive dimension to the character of Trip, who gives his life for a larger cause and is ultimately buried next to the white officer, one he regarded with skepticism, in a brotherhood of death. One reason this prestige performance mattered to Washington is that it allowed him to begin sculpting a religious sensibility alongside other kinds.

On the night he won his Academy Award for *Glory*, Washington attended the legendary party annually thrown by agent Irving "Swifty" Lazar, where he met the highly commercial producer Joel Silver. Silver offered Washington any one of eight starring roles in films he was developing. Much to Silver's surprise, Washington chose *Ricochet* (1991), in which he plays a detective tormented by the escaped convict he had put in jail.[30] By just about any standard, *Ricochet* is among the weakest works in Washington's canon, and downright mediocre by the standards of its genre. But its graphic violence has a distinctly Old Testament eye-for-an-eye mentality. One suspects, of course, Washington's primary motive for taking the part was neither religious nor artistic, but rather commercial in terms of building a career as a star. However, he would show a perhaps surprising affinity for such roles for a good two decades after *Ricochet*, which suggests a bona fide interest in such films and the values they represent.

One need not stretch, infer, or speculate about what can plausibly be termed Washington's signature role of Malcolm X. That's *Minister* Malcolm X. Secular liberals sometimes forget that Malcolm—like the *Reverend* Martin Luther King Jr.—was at his core a man of faith and that the very essence of the civil rights movement was religious. One of the reasons Washington is so unforgettable in this movie is his ability to capture the rhythms and language of Malcolm's preaching, and while that preaching was Islamic, it was rooted in the evangelical style of Malcolm's own father, who, like Washington's, was also a black Protestant minister. Because it is a great work of art, *Malcolm X*, like its original source material, is about a great many things. One of those things is surely a spiritual quest, a quest that dominates the last part of the movie.

Another indication of Washington's interest in African American religious culture surfaces in *The Preacher's Wife*, the first film he made with his own production company, Mundy Lane Entertainment (named after the street where he grew up in Mount Vernon). In *The Bishop's Wife*, the original on which *Preacher* was based, the cleric in question was a white Episcopal minister looking to build a new cathedral. The remake relocates the movie in a middle-class urban black community beset by much more mundane problems like a broken heating system. Both films are sentimental and predictable, but *The Preacher's Wife* offers a more authentic view of the kind of community not often represented in Hollywood, either in its religious values or its culture. (The gospel choir led by Whitney Houston, a decent actor as well as an extraordinary singer, helps a great deal in this regard.)

In the final analysis, however, Washington's ability to embody the archetype of a man of faith is most effective when it emerges organically out of characters who are not explicitly religious, but who say and do things over the course of a story that reveal such a dimension in their lives. A very good example is Jonathan Demme's *Philadelphia*. At the start of the movie, Washington's character, Joe Miller, loses a case to his gay competitor, Andrew Beckett (Tom Hanks). Unable after multiple previous attempts to get an attorney to represent him in a wrongful termination suit, Beckett turns to Miller, who also says no. Miller later tells his wife of his contempt for homosexuals, mocking them with facial and body gestures. "I admit it. I'm prejudiced," he replies after his wife notes his bias. "I don't like homosexuals. There. You got me."

A turning point for Miller occurs when he spots Beckett at a law library and secretly witnesses the attempt of a clerk to segregate him from the rest of the researchers. Visibly if silently appalled by this, he steps forward to greet Beckett and break the tension. Though Miller never says he acts as a black man conscious of centuries of discrimination, the racial optics are evident. Miller takes on Beckett as a client and befriends him as AIDS takes its toll.

The spiritual power of the movie intensifies as it moves toward its conclusion. At one point Beckett collapses in the courtroom, and Demme's camera suddenly sweeps up to view the scene from above, as if through the eyes of God. We then see Beckett surrounded by friends and family in the hospital, moving gently but inexorably toward what in the nineteenth century would have been called "a good death."[31] Having won the lawsuit, Miller comes there to visit Beckett, who, in a comic gesture that alludes to Miller's awkwardness over a handshake earlier in the movie, beckons Miller to sit beside him. This time Miller does so without hesitation.

When Beckett falters after telling a joke, Miller carefully puts Beckett's oxygen mask on his face. The next lines are worth quoting:

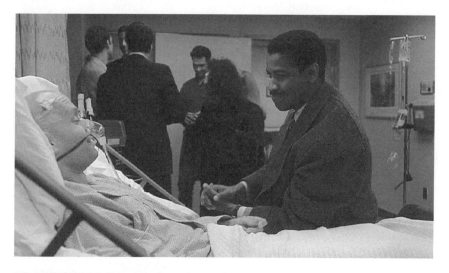

BROTHERHOOD: Washington and Tom Hanks in *Philadelphia* (1993). The experience of family ties finally connects Washington's character, hostile toward gays, with his erstwhile rival and legal partner, dying of AIDS. *(Tri-Star Pictures)*

MILLER: See you later?
BECKETT: Thanks for stopping by.
MILLER: I'll see you again.

Quotidian dialogue, perhaps. But in the stillness of this scene, which cuts between intense close-ups of the two men's faces, it's not hard to hear a transcendental subtext. The "stopping by" Beckett mentions can also be heard as gratitude for Miller's earlier decision to intervene, like the Good Samaritan who paused to help the fallen Jew on the road to Jericho (Luke 10:25–37). And as Miller can't help but be aware by that point, his best hope for seeing Beckett again may well be in the afterlife (note that Beckett does not say he *will* see Miller later, but Miller affirms he will). The scene is almost overwhelming in its understated simplicity.

Another Washington movie with a powerful, and specifically Christian, dimension is *Hurricane*. Like *Malcolm X*, *Hurricane* is many movies—among them a civil rights story, a legal drama, and a celebrity biopic. But prominent among them is a resurrection story. While no one is going to mistake Rubin Carter for a choirboy, he is Christ-like in that he was unjustly condemned to a life sentence, a death in all but name. So it is that he determinedly insists that his wife cut him off so that she can get on with her own life. Yet he persists in believing that he will be born again. His redemption arrives in the unlikely form of an adolescent child named Lesra Martin, a foster adoptee of a group of Canadians. Martin's fascination with Carter's case draws these Canadians in, and they shoulder the struggle to overturn his conviction.[32] At one point during a pause in his retrial, Martin sits alone with Carter as he waits in a holding cell. A grateful surrogate father speaks to a faithful son in slow, measured, biblical terms:

> Lesra, short for Lazarus: "He who has risen from the dead." Rubin, Genesis, Chapter 29, Verse 32: "Behold a son." You put the two together and you behold a son who has risen from the dead. That's no accident. Hate put me in prison. Love's gonna bust me out.[33]

Love also redeems the character of John Creasy in *Man on Fire*. The Creasy we meet at the start of the film is an alienated alcoholic, albeit one who still has enough discipline to take what for him is clearly a second-rate job as a bodyguard for a wealthy Mexican, his Anglo wife, and their daughter. One crucial moment in the melting of Creasy's heart takes place when Dakota Fanning, who plays the child, presents him with a medallion of St. Jude, the patron saint of lost causes, which the preternaturally perceptive girl recognizes is apropos. At another point, the child's mother takes note that he's reading the Bible. When, thanks to the perfidy of the child's father—we come to see there's a reason why he hired an alcoholic—the girl is kidnapped, Creasy becomes utterly remorseless in his quest to rescue her in the classic eye-for-an-eye mentality typical of thrillers. But at the end of the film he makes the ultimate sacrifice for the child—shot and bleeding to death, with blood on his hands reminiscent of stigmata—and our last view of him alive has him rubbing the St. Jude medallion.

Again, I feel compelled to repeat: Washington is not what a skeptical secularist would call a Jesus freak. He has become a movie star of global proportions precisely because he seems, for all his glamour, like an ordinary (black) guy. Since the overwhelming majority of us are believers in one form or another—and African Americans are among the most religious of all Americans[34]—it's not especially surprising that God is in the picture. So it is that in *The Book of Eli* we in effect get to have it both ways: Washington plays a (blind) hero who can dispense thugs with a mere sweep of his terrible swift sword and a pilgrim with a self-appointed mission to keep civilization alive by delivering a Braille Bible to the asylum that once was Alcatraz.

Which brings us back to where this whole discussion started: *Fallen*. "Let me tell you about the time I almost died," we hear Washington say in voice-over before we see anything, and the first image we get is of his desperate figure clawing his way through snowy woods, apparently lunging away from danger. We're informed that what we're about to see is a flashback that begins the night his character, Detective John Hobbes, pays a visit to the jail where the serial killer he captured is about to be executed. The condemned man is oddly ebullient on the cusp of death, singing "Time Is on My Side"[35] and making lots of cryptic allusions and speaking an incomprehensible language. We come to understand that he has been the repository for Azazel, a satanic spirit that leaps across bodies. Hobbes sets up a situation in which he will have a final confrontation with Azazel deep in the woods, so that when Hobbes kills his current host—Hobbes's partner, the otherwise genial John Goodman—the devil will have nowhere to go, because Hobbes has poisoned Azazel's only possible refuge: himself. So when the movie climaxes back where it started, we realize that it's Azazel, not Hobbes, who says, "I want to tell you about the night I almost died," frantically trying to escape Hobbes's body before it expires. In the end, Hobbes's gambit is not entirely successful: a tabby cat circles the dying body and gives Azazel a new lease on life, allowing evil to resume its course on earth.

Recall Roger Ebert's complaint about Washington in *Fallen*: he "doesn't internalize the evil." In a way, this is the point of the movie—though his character cannot vanquish evil entirely, Hobbes nevertheless foils Satan's attempt to steal *his* soul. It's a weirdly optimistic message embedded in a fatalistic film. Ebert is right that it doesn't really work in *Fallen*, but it still reflects the essential optimism at the heart of Washington's work, his confidence that with good faith between generations amid ongoing realities of oppression, time *is* on his side—and that *we're* on the same one. It amounts to a vision of American history that's difficult to resist because it just might be true. And it brings you cheer at the prospect that you'll see him again.

CHAPTER 5

—————

Team Player

Tom Hanks, Company Man

Master narrative: U.S. history as a
saga of collective enterprise

There are lots of ways to talk about Abraham Lincoln, and historians are always finding new ones. The early twenty-first century witnessed book-length efforts to portray him as a gay man, clinically depressed, and a proto-Darwinian in his thinking (Lincoln and Charles Darwin were born on February 12, 1809, spawning bicentennial commentary).[1] But here's a simple way of thinking about Lincoln that I'd like to deploy in the pages that follow: quintessential institutionalist. No man had more confidence in the power of formally constituted organizations as a means to make life better.

The most obvious, but by no means only, manifestation of this institutionalism was his confidence in the positive power of the federal government. Lincoln devotees of the liberal stripe are fond of quoting his famous maxim that "the legitimate object of government is to do for a community of people, whatever they need to have done, but cannot do, *at all*, or cannot, *so well do*, for themselves—in their separate, and individual capacities." One can argue about what really constitutes *legitimate*, and press hard on *need*. Lincoln himself went on to note in this fragment, unpublished in his lifetime, that "the best framed and best administered governments are necessarily expensive; while by errors in frame and maladministration most of them are more onerous than they need be, and some of them very oppressive." But he was able to offer some core examples that remain as cogent as ever: "making and maintaining roads, bridges and the like; providing for the helpless young and afflicted; common schools; and disposing of deceased men's property."[2] If these are not legitimate needs, then nothing is.

Quoting such a passage is a great tool for aligning Lincoln with Franklin Delano Roosevelt, and ever since poet Carl Sandburg's multivolume biography of the 1920s and 1930s, many have done so.[3] But Lincoln can be stretched in plenty of other directions, too. For example, he was a fervent apostle of industrial capitalism, who, as a wealthy lawyer, frequently represented large corporations with a clear conscience. He was an Illinois man, a devoted Republican Party man, and a man whose faith in a government that would provide for "the helpless young and afflicted" also led him to command the largest military the world had ever seen, which he used to prosecute a war of unprecedented scale and unprecedented destructiveness.

Interestingly, about the only institutions Lincoln seemed to lack real zeal for were religious ones. While many historians have noted a deep spiritual vein in his thinking, and believe it increased in intensity over the course of his life, Lincoln was an indifferent churchgoer at best.[4] Born a Baptist, he rented a pew at a Presbyterian church, largely at his wife's insistence. But Lincoln took rumors of his infidelity during his first congressional campaign seriously enough to publish a rebuttal saying that he himself could not support a candidate he knew to be "an open enemy of, and scoffer at, religion."[5] (Now *that's* politics.) True to his word, Lincoln frequently invoked traditional Christian language for the rest of his life while actively sidestepping doctrinal issues or professions of denominational loyalty. He wasn't opposed to organized religion. He just wasn't as enthusiastic about it as he was about most other institutions in American life.

Perhaps this makes Lincoln sound like a pretty conventional, even bland, guy. But it's worth pointing out that there were plenty of people of his time—and ever since—with decidedly different values. Lincoln came of age in a decidedly Jacksonian political culture in which government was widely seen, in Illinois and much of the rest of the country, as a problem, not a solution. Corporations were tools of oppression. Political parties were (newly) acceptable, but the dominant party was that of latter-day Jeffersonians, the Democratic Party, and Lincoln was a Whig, only reluctantly becoming a Republican long after it was clear to many of his peers that the Whigs were no longer a viable political organization. Lincoln's youth also corresponded with a major theological upheaval known as "the Second Great Awakening," in which emerging evangelical churches and doctrines pushed aside established ones and edged their way into social and even political debates. Insofar as Lincoln's religious thought reflected any religious tendency, it was the Calvinism of the New England branch in his ancestry.[6] So it's safe to say that on the major public issues of his time, he was always a bit out of the mainstream.

And yet he managed to win just about every popularity contest he ever entered. That included four terms in the state legislature, a term in the U.S. House of Representatives, and election to the captaincy in the state militia during his military service, an honor he described decades later as "a success which gave me more pleasure than any I have had since."[7] The one major election he lost, his U.S. Senate race with Stephen A. Douglas in 1858, proved closer than any informed observer could have safely predicted at the outset. The point bears emphasizing: Lincoln was not simply respected and admired; he was deeply *liked* by a great many who knew him personally and a great many who did not. The stories attesting to this are legion, as are the jokes, many grounded in self-effacing humor, that have been attributed to him. ("I suppose God loves ugly people," he reputedly said. "That's why he makes so many of them.")

Of course, many people hated Lincoln, too, one enough to kill him. Lincoln took significantly less than half of the popular vote in the divisive presidential election of 1860. Even now, when he comes close to being loved by all of the people all of the time, he can still provoke bitter polemics over his racism or his big-government policies.[8] But no one has embodied the pursuit of individual happiness through the common good more vividly than Lincoln, so much so that he is perhaps the inevitable standard of measurement for the American apostle of the common good.

Like his distant relative Tom Hanks. That's Hanks as in Nancy Hanks, the maiden name of Lincoln's mother. She was one of eight Nancy Hankses born during the 1780s; Lincoln himself, who believed he inherited his ambition, alertness, and powers of analysis from his mother, considered her illegitimate (he understood her to be the child of Lucy Hanks and "a well-bred Virginia farmer or planter"). The Tom Hanks branch of the family tree emerges with his great-grandfather Daniel Boone Hanks, who left his native Kentucky and migrated to California in 1873.[9]

Hanks has made allusions to his famous ancestor. As generations of children know, he is the voice of Woody the cowboy in the *Toy Story* saga. In *Toy Story 2* (1999), Woody meets his love interest in Jessie the Yodeling Cowgirl (voice of Joan Cusack), who exclaims "Sweet Mother of Abraham Lincoln!" upon meeting him. In a 1990 episode of *Saturday Night Live*, Hanks, who's hosting, pretends to limp onstage with a bad knee and is recounting his recent triumphs when he's suddenly confronted by the Great Emancipator, who calls him "an incredible pussy."[10]

Of course, it would be foolish to make too much of this connection. Or the two men's affinity for Shakespeare. Or difficult childhoods in blended families that led both to leave them decisively behind. Or even their submerged religiosity and tendency to go along with their wives' traditions. Nevertheless, at least one affinity matters: they both symbolized, for millions of Americans of their time, the viability and decency of national institutions when they were being called into question. Neither man is typically described in these terms, but to a great extent, their institutionalism lies at the core of their appeal.

As with Lincoln, one can begin to appreciate what makes Hanks popular and distinctive by comparing him with his peers. Clint Eastwood's entire career has been premised on skepticism toward big institutions. Denzel Washington's vision of history is conceived in terms of families, literal and figurative; in his vision of republican fatherhood, good parents and mentors make good public servants. Even more than Eastwood, Daniel Day-Lewis plays rugged individualists whose attempts at solidarity almost always fail.

Hanks is different. Fathers, children, and lovers have always figured in his work, particularly his early work, yet they've never really been central, and are as likely a hindrance as a help. Families are often part of the story. But *teams*, broadly construed, are close to his heart. No less than Day-Lewis or Eastwood, Hanks has an ego, and his characters typically occupy some kind of leadership position. They nevertheless operate within a *system* of some sort and are committed not only to working within it but to making it better. There's an emphatic spirit of republicanism at large in Hanks's America: his characters represent, serve, and act on that basis.

It's a powerful vision, and it's made him a powerful man. By the early twenty-first century, Hanks was the single most successful actor in U.S. history, with box office grosses that will have crossed $4 billion by the time you read these words.[11] A surprising number of lines from his movies— "There's no crying in baseball!"; "Houston, we have a problem,"; "Life is like a box of chocolates"; "Stupid is as stupid does"—have become pop culture slogans. He has also become an entertainment impresario with his own production company (Playtone, named after a fictional record label he created for the 1996 film *That Thing You Do!*) and an active producer whose programming ranges across movies, television, and the Internet. Hanks makes mocking references to his "crack team of show-business experts," but the irony of the phrase can't quite hide the reality of his circumstances.[12]

Amid his wide-ranging interests, history is central. In addition to his lead role in *Saving Private Ryan* (1998), Hanks was executive producer of the 2001 World War II miniseries *Band of Brothers* and a producer of its successor, *The Pacific* (2010). His lifelong interest in the space program— and star turn in the 1995 film *Apollo 13*—led to the 1998 cable series *From the Earth to the Moon*, which he helped write, produce, and direct, as well as appeared in as an actor. As of this writing, he is developing a series on the Kennedy assassination. These are among the reasons the esteemed journalist and historian Douglas Brinkley wrote a 2010 essay on Hanks as historian.[13] Here, though, our focus will be on Hanks the actor, as he was when his vision first crystallized. It's a vision that's surprisingly clear—and just plain surprising in having materialized at all.

———————

Tom Hanks was not born in a log cabin, but his beginnings were modest enough. He arrived on July 9, 1956, in Concord, California. His father, Amos, worked as a chef; his mother, Janet, was a housewife who bore three other children (Tom was the third of the four). Two major developments destabilized his family life. The first was the itinerancy of his father's job, which led to frequent moves around California and to Reno, Nevada. The other was a string of blended family arrangements that began when his parents divorced when Hanks was five years old. The tenor of childhood recollections is melancholy. "There's no denying I had an unhappy childhood," he said in 2010. His father was frequently absent and remote, though the two were relatively close by the time of Amos's death in 1992. He remains in touch with his primary siblings, as well as his biological mother, whom he typically saw on holidays while growing up. But scars linger. "I am not as close to my mom as other kids are, but that doesn't stop the fact that I love her," he has said. "I say to my mom, 'I love you, but I don't know you because I didn't live with you.' "[14]

Hanks attended high school in Northern California, where he kept a relatively low profile and earned middling grades. Though he was raised as a Catholic, an evangelical Christian group was an important basis of his social life ("It beat smoking pot," he explained, with a wry tone that would become a staple of his interview mode).[15] He also started acting in school productions. His relationship with his acting teacher, Rawley Farnsworth, caused an unintentional stir in 1994 when Hanks inadvertently outed him as a homosexual by way of thanking him in his Oscar acceptance speech for *Philadelphia* (1993). The incident became the basis for the 1997 Kevin Kline movie *In and Out*.[16]

Upon his graduation in 1974, Hanks deepened his study of theater by enrolling in Chabot College, a large community college in the Bay Area. He later transferred to Sacramento State, where he earned a scholarship. His immersion in all aspects of theatrical production led to a focus on acting. It was at Sacramento State that Hanks met his first wife, Susan Dillingham (stage name Samantha Lewes), whom he married in 1980. He was also noticed by the artistic director of the Great Lakes Shakespeare Festival, who invited him to work as a summer intern. Hanks and Lewes eventually moved (six months shy of graduation) to Cleveland, where he landed a series of leading—and paying—roles.[17]

With Lewes and their infant son, future actor Colin, in tow, Hanks headed to New York in 1978, where the couple hoped to make their breakthrough. Lewes did not; Hanks struggled long enough to win a small role in the third-rate slasher film *He Knows You're Alone* (1980). A few months earlier, amid an increasingly desperate economic situation, marital tension, and a brief flirtation with drugs, Hanks had been invited to Los Angeles to audition for a new ABC sitcom, *Bosom Buddies*.[18] The show, in which he would be paired with Peter Scolari, was a running gag about a pair of men who cross-dress in order to live in a cheap New York residential hotel. *Bosom Buddies* was a moderate success after it went on the air in late 1980, but it ran out of ratings steam and was canceled after two seasons. It was during this period that he met actor Rita Wilson, who became his second wife in 1988. Hanks had two more children by Wilson in addition to the two he had with Lewes.

Bosom Buddies showcased Hanks's comic gifts. Though he lacked the chiseled good looks of Eastwood, Day-Lewis, or Washington—all of whom also got their start in (dramatic) television—his manic, yet subtly controlled, personality attracted the attention of other television producers, resulting in a 1982 performance on the long-running hit series *Happy Days*. Hanks's work in that episode intrigued Ron Howard, whose lifetime of acting on *The Andy Griffith Show* and *Happy Days* had just culminated in his directorial debut, *Night Shift* (1982). A shrewd judge of talent, he cast Hanks in the lead for his next film, *Splash* (1984).

Splash boosted multiple careers, among them Daryl Hannah's and John Candy's; for Howard it marked the burgeoning of a film empire. But its box office success was grounded in low-budget charm. Hanks plays Allen Bauer, who with his brother Freddie (Candy) runs a produce business in lower Manhattan. As a child we see in an opening prologue, Bauer creates an alarming incident when he jumps off a vacation vessel near Cape Cod in pursuit of a mermaid, which of course no one believes. As an adult Bauer is a likable fellow, but one with a persistent vein of melancholy who cannot sustain a romantic commitment. Into his life returns the mermaid, who visits New York on a temporary set of legs. She chooses the name "Madison" for herself from a street sign during a midtown jaunt, and the two begin—or, perhaps more accurately, resume—their romance.

Splash generated a lot of momentum for Hanks, but he was unable to build on it. Over the next four years he released a string of movies— *Bachelor Party* (1984), *The Man with One Red Shoe* (1985), *Volunteers* (1985),

The Money Pit (1986), *Nothing in Common* (1986), *Every Time We Say Goodbye* (1986), and *Dragnet* (1987)—that suggested stasis at best. By the end of the decade, Hanks was an established B-actor.

Then came *Big*. This 1988 high-concept film, in which a child inhabits an adult's body, was developed with a strong Hollywood pedigree that included Anne Spielberg, sister of Steven, as co-writer and Penny Marshall as director. Robert De Niro, Harrison Ford, and Warren Beatty were all in serious discussions for the lead, but all three finally declined. Hanks himself took some persuading, but eventually signed on to appear in what became his first blockbuster movie.[19]

Big was also truly a *Tom Hanks* movie. One can see why a Beatty, De Niro, or Ford would have been interested in playing thirteen-year-old Josh Baskin; the role brought with it technical challenges that would appeal to serious actors. Yet, talented as they are, in retrospect it's hard to imagine them playing the part with the unself-consciousness Hanks achieves. By design, *Big* is a simple story: suburban New Jersey boy gets wish to be "big"; becomes an executive for a Manhattan toy company; gets enmeshed in corporate politics and a love triangle; finds his way back to childhood again. The performance rests on nuances of facial expression and bodily movement, reflecting a simplicity both inherent and achieved. It earned Hanks his first Oscar nomination.

The movie also gave him a second chance for top-tier stardom. Even before *Big*, Hanks had taken the part of a stand-up comedian in *Punchline*, which was released shortly after *Big* in 1988 and thus widely viewed as a follow-up. He portrays an edgy, competitive person who never becomes completely unlikable, and it ranks among his best work. Nevertheless, while *Punchline* may have been an artistically ambitious undertaking, it was part of another string of less-than-stellar movies—one that included *The 'Burbs* (1989), *Turner & Hooch* (1989), and *Joe Versus the Volcano* (1990)—that once again threatened his standing.

Moreover, his next move, while thoroughly understandable, was a thorough fiasco: Hanks took the lead role in *The Bonfire of the Vanities*, the 1990 movie directed by Brian De Palma and based on the 1987 novel by Tom Wolfe about a Wall Street trader embroiled in a racial firestorm after a hit-and-run accident in the Bronx. A plum role for just about any actor, it held special promise for Hanks in terms of establishing serious dramatic chops, and one he was in a good position to exploit given the status he had gained from *Big*. The rise and fall of this once-hot Hollywood property has been brilliantly documented by journalist Julie Salamon, who did the research on it in real time and subsequently published *The Devil's Candy*, one of the best books ever made about the movie business.[20] The conventional wisdom is that *Bonfire* was hobbled by a number of problems, among them a storyline that couldn't effectively encapsulate Wolfe's novel, a saccharine sermon in its conclusion (after late rewrites and ethnic shuffling within a script that preview audiences considered racist), and, above all, poor casting choices, among them Melanie Griffith as a southern belle and Bruce Willis as an alcoholic journalist who is simply impossible to take seriously. Many reviewers also believed Hanks was miscast as the blue-blooded Sherman McCoy. But he had already done a good, albeit comic, turn as a boozy 1960s Yale graduate who escapes angry bookies by joining the Peace Corps in *Volunteers*, and nothing in his *Bonfire* performance rings particularly false. Had the movie been a success, it might well have entered his personal pantheon.

He managed to walk away largely unscathed—indeed, he's one of the few major players who emerges from Salamon's book with his dignity intact—but also tried to take stock. He'd appeared in fourteen films in the space of six years and decided that was too many. "Part of it is the insecurity factor," he reflected later, in a comment that would be permuted a series of ways in subsequent interviews. "Every time, you feel like you're never going to get another opportunity again."[21] Another aspect of this personal reassessment involved getting a new agent, Ron Meyer of Creative Artists Agency, one of the most powerful in the industry. Meyer advised Hanks to take a role he had rejected multiple times already: a small part as an alcoholic manager of a 1940s women's baseball team.[22] Hanks took that advice and began making history.

———

Julie Salamon does not devote much space to Tom Hanks in *The Devil's Candy*—her protagonist is really the director, Brian De Palma—but the portrait that emerges of Hanks, one that's important to the degree to which it was unmediated by the usual show business filters, is intriguing. We see him at the start of the book quietly but firmly advocating Melanie Griffith over Uma Thurman as his onscreen love interest for *Bonfire of the Vanities*, a clear case of a star exercising his leverage. For the most part, however, he is determined to be a stand-up guy. "He believed, and wanted everybody else to believe, that he was just a guy doing his job," Salamon reports. In contrast to Method actors who undergo a flashy personal transformation (think Daniel Day-Lewis), "Hanks, a pragmatic man, actually believed stars could simply *pretend* to be somebody else." When Hanks goes down to the World Trade Center as part of his research on how to be a bond trader, he refuses to take the stretch limousine the movie studio provides, insisting on the plain black sedan the traders use—only relative slumming, to be sure, but an act of moderation nonetheless.[23]

Salamon was probably right to be skeptical about Hanks's modesty (even if that skepticism was partly a matter of frustration about how guarded her subject was), and the passage of time and the growth in Hanks's clout have probably made him both more guarded and quite possibly more imperious when there's nobody around to report it. But there are at least two reasons to take his self-presentation seriously. The first is how much better he comes off relative to his co-stars. Salamon depicts a Bruce Willis justifiably insecure about his acting abilities; compared with him, she writes, "Hanks was diligent and uncomplaining—and he had talent." Griffith, for her part, was downright embarrassing. At one point she "totters" over to a seated Hanks and plops herself on his lap. She wants to know if he's uncomfortable at the prospect of their upcoming love scenes. "Not at all, no," he replies, pulling his head back stiffly. Hanks then makes a genial but pointed joke about having seen Griffith's husband, Don Johnson, on TV recently. Griffith apparently takes the hint and moves on.[24]

The other, and really more important, reason to take Salamon's portrait seriously is that it comports with the choices Hanks began to make now that he had finally attained a durable degree of power in the movie industry. He not only slowed down his pace but began to pick parts that had a more emphatic collaborative dimension. If filmmaking is among other things a form of politics, Hanks now began to reveal real talent in the way he got things done. And at the heart of that talent was what might be termed characteristically Lincolnian skills of discipline and plainspoken eloquence.

One early indication of this, and a real turning point as it concerns Hanks's historical vision, is *A League of Their Own* (1992). *League* was another Penny Marshall project, a plum assignment for a female director at what could be termed a feminist moment. (As we've seen, this was the same moment when Meryl Streep was actively deconstructing portrayals of women in the films she was making.) The Clarence Thomas–Anita Hill controversy of 1991 generated new awareness of sexual harassment in the workplace, and the optics of a row of older white males sitting in judgment of a female sparked the so-called Year of the Woman that brought fresh faces, like U.S. Senator Patty Murray, to Congress. This was also the year of *Thelma & Louise*, a cinematic feminist manifesto by screenwriter Callie Khouri. It was, moreover, a moment when a new wave of feminist scholarship committed to documenting the lives of ordinary people began trickling down into popular consciousness. And Title IX, a 1972 law that promoted equity in sports, was reaching critical mass in the nation's schools. All these currents converged to create an audience for a film loosely based on a real-life All-American Girls Professional Baseball League founded by Chicago Cubs owner Philip K. Wrigley, which operated from 1943 to 1954. Players in the league are honored in the "Diamond Dreams: Women in Baseball" exhibit installed in the Baseball Hall of Fame in Cooperstown in 1988.

A League of Their Own is an ensemble piece whose novel cast includes Madonna and Rosie O'Donnell as ballplayers. Their team, the Rockford Peaches, resembles the quintessential platoon in a typical Hollywood World War II movie: you got your wiseacre city kid, your hayseed, your nerdy intellectual, etc. There's also a sibling rivalry between two sisters that serves as the plot engine of the story. The presiding spirit of the picture is Geena Davis, who plays Dottie Hinson, star catcher of the Peaches, and she carries the film with understated grace.

Hanks, who doesn't appear until a half hour into the movie, plays the manager of the Peaches, Jimmy Dugan. His entrance is a bit startling: boozy, overweight, and unshaven, he's pretty much the antithesis of any previous Hanks character. Dugan's haplessness is also contextual: a former slugger who's blown out his knee, he's unsuited to join the war effort, much less play ball himself ("How did I get so useless so fast," he laments under his breath at one point). Nor is there any charm in his loutishness, as there had been in previous Hanks characters. Dugan is prone to humiliate his players publicly when he's sober enough to notice them. "Are you crying?" he asks a player after chewing her out in the movie's signature moment. "There's no crying in baseball!"

Naturally, Dugan begins to change—but only when he begins to follow the example of his catcher. At one point early on in his tenure as manager, Dugan looks up from his newspaper to realize that Hinson, who has been functioning as a de facto coach in response to Dugan's de facto absence, is foolishly signaling for a bunt. "What are ya, stupid?" he says to her. Dugan demands that another player—"blond girl"—tell him what the signal is to swing away. What follows is a comic tug-of-war with a bemused batter trying to figure out which set of touched noses, pulled earlobes, and doffed caps she should follow. "Who's the goddamn manager?" Dugan finally asks, answering his own question in exasperation: "I am!" An angry Hinson responds, "Then act like it, you big lush!" She steps aside, Dugan prevails, and his judgment proves sound: the batter responds with an extra-base hit that scores a run. Dugan naturally struts at this. Hinson turns away in the dugout but can't hide her smile: she's happy about the hit (and perhaps that she's nudged Dugan to do his job).

Hinson and Dugan gradually become more friendly, though any romantic relationship is blocked by the fact that Hinson is married to a GI

MIXED SIGNALS: Tom Hanks and Geena Davis compete to coach a batter in *A League of Their Own* (1992). The film marked a turning point in Hanks's career and his institutional vision of U.S. history. *(Sony Pictures)*

fighting in Italy. The fear of permanent separation from loved ones looms over the women's lives, and it's in response to this that Dugan finally turns a corner and achieves a sense of maturity. He's in the process of a self-serving locker-room pep talk, noting that he'll get a bonus if they win the championship, when a mail carrier arrives with an ominous telegram from the War Department. The mailman clumsily notes that this is bad news, but then realizes he lacks the paperwork to deliver it to the right party. (Hinson braces herself to be informed that her husband is dead.) Dugan, angered by the carrier's insensitivity, literally manhandles him, yanking the telegram away, ripping it open, and gently delivering the bad news to another player. In so doing, he's taken a significant step toward becoming a supportive man who takes care of his team.

Hinson's husband unexpectedly returns from the war, and she quits the squad. Dugan is upset, in part because he believes she doesn't really understand just how much being a ballplayer has meant to her, how central it really is to her identity, whether or not she happens to be somebody's wife. The movie manages to orchestrate her return, resolve her sibling rivalry with her less talented younger sister, and set up a future for Dugan as a committed manager (where he can be a father figure in a way that's a bit reminiscent of Denzel Washington). It ends where it began, a half century later, with the now-widowed Hinson making a trip to visit her teammates in Cooperstown. Dugan is dead by that point. But a paradigm for Hanks has been established. From this point on, he will be a team player. Many, as they were for Lincoln, are teams of rivals.[25]

"I had any number of people saying 'What the hell are you doing?'" Hanks told *Entertainment Weekly* after the movie's release. "'It's not even your movie, you're just a guy passing through.'" But, he explained, *League* was a more compelling option at this point in his career. "I could have done *Popo Goes to the Big Town* and *Oops, I Tripped on a Lawn Chair.* Things like that. I was looking for something to do different and I think the message got out that he'll [Hanks is referring to himself] do anything. Which is a good thing. He'll get fat. He doesn't have to be the cute guy. He will cut his hair in an unattractive manner. He will be disgusting and sit there. He doesn't have to be the king of every scene that he is in. Well, that's a marvellous message to put out there."[26]

A League of Their Own was a surprise box office success, breaking the $100 million benchmark for a hit at the time. Hanks basked in this group triumph—Madonna and Davis were at the zenith of their careers; Rosie O'Donnell would soon have a hit TV show—and then moved on to a more decisively starring vehicle. This was *Sleepless in Seattle* (1993), co-produced, co-written, and directed by a woman (Nora Ephron, of *Heartburn* fame with Meryl Streep). The "team" in this case is a family that consists of the widowed Hanks and his son. This storyline converges toward that of Meg Ryan's character, an engaged woman in Baltimore, culminating in a finale strongly reminiscent of the 1957 Cary Grant–Deborah Kerr classic *An Affair to Remember*. *Sleepless in Seattle* consolidated Hanks's status as a romantic lead. His appeal was that of Everyman: He makes it plausible for any guy to imagine that he, too, might land Meg Ryan.

Hanks's next movie, *Philadelphia* (1993), ranks among the most important in his collaborative vision. I've already discussed this film from the point of view of Hanks's co-star, Denzel Washington, and the way it reflects Washington's career-long engagement with issues of family and faith. Here, though, *Philadelphia*'s importance is somewhat different: as a story about one of the more hallowed institutions in American life—its legal system—and what happens when it becomes an instrument of oppression, a refuge for the wicked.

Philadelphia opens with Hanks's character, Andrew Beckett, as a rising star in a powerful corporate law firm in Philadelphia. The first scene shows him dispatching a restraining order sought by Washington's character, clearly a lower-rent attorney, who is waxing rhapsodic with a judge about how the limestone powder at a construction site is essentially a form of environmental racism. Hanks, however, can also wax with the best of them, noting that the construction site is responsible for more than 750 jobs, and that the injunction is "an example of the rapacious litigation that today is tearing at the fabric of our society." His little speech is something of an inside joke that both his opponent and the judge recognize as frothy, as evidenced by their facial expressions, and she chastises the lawyers for their inflated rhetoric before ruling in Beckett's favor. The sequence is almost a piece of legal Kabuki theater in which social conflict is resolved in terms of linguistic posturing.

But more serious issues lurk. We get a foreshadowing of this in the next scene, which begins with both attorneys entering an elevator with an injured man. As the elevators doors close, we see (as they do not) graffiti bearing the famous words long associated with the civil rights movement: "No justice, no peace!" We also see Beckett going to a clinic for treatment of AIDS, a condition he is hiding from his employers. When they find out, they frame him for the misplacement of an important document, which then becomes a pretext for firing him. Professionally, Beckett goes from *Bonfire of the Vanities*–style Master of the Universe to pariah of the firm.

The rest of *Philadelphia* is essentially a process whereby Beckett creates a new team with his erstwhile rival, as they launch a wrongful termination suit against Beckett's former employer that rests on their interpretation of the Americans with Disabilities Act. To put it another way: he pursues an institutional remedy for an institutional wrong. Allegorically speaking, Beckett is a bit like his namesake, Thomas Becket: a bishop (which is to say agent of church law) who ran afoul of his powerful patron, King Henry II of England, and was murdered for his resistance. The assassination here is figurative; the canonization artistic. But both men died true believers in their respective systems. So, of course, did Abraham Lincoln, who was also a lawyer.

Philadelphia was a complete triumph for Hanks, part of a string of unbroken critical and commercial successes that culminated in his first Academy Award for Best Actor in 1994. Even more remarkable, he followed it up later that year with *Forrest Gump*, among the most commercially successful movies of all time. Hanks also scored a second Oscar for Best Actor—one of only two serial winners (the other was Spencer Tracy). The one-two punch of *Philadelphia* and *Forrest Gump*—a combination all the more powerful for Hanks's markedly different performances—completed his transformation from promising-but-wobbly journeyman actor to Hollywood phenomenon.

This does not mean *Forrest Gump* is a good movie. Certainly, the special effects, which show Hanks's title character spliced into any one of a number of historical scenarios, were positively amazing in the age before computer-generated imagery, of which Robert Zemeckis, the director of *Forrest Gump*, was a pioneer. But there are plenty of reasons to regard it with skepticism, beginning with its source material, Winston Groom's 1986 novel of the same name.[27] The filmmakers took the core of the novel for their plot: mentally handicapped mid-century Alabama man stumbles into a series of famous historical moments while pining for his childhood sweetheart. But in an unusual reversal from what one typically expects, Forrest Gump is a far more nuanced character on the screen than on the page. Even with a dead-pan expression, Hanks manages to endow the character with more psychological complexity than Groom does. The novel's opening line, "Let me say this: bein a idiot is no box of chocolates," was refashioned into the still trite, but more resonant, "My mama always said life was like a box of chocolates: you never know what you're gonna get." The signature line of the novel is variations on "I am tryin to do the right thing." But "Stupid is as stupid does" has a lot more zing. Both versions note that Forrest's name, derived from Ku Klux Klan founder Nathan Bedford Forrest, was given him by his mother as a cautionary tale, but the movie hits this irony more cleanly.

Similarly, the filmmakers took many plotlines from the book but spruced up the story by leaving others, like Forrest's stint as a professional wrestler, behind. And they dropped his sweetheart marrying another man, instead having the joylessly sybaritic Jenny Curran (Robin Wright) die of AIDS, a more dramatic choice that gives the story more relevance even as it somehow makes her a more pure character. They also replaced the hulking figure of the novel and clapped braces on his legs that he only sheds when fleeing bullies—hence Jenny's famous line, "Run, Forrest, run!" With the proper support, the film suggests, weak children can still make strong adults. So it is that Sally Field's Mama Gump resorts to sexual barter so that her son can attend the local public school rather than be sent away to a special ed program. The overall effect of these changes makes the movie more deft, but also more sentimental.

I was teaching freshman composition at Harvard at the time of *Forrest Gump*'s release, and at one point included it on a list of possible essay topics. But I could never resist offering my own one-line review: "This is a movie a fascist would love." I'd explain that Forrest is a man who simply does what he's told, an utterly passive figure who makes no real contribution to the world-historical events—the civil rights movement, Vietnam, Watergate, Alabama football under Bear Bryant, et al.—with which he accidentally intersects, like the allegorical feather in the wind that flutters across the opening and closing frames of the movie. This effect gets reinforced by the filmmakers' attempts to strive at ideological balance. Forrest braves an angry crowd of racists to pick up the dropped books of an African American student at the University of Alabama, but the hippies with whom Jenny throws in her lot come off as a narcissistic, even hypocritical, bunch. Forrest stumbles his way to the microphone at a war protest at the Lincoln Memorial while wearing his army uniform, but the power gets cut so that no one can hear what he says—a moot point once he spots

Jenny in the crowd and splashes his way into the reflecting pool. Though drenched in the recent history of the United States, the movie is a dispiriting experience for anyone who considers the social upheavals of the late twentieth century as more than a set of costume changes in a movie that floats from one scenario to another. Insofar as there is one beyond the moment at the memorial, the Lincoln connection in the movie takes the form of a sentimental fanfare for the common man.

It was my oldest son, on the cusp of taking a first-year writing course himself, who forced me to revise this view of *Forrest Gump*. He pointed out that Forrest does not only observe but takes action, and has a specific contribution to make in the various institutional settings in which he finds himself: his speed. However dull-witted he may be, his natural physical quickness allows him to return kicks for the Crimson Tide, to win the Medal of Honor rescuing his comrades in Vietnam, to go on a global goodwill tour as a Ping-Pong champion, and to inspire a legion of followers when he takes up cross-country running. His speed is both comic and moving when he senses, not always accurately, any harm to Jenny, the only time he resorts to physical force.

My son makes an important point. But it should also be noted that Forrest lacks any particular feeling or loyalty for the various institutions he joins—educational, military, commercial—*as* institutions. In all cases, he comes and he goes. His loyalties—to Jenny, whom he meets on a school bus; to Lieutenant Dan, his former commanding officer; to his late comrade, Bubba, in whose name he starts a shrimping business—are personal. While such connections are the foundation of any abstract sense of institutional loyalty, abstraction is not Forrest's strong suit.

Still, one can begin to appreciate what institutions do for Forrest when one considers that Jenny's tragic fate can be explained precisely by their absence: she's rootless, and that begins with the institution of the family. The script strongly hints that Jenny is a victim of abuse at the hands of her father and effectively spends her life running away, including running away from the one man who can heal that psychic wound. In an ironic act of compassion, Forrest later sees to it that her house is torn down.

Perhaps there is a historiographic argument embedded in the movie after all: Jenny's rebellion is a dead end because she lacked functional social institutions into which to channel any hope for change, instead drifting in and out of casual relationships, personal as well as collective. Forrest may have been dim-witted, but he always had a home. He also always had some other place to belong, a real community to join. Institutional communities have limits. But it's only within limits that possibilities can take shape.

Hanks's next project, *Apollo 13* (1995), in which he again teamed up with director Ron Howard, represents his most full-throated expression of affection for a government institution: the large bureaucratic federal agency known as the National Aeronautics and Space Administration (NASA). Hanks's childhood passion for the U.S. space program has been well documented; what's worth emphasizing here is that this formative hobby took root at the very moment in American history when collective confidence in the federal government was at an all-time high, and one in which vast public projects—the interstate highway system and the early Internet, to name two other examples—were undertaken in a can-do spirit. Though *Apollo 13* is a chronicle of a real-life near-disaster, the filmmakers don't blame individual government workers or the agency generally. Indeed, we learn that the mysterious problem that endangers the lives of the three astronauts on board the spacecraft was caused by equipment malfunction—which is to say, it was the *private* sector to which such tasks were subcontracted that screwed up. *Apollo 13* is an unabashed story of heroism on the part of thoroughgoing organization men.

At the center of this heroism is Hanks's character, astronaut Jim Lovell, who led the mission. But for all the excruciating planning that goes into moon exploration, much remains a matter of chance. Indeed, Lovell only leads the mission because the team slated to go is unexpectedly scratched, and he subsequently makes the reluctant decision to scratch a member of his own team because it's believed he's coming down with measles. So when crisis erupts on the very cusp of success, a third member of the trio cannot repress his suspicion that the replacement precipitated the crew's problems. In a crucial scene in the movie, Lovell shuts this carping down. By virtue of his disciplined leadership, the three men maintain their emotional equilibrium under extremely stressful conditions. Meanwhile, the crew on the ground strains its own internal resources to bring these men back safely. *Apollo 13* is thus not a story of systemic breakdown, but rather of systemic success.

Hanks reaffirmed his commitment to his vision of teamwork with his participation in the now-classic Pixar Studios animated *Toy Story* trilogy, the first installment of which was also released in 1995 (two others followed in 1999 and 2010). He is the voice of Woody, the TV tie-in cowboy figure and beloved companion of Andy, a suburban child unaware that the toys that populate his room have a life of their own. Like a lot of communities, this one is populated by a diverse collection of individuals (loosely defined, in that many are reproductions, like the Mr. Potato Head), who did not necessarily arrive there by active

PROGRAM MANAGER: Hanks as astronaut Jim Lovell in *Apollo 13* (1995). The film was a paean to a federal government bureaucracy, something that had almost become inconceivable in the conservative climate of the 1990s. (*Universal*)

choice, and who must—in any number of meanings of the term—find their place.

Andy's toys are fortunate in this regard in that they are led by Woody, who governs—and here it's worth noting that he's a sheriff and as such an upholder of institutional order—this motley crew with a notably graceful hand: he's smart, funny, and genuinely appreciative of the specific skills individuals contribute to the community (like the reconnaissance missions performed by toy soldiers). Woody's Achilles' heel is his vanity, which gets wounded by the arrival of a rival for Andy's affection: the outer-space action figure Buzz Lightyear (voiced by Tim Allen). Buzz is genial and generous, but has an elevated view of himself, which irritates

Woody, who ultimately succeeds in puncturing his illusions by showing him a television advertisement for other versions of himself. "You are a *toy!*" he shouts at Buzz. "A child's plaything!"

Woody pays for this transgression by forfeiting the goodwill of his fellow toys, which leads to his falling into the clutches of the evil Sid, the boy next door who brutally rips apart and reconstructs toys in the service of his own imagination. Only when Woody and Buzz achieve some sense of clarity about themselves—and, most crucially, only when they demonstrate a willingness to collaborate—can they and the other toys overcome the series of crises in these movies that include covetous toy collectors, a dastardly toy cabal at a child-care center, and near-incineration, not to mention the tragic inevitability of Andy growing up and leaving them behind. In *Toy Story 3,* Woody, who still holds a place of honor in Andy's heart, is slated to go to college with him. But the moving conclusion of the saga suggests that a meaningful life is best found with one's colleagues in the service of the next generation.

Though the *Toy Story* saga was in fact an enormously complex undertaking to bring to the screen, Hanks's participation, while prominent, was relatively minor. *That Thing You Do!* (1996), by contrast, was his most demanding project to date: a film he wrote, produced, and directed, in addition to appearing as a supporting actor. This story of the rapid rise and fall of a one-hit rock band in the 1960s is a small masterpiece, a perfectly pitched paean to the golden age of pop music. The film also featured some up-and-coming talent, including Charlize Theron, Liv Tyler, Giovanni Ribisi, and Steve Zahn, all of whom would go on to greater prominence. While one should always take the promotional materials for movies with a grain of salt, the seemingly genuine affection a good chunk of the cast expressed for this production in general and Hanks in particular at a video-recorded ten-year reunion gathering suggests a deft managerial hand.[28]

That Thing You Do! is also a compelling document in Hanks's evolving vision of the way organizations shape history, in this case cultural history, and a growing sense of the ambiguities involved. We witness the birth of the Wonders, four young men from Erie, Pennsylvania, who join forces in a somewhat improvised fashion when drummer Guy Patterson agrees to sub for a band member who has broken his arm. The Wonders are led by a talented, driven, and callous songwriter who neglects his girlfriend. His song "That Thing You Do!" generates some spontaneous attention, eventually attracting that of the somewhat mysterious "Mr. White," who signs the band to his label, Playtone Records.

Hanks plays Mr. White with an inscrutable, and just possibly malevolent, air. He's eagle-eyed, something the band members don't seem to

MAKING A POINT: Hanks as the enigmatic Mr. White, manager of the Wonders, issuing a directive to band member Guy (Tom Everett Scott) in *That Thing You Do!* (1996). The film, Hanks's directorial debut, reflected his ensemble sensibility. *(20th Century Fox)*

notice when he engages them in not-quite-casual conversation. They follow his commands largely without question, though the bandleader becomes increasingly anxious and insistent that the group go into the studio, while the evocatively named White blandly informs them they will continue their tour and milk "That Thing You Do!" for all it's worth. Which, as it turns out, is a lot. The song rides up the charts, culminating with the band's appearance on an Ed Sullivan–type variety show and a stint at the Ambassador Hotel. Most band members consider the whole experience a lark, Guy included, though we in the audience and White suspect he has more substance, as indicated by his love of jazz.

That Thing You Do! is a creampuff of a movie. Hanks's next, *Saving Private Ryan* (1998), is as substantial a film as he has made. *Ryan* is a landmark in many ways; widely regarded as the most graphic World War II movie ever produced, it ranks with *Schindler's List* (1994) as among director Steven Spielberg's greatest accomplishments. For Hanks, who played the role of Army Ranger John Miller, *Ryan* further affirmed his place as the premiere American actor of his generation.

Ryan represents a turning point in Hanks's vision. At first, his primary objective had been simply to establish a career. Upon doing so, he began to make a series of movies that affirmed the power of institutions in the lives of ordinary people—pretty much the only kind Hanks ever plays. He sometimes has shown us what happens when people fail to play a productive role within them, as in *Philadelphia*, *Toy Story*, and *That Thing You Do!* Then, starting with *Ryan*, Hanks began to explore the moral dilemmas and problems *inherent* in the nature of institutions them-selves—in this case a vast and mighty institution known as the U.S. Army. It is a preoccupation that has marked his work ever since. This emerging spirit of critical inquiry, it is important to add, is one of engage-ment, not skepticism.

After a brief opening scene in which we see old war vet James Ryan (Matt Damon) visiting an American military cemetery in Normandy with his family, *Saving Private Ryan* proceeds to one of the most grueling experi-ences in cinematic history: a twenty-minute sequence depicting the Allied landing of June 6, 1944. Having demonstrated an almost ruthless ability to induce awe, Spielberg indulges what many consider his signature vice: sen-timent. The action shifts to the War Department in Washington, where we see an observant secretary come to a sudden realization, and we learn that three brothers from the same family have been killed and a fourth is missing in action. Deliberations about whether to try to rescue the missing brother head up the food chain to U.S. commander George C. Marshall, who goes to his desk and pulls out what turns out to be one of the more famous documents in Lincoln lore, the so-called Bixby letter that Lincoln wrote a Union woman who lost four sons in the Civil War. Because it's such a masterpiece ("I feel how weak and fruitless must be any words of mine which should attempt to beguile you from the grief of a loss so over-whelming"),[29] you kinda wish Spielberg would let up on the Coplandesque soundtrack. Marshall's position is clear: the mission will go forward.

That mission falls into the lap of Hanks's Captain John Miller, whom we see earlier in the film moving his men successfully up the beach to disable a Nazi pillbox. (We also see some atrocities committed by Amer-icans who shoot surrendering enemy soldiers.) Miller puts together a team of eight men who will go into the German-infested countryside in search of Ryan.

As all these men—who, again, per classic Hollywood war movie conven-tion, are the usual mix of southern boy, wiseacre Brooklynite, nervous intel-lectual, etc.—recognize, this is a hideous undertaking. The intellectual, Upham (Jeremy Davies), an outsider to the company recruited as a transla-tor, tries to fit in by engaging his new comrades, who regard his innocence as dangerous. When another soldier, Private Richard Reiben (Ed Burns) points out the crazy math of sending eight men to rescue one, Upham invokes Rudyard Kipling, which only invites greater scorn. When the medic (Giovanni Ribisi) points out that Ryan has a grieving mother, Reiben replies that they all have mothers—even, just possibly, Captain Miller.

(REALLY) BIG GOVERNMENT: Hanks in *Saving Private Ryan* (1998). In portraying public sector institutions as deeply flawed and yet worthy of collective allegiance, Hanks kept alive a cultural vision of liberalism even as it was in political retreat. *(DreamWorks)*

These soldiers seem to like and respect their commanding officer, whom they treat with teasing that might well be regarded as insubordination by another man. But Miller spends some of his credibility with them by suggesting that the callow Upham might have a point:

> MILLER: Upham's talking about our duty as soldiers. We all have orders and we have to follow them, and that supersedes all, including your mothers.
> UPHAM: Yes sir, thank you sir.
> REIBEN: Even if you think the mission is FUBAR [fucked-up beyond all recognition]?
> MILLER: Especially if you think the mission is FUBAR.

Hanks delivers this line with a puckish grin, which matters a great deal. The officer is making clear that he doesn't agree with the mission any more than his subordinates do. His manner builds credibility among his men (and, perhaps, the audience). This is all the more important because, strictly speaking, Miller's logic could be invoked by Nazis no less than by their Allied adversaries. His gestures—the easy humor, the facial expression, the willingness to tolerate a small but real deviance from strict military orthodoxy, all of which contribute to a powerful democratic spirit—make the difference. The captain's gracefully calibrated measure of deference, to his orders by men above him as well as to the feelings of men below him, make Miller a talented leader. And a good American.

This reservoir of goodwill and respect becomes crucial later in the movie when Miller faces a serious challenge to his authority. He orders the reluctant men to lead a successful attack on a German gun emplacement, but this sideshow results in the death of their medic. Miller antagonizes them further when he subsequently releases a German they capture. Appalled and angry, Reiben announces he's going to desert, which leads to a series of overlapping recriminations and threats. Amid the noise, Miller chooses this moment to address questions that have been matters of such feverish speculation that the men had started a pool betting on the answers: where he's from (Pennsylvania) and what he does for a living (high school English teacher). This stops them in their tracks, as do his memories of his former life, his desperate desire to go home, and his hope that an act of mercy will make that possible—if not in any direct sense, than in allowing him to maintain a measure of humanity so that he will be able to return to his wife reasonably whole.

Miller will pay for that act of mercy—it happens so quickly amid so much other action at the end of the movie that it's easy to miss—and the Parkinson-like hand-shaking he exhibits throughout the movie casts doubt on whether he really ever will be able to go home again. Moreover, it's one thing to pledge your own life; it's another to pledge the lives of others. Some of Miller's charges pay for their loyalty to him with their lives. This is why, in the end, Miller commands the lost Ryan (Matt Damon) to "earn this"—to be worthy of the lives of these men, and by implication all the casualties of World War II, so that we, their heirs, may experience a new birth of freedom in the postwar world.

In a 2001 essay on *Saving Private Ryan*, John Bodnar, a pioneering figure in the study of collective memory, argued that the film's emphasis on patriotic sacrifice invoked the spirit of early World War II movies. He also argued that *Ryan* effaced more recent cinematic history, which tended to focus more on the personal cost of war and the fate of the individual.[30] Yet what Bodnar termed a form of forgetting might be better described as a bid for resurrection. In recent decades, the economic libertarianism of the Right and the cultural libertarianism of the Left have made it hard to even grasp, much less take seriously, the idea that individuals might take personal risks, and experience unrealized hopes, in the name of collectivities greater than themselves.

Saving Private Ryan is not only haunting because we see many people die what can plausibly be considered senseless deaths. It's also haunting in ways that the filmmakers themselves may not intend: I have to confess I found myself wondering, right along with old James Ryan, whether, on the basis of his well-scrubbed but not especially distinguished-looking family, he really did "earn this" by living the life Miller demanded of him. To the degree that Spielberg & Co. wants us to believe this and we don't buy it, we may say the movie fails. But our very desire, even urgency, to see a life as a good buy may itself be part of our collective existential malaise. Perhaps we can take solace that in a world of random violence, *any* life, even that of the unremarkable Ryan, is precious. Either way, the movie asks us to remember—amid justified skepticism that may lead us to make different choices than these people—that our lives are shaped by forces that matter more than our wishes or our will. By the end of his life, so vividly evident in his Second Inaugural, in which he noted that "the Almighty has his own purposes," Abraham Lincoln knew this. By the time his career reached its apogee, Tom Hanks did, too.

In an important sense, Hanks has never scaled these heights again. Perhaps not surprisingly, his next movie was a light romantic comedy, *You've Got Mail* (1998). Yet even here Hanks continued to show himself as a company man, albeit a different kind of company: the institution in question is a commercial one. *Mail* is a remake of the 1940 classic *The Shop Around the Corner*, which starred Jimmy Stewart and Margaret Sullavan as rival employees of a Budapest retail store unaware that their respective pen pals are in fact each other. The clever conceit concocted by writer/producer/director Nora Ephron, who worked with Hanks and co-star Meg Ryan in *Sleepless in Seattle*, involves setting their scenario on the Upper West Side of Manhattan, and substituting the anonymity of postal correspondence with the anonymity of the Internet. This time Hanks and Ryan are rival bookstore owners—he a big chain, she a small independent—who meet in a chat room and conduct a relationship via e-mail. A film truly of its moment, *Mail* quickly became dated in surprising but intriguing ways: America Online (AOL), e-mail, and chat rooms have all become relics, at least in their original form, and chain bookstores, once commercial juggernauts that steamrollered all in their path, have themselves become endangered species thanks to online retailing and e-books.

In a gentle but unmistakable fashion, *You've Got Mail* satirizes the righteous indignation of the small businessperson when faced with a corporate challenge. Meg Ryan's character is utterly charming, but increasingly embittered by her inability to compete with the new chain. Hanks's character, for his part, is (like Lincoln, who also worked on behalf of large corporations as a wealthy railroad lawyer) an unapologetic capitalist who sees himself as providing a real service to consumers. He reacts with unfeigned sticker shock when he takes the children from his father's second marriage (his father is Dabney Coleman, playing his customary role as roué to perfection) to Ryan's shop and pays full retail for the books they buy. Ryan eventually comes by Hanks's store, and we viewers recognize—as she silently appears to—that its coffee shop, winding staircase, and vast inventory really represent a bona fide booklover's dream, even if a clueless clerk can't provide a customer with the name of a prominent children's author (a service she renders as a bystander). It's worth emphasizing that in the carefully calibrated character calculus of the romantic comedy, of which this is an exemplar even more deft than its original source, Hanks's character never pays a price for corporate sin. Which, coming from an Upper West Side liberal like Ephron, is really saying something. Yet it's of a piece with the character of Hanks characters.

One could say that the greatest punishment for the Institutional Man is not defeat—military, commercial, or otherwise—but rather isolation. This is the premise of Hanks's 2000 film *Cast Away*, in which he plays yet another company man, this time a time-obsessed FedEx systems analyst, who becomes the sole survivor in a plane crash and is forced to live on an uninhabited Pacific island for four years. Deprived of companionship, he resorts to inventing it in the form of a volleyball he names after its manufacturer: Wilson. Hanks, who earned an Oscar nomination for some of the best acting of his career, conveys just how deeply his castaway bonds with Wilson; one of the saddest moments in the movie comes when he finds himself separated from this cherished friend. But what may be the most truly wrenching aspect of his ordeal is his return to society and his only partially successful attempt to recover what he has lost. Perhaps not surprisingly, his work life affords him more solace than his personal life, in particular his relationship with the fiancée played by Helen Hunt.

Hanks continued to deepen his inquiry into the nature and problems of institutional life with a set of films—*The Green Mile* (1999), *Road to Perdition* (2002), *Catch Me if You Can* (2002), and *The Ladykillers* (2004)—from a new angle: crime and punishment. *Mile* (based on a serialized Stephen King novel) and *Catch Me* (based on the memoirs of master criminal Frank Abagnale) depict the surprisingly symbiotic bond between law enforcement officers and those they pursue and/or incarcerate as conjoined members of a larger criminal justice system. In the case of *Mile*, we have a community of cops and death-row convicts at a Louisiana prison in the 1930s. That community is hardly idyllic; the title of the film refers to the long path convicts take on their way to the execution chamber where they will be electrocuted. Nevertheless, there is a measure of normalcy in the lives of these people in small acts of decency, notwithstanding the malice of two characters, one a cop and the other a murderer, who disrupt the lives of all around them. The compassion of Hanks's corrections officer Paul Edgecomb finds its foil in the character of Coffey (Michael Clarke Duncan), the African American inmate who may or may not have been rightly condemned to death for the murder of two little girls. *Mile* is an unusual Hanks movie by virtue of its supernatural content; Coffey cures Edgecomb of a painful urinary tract infection, brings a dead pet mouse back to life, and goes on to cure the cancer of the warden's wife. For all its Gothic qualities, *The Green Mile* is at heart a sentimental story, marred by the tiresome trope of the Magic Negro who by virtue of some special power aids a white protagonist. The film is nevertheless a useful snapshot of Hanks's ongoing interest in stories about institutions that do not define membership solely on the basis of paid employees.

In the most obvious sense, *Catch Me if You Can*, which reunited Hanks with Steven Spielberg, is a story about a child prodigy of fraud, played by Leonardo DiCaprio. Hanks, who took second billing to his co-star, plays an FBI agent who repeatedly fails in pursuit of his quarry. But their relationship is not that simple. As the movie makes clear, DiCaprio's dysfunctional behavior is patterned on that of his father (Christopher Walken), whom he loves but whose failures as a husband and productive member of society become increasingly impossible to ignore. Though far more competent, Hanks's character is also a failure as a husband and father, deficiencies that are implicitly depicted as part of the man's commitment to his career. Yet over time, Hanks becomes a father figure to DiCaprio, his very commitment to his job a form of male role modeling that turns the movie into a quest for redemption and rehabilitation. Significantly, the film is set in the late 1960s and early 1970s; although DiCaprio's character is not really a hippie, his countercultural behavior is a form of permissive self-indulgence corrected by a straitlaced man who belongs to a large and powerful establishment. *Catch Me if You Can* thus becomes one more example of Hanks's cultural conservatism that can be traced as far back as *Forrest Gump*.

For the second set of these movies, *Road to Perdition* and *The Ladykillers*, Hanks chose the role of robber rather than cop. These are two very different films; *Perdition* is a family drama set in the 1930s, and *Ladykillers* is a contemporary remake of a British Ealing Studios black comedy of the 1950s. In terms of this discussion, however, both movies become cautionary tales of how personal weaknesses compromise the integrity of organizations.

In *Perdition*, Hanks plays the role of Michael Sullivan, 1930s Chicago-area mob enforcer for John Rooney (the legendary Paul Newman, in his final movie role). Rooney regards Sullivan, a married man with two sons, as family. The problem is that Rooney has an actual (ne'er-do-well) son, Connor (Daniel Craig). When Connor does Sullivan irreparable harm and blood proves thicker than water, Sullivan finds himself on the run with his older son. They make their way to the Windy City, where Sullivan seeks license for revenge from Frank Nitti (Stanley Tucci), the real-life lieutenant of Al Capone. But Nitti is unwilling to sanction this, and we subsequently see him aid Rooney by providing a hit man (Jude Law) to get rid of Sullivan. Sullivan succeeds in saving his son. But there is nevertheless a price to be paid, less for crimes we never quite see Sullivan commit—a way in which the film pulls its punches, as Hanks is never fully credible as a gangster[31]—than for his casting his lot with an organized crime outfit that lacks the integrity to properly police its own members.

Hanks is a far different character, a silly one, in *Ladykillers*, directed by Ethan and Joel Coen (a rare case of Hanks making a foray into the realm of independent filmmaking perfected by the brothers). He presents himself as a foppish southern professor at the Mississippi home of an elderly black woman (Irma P. Hall), from whom he rents a room along with the right to use the basement for rehearsals of "recitals" by his musical ensemble. The ensemble is in fact a group of criminals who hope to tunnel their way into the nearby vault of a casino. They encounter a series of complications, which includes their own ineptitude and internecine quarrels. Their biggest obstacle proves to be the old woman, who discovers their ruse and vows to tell the police unless they return the money and repent their sins. They respond by trying to kill the lady (hence the title), a scheme that goes comically awry. In the end we see not only a set of people who fail because they lack sufficient camaraderie, but also an object lesson in the power of a woman who is, however comic or exasperating to those around her, securely grounded in her community. She has the resources, institutional and otherwise, to challenge malfeasance and prevail.

In addition to this cluster of crime films, Hanks explored other side streets of institutional life in the first decade of the new century. In *The Terminal* (2004), yet another Spielberg film, he plays Viktor Navorski, a tourist stranded when revolutionary violence in his fictive home country of Krakozhia renders his passport invalid, leaving him marooned in the confines of New York's JFK Airport. In effect, we get a warped immigration saga, in which a man who is pushed into the antiseptic institutional setting of an airport is forced to make a life for himself as a permanent resident of what was made to be a liminal space. He must do so amid a series of challenges, not the least of which is a petty federal official (Stanley Tucci) desperate to get rid of him and eager to punish him when he finds he can't.

Whatever his legal status, the movie strives to establish Viktor Navorski as an honorary American. He's a jazz aficionado, a hobby that we learn is an act of filial piety to his now-dead musician father, in whose honor Viktor has made the trip. He also befriends a multicultural array of airport employees, making substantial contributions toward forging them into a real, albeit improvised, workplace community. Perhaps most importantly, Navorski becomes the quintessential American dreamer when he sets his sights on an airline employee (Catherine Zeta-Jones) who passes through JFK every few weeks. Though there's a seemingly inevitable Spielbergian sentimentality in *The Terminal*, it's nevertheless a credit to the filmmakers, especially screenwriters Sacha Gervasi and Jeff Nathanson, that the story is not quite predictable. Hanks, however, is once again a regular guy with a heart of gold.

He made a serious attempt to challenge that perception with *Charlie Wilson's War* (2007). This movie, which closely tracks the 2003 book by CBS producer George Crile, tells the story of how a randy Texas congressman teamed up with a maverick CIA agent (Philip Seymour Hoffman) and a wealthy Republican socialite (Julia Roberts) to quietly engineer the successful U.S. effort to aid rebels in the overthrow of the Soviet-backed regime in Afghanistan and catalyze the end of the Cold War. Hanks plays the title character, and never quite musters quite enough sleaziness to be truly believable in the part. Still, the movie does a remarkably good job of illustrating the book's argument, which is to show how a few knowledgeable people can demonstrate enormous leverage in redirecting the entire federal government if they have the knowledge, will, and social skills to get the job done.

There is a flip side to this story, which the movie acknowledges, albeit halfheartedly. This very success in the ouster of the Soviets created a power vacuum that ultimately led to the success of the Taliban in taking control of Afghanistan, thus giving Osama bin Laden the base of operations he needed to launch 9/11 a little more than a decade later. We see Hoffman's character express concerns about such an outcome late in the story and see Wilson lobby unsuccessfully for small allocations for schools in

Afghanistan, making him seem prescient rather than an enabler of what was to come. As ever, Hanks is finally a good guy. Apparently the original screenplay had a darker ending, but it was reputed that Hanks "couldn't deal with this 9/11 thing," according to a source close to the production.[32]

Indeed, by the second half of the decade, it seemed Hanks was having difficulty choosing material and rendering performances that had quite the freshness and power of his nineties heyday. Whatever their artistic merit, *The Terminal* and *The Ladykillers* failed to gross $100 million at the time of their release—two successive disappointments and Hanks's first in more than a decade.[33]

No such commercial problems afflicted *The Da Vinci Code* (2006) and its sequel, *Angels and Demons* (2009), two blockbuster movies based on the hugely commercial novels of Dan Brown. But the kind of critical praise that had been routine since the time of *Philadelphia* was conspicuously absent for Hanks's portrayal of Harvard "symbology" professor Robert Langdon. Though both stories are nominally institutional critiques—one negative, the other more positive—of the Catholic Church, both are relatively uninteresting. The book and film versions of *The Da Vinci Code* generated enormous controversy at the time of their respective release, owing in part to their sensational argument that Jesus Christ married Mary Magdalene, who gave birth to a daughter. The film version of *Da Vinci* is all too faithful to the book in its tedious—and historically dubious—lectures on Church history. Insofar as Hanks, himself a lapsed Catholic, participates in a project critical of the Church, he's hardly outside an American mainstream with plenty of reasons to be unhappy with it; one fantasy element of *Angels and Demons* is that it's a progressive pope who dies at the movie's outset. In any case, it can't really be said that Professor Langdon is hostile to organized religion per se. While he confesses to his clerical ally in *Angels and Demons* that he's not a believer, both he and the filmmakers depict belief as a gift he lacks rather than credulity he indulges.

Further evidence of Hanks's commercial fade, but ongoing institutional commitment, is apparent in *Larry Crowne* (2011), a movie in which he again teams up with Julia Roberts and also directs. It marks a shrewd foray into yet another dimension of institutional life: higher education (he's the middle-aged student, she's the burnt-out professor). Rather than focus on elite schools that represent a shrinking minority of collegiate experience, *Larry Crowne* is set in the much more common, yet rarely explored, environs of a community college. The title character, a successful big-box employee who loses his job because he lacks an undergraduate degree, finds himself going back to school amid a motley crew of adults—some young, some not—who are trying to find traction in an often alarmingly fluid economy in which a comfortable middle-class life looks increasingly exotic. A project of modest scope, the movie implicitly mocks the idea of Hanks, whose charm in the film is a function of his goofiness, as a screen idol. More explicitly, in the story arc if not in so many words, it endorses public higher education as a vehicle of upward mobility, much as Lincoln did in signing the Morrill Act of 1862, which created the modern state university system in the United States.

Hanks is a presence of an altogether different kind—a ghostly one—in the 2011 film *Extremely Loud & Incredibly Close*, based on the 2005 novel by Jonathan Safran Foer. Here he plays a Manhattan jeweler killed in the World Trade Center on 9/11, who reappears in flashback as his young son (Thomas Horn) grapples with his grief. Here Hanks's role seems to be as an embodiment of national tragedy, a husband and father whose decency became the basis of a productive memory. Though Hanks received praise for his performance, the film was tepidly reviewed and in any case shows his ongoing evolution toward a supporting role in terms of his onscreen presence.

Indeed, even if one assumes he will go on acting, Hanks's role as a showbiz magnate will likely dominate his future. In 2008, he and long-time business partner Gary Goetzman produced *The Great Buck Howard*, a movie starring his son Colin, who in recent years has begun to make his own mark as an actor. The elder Hanks makes a pair of appearances as the disapproving father of a son who goes to work for a magician (John Malkovich). It's a movie that says little, if anything, about the nature of institutional life. Which is a relief: not everything *is* about that. Even for a guy whose career has, perhaps unwittingly, rested on it.

Other than noting that the two men held parallel roles in *The Shop Around the Corner* and *You've Got Mail*, I have thus far avoided making a direct comparison between Tom Hanks and another figure who dominated U.S. cinematic life for much of the twentieth century: Jimmy Stewart. Type the two actors' names into a typical search engine or periodical database and you will find dozens of hits that do not merely contain their names but make explicit connections between the two. There are lots of obvious similarities: Both enjoyed long careers as Everyman, albeit of an idealized kind. Both were unremarkable in their looks but attractive to women in their demeanor, language, humor, and understated intelligence. Both were widely known and liked by their peers, and worked repeatedly with the best directors of their time. And both played a variety of roles across genres, their versatility obvious and important, but never able to overcome a star persona that made it impossible for their characters to really be seen as villains.

There are more subtle similarities, too. Both men had complicated and difficult relationships with their fathers. Both men had relatively long apprenticeships, the memory of their many flops largely erased by a few early big hits (for Stewart, these were *Mr. Smith Goes to Washington* in 1939 and *The Philadelphia Story* in 1940, for which he won his only Best Actor Oscar). Margaret Sullavan, the blond beauty with whom he appeared a number of times, was Stewart's Meg Ryan.

Hanks, aware of these similarities, has aptly distilled Stewart's appeal in ways that capture his own as well. "Sure I would like to have the class of a Cary Grant. I would like to have the enthusiasm of a Jack Lemmon. But above all I would like to be Jimmy Stewart," he has said. "He's not the most handsome man in the world, and he has kind of a geeky voice, but it doesn't matter—there are women out there who are rabidly in love with him, and men who admire him. Mostly, without a drastic altering of look or personality, you believed him in everything he did."[34]

Less commented upon are the two men's differences. Stewart came from an illustrious East Coast family; Hanks from an unremarkable one (other than that Nancy Hanks pedigree, an ironic distinction given the lowliness of her origins). Stewart attended a prep school and then Princeton; Hanks a pair of relatively undistinguished California public colleges. In addition to portraying military men, Stewart in fact served with distinction in the Army Air Corps, a forerunner of the U.S. Air Force; Hanks never got closer to combat than the set of *Saving Private Ryan*. Stewart was a lifelong Republican; Hanks, notwithstanding the conservative currents that run through many of his movies and his widely reported unhappiness with Bill Clinton after the Monica Lewinsky affair, is a lifelong Democrat (and at one point in the nineties was a bona fide Lincoln-bedroom-visiting Friend of Bill).[35]

For our purposes, though, there's one core similarity and one core difference that really matter in the juxtaposition of Stewart and Hanks. The similarity is that as actors, both men carried the torch of institutionalism. The difference is that they did so at different times.

This is not the place to rehearse Stewart's vast output in any detail; suffice it to say that from early pictures like *Mr. Smith Goes to Washington* to middle-period ones like *It's a Wonderful Life* (1946) to late ones like *The Man Who Shot Liberty Valance* (1962), he was almost always cast as the upholder of community values. (In those rare cases when this was not true, like Alfred Hitchcock movies such as *Rear Window* or some of the

Anthony Mann Westerns, it was precisely the friction between this image and those roles that gave such movies their power as exceptions that prove the rule.) As with Hanks, the institutions he represented ranged from the U.S. government to businesses like the fabled savings and loan of *Wonderful Life*, often in contrast to gunslinging contemporaries who prized their autonomy. Stewart was a fixture of the Western—something Hanks has not been—and here, too, he is typically the lawman, or, at the very least, the promoter if not enforcer of shared ideals, particularly in the string of psychologically complex Westerns he made in the 1950s.

As such, Stewart was the Lincolnian figure of his generation and was recognized as such by his contemporaries and those who followed. As Stewart biographer Marc Eliot has observed, "Henry Fonda may have played Abe Lincoln on screen [in *Young Mr. Lincoln*, 1939], but in real life it was Stewart who was far more Lincolnesque: tall, awkward, soft-spoken, real-life heroic." Film scholar James Naremore notes his "lanky awkward diffidence suggestive of Lincolnesque virtue."[36] Stewart got one of his first assignments as an MGM contract player in *Of Human Hearts* (1938), a Civil War movie about a man who rebels against his father's strict religious upbringing and becomes a battlefield surgeon. There's an unintentionally hilarious scene when Stewart's character is summoned to the Oval Office by President Lincoln, who reveals that he knows the young man has failed to write his long-suffering mother and demands the lad do so at his desk immediately (we get a close-up of Stewart writing on Executive Mansion stationery).

A far more famous example of Stewart's intersection with Lincoln comes from Frank Capra's *Mr. Smith Goes to Washington*. At the start of the movie we see the naive boy senator awed by the Lincoln Memorial, hoping that he will be worthy of the Great Emancipator. Later in the movie, disillusioned and in despair over the betrayal by his father's old friend Senator Paine (Claude Rains), he makes a night pilgrimage to the memorial alone. He's joined by the once-cynical Jean Arthur, who has gone from skeptical to charmed to moved by Smith, and now seeks to prop him up. "You didn't just have faith in Paine, in any other living man," she counsels him. "You had faith in something bigger than them. You had plain, decent, everyday common rightness. And this country could use some of that."

Tom Hanks could never appear in such a movie, whose widely noted sentimentality—"Capracorn," in the lingo of cineastes—would be laughable today (though as some have noted, *Mr. Smith* was far more controversial in its depiction of government corruption than a contemporary viewer would realize).[37] Which is what brings us to the key difference between the two men. Stewart's career corresponded to a time of global crisis, from the Great Depression to the Cold War, when it was self-evident to a great many Americans that only large-scale institutions could respond to the huge challenges of the time. This did not mean that all Americans loved big institutions, nor did it mean that Americans turned a blind eye toward their inevitable defects and corruptions. They recognized the need for them, though, and actors like Jimmy Stewart helped ease their accommodation to them. Indeed, the fact that Stewart was a Republican made him all the more credible in this metarole.

Hanks, by contrast, came of age in a very different era, one of suspicion of government on the Right and of just about every other kind of institution, from religion to big business, on the Left. In such an environment, only a much more low-key, even ironic, approach to the kind of institutionalism he represented could be credible, and in *this* metarole, Hanks, who has always had a quicker wit than Stewart, excelled. The real surprise is the degree to which Hanks has been able to smuggle (really) big government affirmations like *Saving Private Ryan* and *Apollo 13* into his body of work. It's not coincidental that the center of gravity for Hanks's vision of American history is precisely that Stewart-era locus of the twentieth century stretching from *Road to Perdition* to *That Thing You Do!* He could only serve this metarole by showing his huge audience that his brand of institutionalism has had a history—a history that worked. And that institutions of the people, by the people, and for the people represented our last, best hope once, and may yet do so again.

The question now is whether we can believe it.

CHAPTER 6

The Brave One

Jodie Foster, (American) Loner

Master narrative: U.S. history
as a pilgrim's progress

For most of my life I've been afraid of Jodie Foster.
 Like a lot of fears, this one is grounded in attraction. Certainly there are plenty of reasons to be drawn to Foster, among them talent, intelligence, and a skillfully managed public persona in which good manners do not quite cloak a certain steeliness she's too smart to think she can entirely hide. I also feel a generational affinity for her; born three weeks before I was, she has always been a presence in my life, a yardstick more compelling and immediate, than, say, Clint Eastwood, who has also always been around, but as a more remote figure. As with a lot of artists who are in it for the long haul, Foster's preoccupations have corresponded to where she has happened to be in the life cycle, and so I can say, not entirely ironically, that we grew up together.

For a long time, the principal source of my Jodie Foster anxiety was rooted in gender difference. Naturally, many a geeky heterosexual white guy could not help but be attracted to her—those piercing blue eyes!—and for that very reason be content to regard her from the anonymous safety of a movie theater. Such is the intimidating allure of a certain kind of movie star. But as everyone of her generation knows, Foster had the unhappy experience of being stalked by a presidential assassin, and ever since I've always regarded my interest in her with inner suspicion, a nagging fear that it amounts to a manifestation of the dark impulses that lurk in my psyche, whether I'm conscious of them or not. I attribute this fear in part to a Catholic upbringing, and in part to coming of age in a feminist era in which the people who educated me went to great pains to emphasize the predatory character of the male gaze. Interest in Foster was akin to stalking her, and I came close at one point in planning this book to concluding that to even write about her would be a form of disrespect and I would thus not do so.

I managed to realize this was a bit extreme. While my fears were understandable, even legitimate, they'd become unduly paralyzing: having dark impulses is not the same thing as acting on them, and having them does not negate any series of others. Moreover, insofar as Foster would care, I'd have to guess that she'd prefer to have a good faith effort to engage her work rather than studied silence about it. After all, she decided to embark on a public career as an actor, long since accepting that the benefits outweigh the costs. It seems rational to conclude that one of those benefits involves attention designed to affirm her significance as an artist in her time, and a claim that this significance will endure after her time.

However, in embarking on this chapter, I've come up against a different, even more discomforting, discovery: Jodie Foster does not really love U.S. history. She's hardly a traitor. My guess is that there have been any number of moments in her life, like the aftermath of 9/11 or a not entirely implausible scenario of her feeling an unaccountable surge of affection during the singing of the national anthem at an L.A. Dodgers game with her sons, where she could cite patriotic feeling. But I get very little sense in looking at Foster's body of work that she has tried to engage the American experience *as* an experience, of thinking of the nation-state as a crucial organizing principle of her work or identity. Clint Eastwood, Denzel Washington, and Tom Hanks have all done so. The fact that these are all men and Foster is a woman may have something to do with this, but Meryl Streep, whose early work was anchored in private concerns, has shown increasing engagement with national life in recent movies. Even a foreigner like Daniel Day-Lewis evinces an abiding fascination with American history. But Foster? Not so much. The phrase is important: Foster doesn't particularly *love* American history, but she doesn't really *hate* it, either. History is just not that important. The subject comes up—she's made a number of period pieces—but her primary preoccupations are not historical. To grapple with her history is, in an important sense, to grapple with an absence.

Indeed, when it came time to think about a historical figure with whom Foster can be paired the way I pair Meryl Streep with Betty Friedan, I found myself stumped. Listening to my dilemma, the esteemed University of Chicago historian James Sparrow immediately suggested Holden Caulfield, the irascible protagonist of J. D. Salinger's classic 1951 novel, *The Catcher in the Rye*. I reflected upon this suggestion for a long time afterward, in no small measure because Foster is an avowed Salinger fan (she particularly loved his 1963 book, *Franny and Zooey*, reputedly an inspiration for her 1991 directorial debut, *Little Man Tate*).[1] It's also arresting to think about Holden Caulfield's stated wish that he could be the protector of children in that field of rye when one considers Foster's most famous role as a rescuer of a senator's daughter in *The Silence of the Lambs*.

Yet I don't finally consider the Foster-Salinger juxtaposition sustainable. As Professor Sparrow pointed out to me, John Hinckley Jr. was also a big Salinger fan—a copy of *Catcher in the Rye* was found in his hotel room after he was arrested in the shooting of President Reagan—and it seems safe to surmise that he considered a Salingeresque sense of alienation as one facet of his imagined bond with Foster.[2] But Hinckley was certifiably insane. So, arguably, is Holden Caulfield. Jodie Foster, on the other hand, is deeply sane, almost unnervingly so. In their very different ways, Hinckley and Caulfield (and, sadly, J. D. Salinger himself) seem to be cases of arrested development. Foster, by contrast, embarked on a career that suggests a much fuller range of human experience.

In an important sense, however, Foster has made her cinematic journey alone. To a striking degree, she plays single women, and even in those frequent cases where her characters experience romance, these relationships are severed by death or other forms of separation. On those occasions when Foster is a parent, it's as a single mother. Even *The Beaver* (2011), a movie that one could regard as an exception because Foster is in a troubled but legally valid marriage, ends with her character on the edge of the frame, observing husband and son from a distance.

Foster tends to live alone in another important respect as well: to a degree that's singular among the other figures of this book, her characters try to live their lives independent of public institutions, particularly government institutions. At best, institutions are ineffectual in meeting their stated aims; at worst, they're menacing, even downright evil. But—and this is really key to the point I'm trying to convey here—this aspiration for autonomy tends to be a pragmatic choice, not a deeply held principle or grievance. Clint Eastwood characters often have chips on their shoulders, even as they try to form communities. Foster characters are tougher: less hostile than guarded, with little inclination to bond. Even in those cases when they *do* work within institutions (as, say, a cop or a nun), they tend to work on their own. They not *anti*-institutional so much as *non*-institutional. As such, they're both harder to resist and harder to embrace. You wonder what Foster lacks, and then you wonder what you do. In a deeply ironic yet apt way, she's a bit like Ronald Reagan: disconcerting in her institutional skepticism and the instinctive confidence with which she embodies it.

It's hard when someone you like and respect apparently just doesn't care about the things that you consider important. Foster is not a radical critic with strong ideas one can comprehend if not entirely accept, and whom any right-thinking liberal would try to understand. I regard her as one of us: for all our obvious differences, she inhabits the same country I do, and she was entertaining me long before I ever considered what that might mean. Yet it's clear that even as Foster has represented American life in ways I recognize, she feels differently about our country than I do. What does she know that I don't?

———

Movie stars are a bit like star quarterbacks in the National Football League: it's very hard to tell which prospect will become a star. Lots of quarterbacks show promise. But sports lore is full of first-round draft picks who disappoint and virtual afterthoughts who get a chance and unexpectedly set the league on fire. Late blooming of the Kurt Warner or Tom Brady variety is proverbial. Yes, there are the prodigious Namaths and Elways, too. But never as many as you might think.[3]

Similarly, when you look at the background of an Eastwood, a Washington, or a Hanks, you typically see signs of talent, or at any rate, distinctive elements of character that retroactively get written as premonitions. But they're rarely at the forefront of their peers. Many show early interest in their craft and real promise. Then again, so do a lot of people. Actually, there's reason to think that early success is more a liability than an asset, whether because of burnout or simply because what's cute in a child does not necessarily carry over into adolescence, much less adulthood. Again, there are exceptions—Mickey Rooney and Drew Barrymore come to mind. But most child actors end up like Buddy Foster of *Mayberry R.F.D.* (1968–71): they get attention in commercials, move on to bona fide celebrity in television and/or films, and are largely finished with show business with the onset of puberty.[4]

Buddy Foster's kid sister, on the other hand, turned out to be a different story. A child of Hollywood in the truest sense, she bucked the odds to have a half-century-long career. It's a little shocking to realize that her collaborators stretch from the grande dame of the theater, Helen Hayes, born in 1900, through screen legends like Robert De Niro, born in 1943, all the way to Kristen Stewart, born in 1990. On the basis of experience alone, Jodie Foster is already a grande dame herself.

Yet her pedigreed background, real as it is, was marked, as many such backgrounds are, by early struggle and subsequent setbacks. She was born Alicia Christian Foster on November 19, 1962, in Los Angeles, the youngest of four children of Evelyn "Brandy" Foster and Lucius Fisher

Foster III, a former air force officer turned real estate broker. The Foster ancestry can be traced back to the famed Pilgrim John Alden, reputedly the first man to step off the *Mayflower* in 1620.[5] Lucius, like his daughter, is a graduate of Yale.

The most salient fact about Foster's father, however, is his absence from her life. Her parents' contentious marriage ended before she was born; her surrogate second parent appears to have been her mother's companion, Josephine Dominguez Hill (1930–84), known as "Aunt Jo," whose bowdlerized moniker, "Jo-D," became Foster's nickname.[6] In any case, the decisive force in her life was Brandy. Driven, controlling, and forced by her divorce to improvise financially, she networked her son into commercials and television, where he became the family breadwinner to the impressive sum of $25,000 a year.[7] Brandy was Buddy's manager, professionally supervising his career and actively seeking to expand it.

But the future lay with Jodie. Walking at six months, talking at nine, she reputedly taught herself to read by the age of three. After elementary school, Brandy enrolled her in the prestigious Lycée Français in Los Angeles, where Foster rapidly became fluent in French. (She served as Robert De Niro's translator at the Paris press conference for *Taxi Driver* as a teenager in 1976, has made French films, and dubs her own movies to this day.) Although actors are not typically gifted or committed academicians, Foster also demonstrated uncanny ability in managing her time despite her manifold professional commitments, all the way through a Yale career that culminated in an honors thesis on the fiction of Toni Morrison. At one point in her life she seriously considered pursuing a doctorate in literature.[8]

Most obvious, though, were her prodigious skills as an actor—among them an ability to memorize lines rapidly—which emerged at a very early age. At three, in 1965, Foster became the so-called Coppertone Girl in TV advertisements for the tanning cream, though in pop culture folklore she's mistakenly considered the inspiration for the iconic print illustration of the child whose bikini bottom is tugged on by a dog. Over the course of the next few years, she became a fixture of the advertising business, appearing in fifty commercials by the time she was ten.[9] I was stunned to come across her doing a 1971 GAF View-Master commercial with Henry Fonda (!), in which Fonda, in grandfatherly mode, chats with a few kids about the virtues of this newfangled toy. Each child has something precocious to say—"extremely interesting," says one; "the three-dimensional color pictures are extraordinary," says another—culminating in Foster's line, delivered with offhanded panache: "I always considered the GAF View-Master an ingenious device of great educational value." Even here, her acting chops were apparent, head and shoulders above her peers.[10] I speak figuratively; the adult Foster is barely five feet tall.

Commercial work led to a string of appearances in now-forgotten TV shows—*The Doris Day Show* in 1969, *Kung Fu* in 1973—along with others of somewhat more significance, like *Julia*, starring Diahann Carroll, notable in the history of television as one of the first shows with an African American lead actor (Foster appears in a 1969 episode and arguably does a better job than the actor cast as her father). It also led to what might be termed an apprenticeship with Disney Studios in which Foster was cast in a series of supporting roles. She proved to be a trouper amid adversity, surviving a moderate mauling by a lion during the filmmaking of *Napoleon and Samantha* (1972).[11]

By the second half of the seventies, it became increasingly apparent that Foster had a distinctive character as an actor, and that her emerging persona—bright, confident, impatient with the strictures of traditional authority—was perfect for the post-sixties zeitgeist. "It was just at the beginning of women's liberation, and she kind of personified that in a child," Brandy Foster recalled in 1988. "She had a strength and uncoquettishness. Maybe it comes from being raised without a father to say 'Turn around and show Daddy how pretty you look.'"[12] That last line is arguably self-serving—plenty of fathers are happy enough with tomboys, or at any rate want more for their daughters than to look good in a dress— but the elder Foster was surely right that her daughter's unself-conscious demeanor was filtered through an ideological lens in ways that worked in her favor.

One of the first people to recognize this was Martin Scorsese, himself at the beginning of one of the legendary careers in cinematic history. Scorsese cast Foster in a small part as a tough-minded tomboy who befriends Ellen Burstyn's son (played by Alfred Lutter III) in *Alice Doesn't Live Here Anymore* (1974). Foster has only two major scenes, one of which involves faking an injury as part of goading Lutter's character into an act of shoplifting. Even so, she's a compelling presence, just as she was in real life. "Jodie just walked into our office on the Burbank lot, and she had total command," Scorsese later remembered.[13] Kris Kristofferson, who starred in the film, was also impressed. "She came right up and shook my hand, all business," he said in the commentary that accompanied the DVD release of the film. "She wasn't like a little girl at all." This poise allowed her to win an important part in the early Alan Parker movie *Bugsy Malone* (1976), a mock gangster musical with an all-child cast.

The turning point in Foster's career as an actor—and a touchstone for her preoccupations as an artist—was her second Scorsese project, *Taxi*

Driver (1976). A signature document in the emergence of independent cinema in the 1970s, the film tells the story of Travis Bickle (Robert De Niro), a deeply troubled Vietnam vet turned cabbie who takes a shine to, and is spurned by, a beautiful young woman (Cybill Shepherd) who works at the Times Square office of a slick but inane presidential candidate. In his extreme emotional isolation, Bickle becomes increasingly paranoid and determined to do something significant, which we gradually sense may be an attempt to assassinate the candidate. But Bickle accidentally encounters a child prostitute named Iris (Foster) and begins an effort to rescue her from her pimp, Sport (Harvey Keitel). The movie climaxes in notorious violence—and irony.

This is not a film many mothers would let their children watch, much less act in as a streetwalker, but there's little indication that Brandy Foster had reservations. Twelve-year-old Jodie herself was eager to take the part; the recipient of a cosmopolitan upbringing, she was already a foreign film aficionado and understood that the part of Iris was more than just another acting job.[14] Child welfare authorities in California, however, were not so sure it was a good idea. Only after an evaluation by a UCLA psychiatrist (who reported that Foster had a very high IQ) and the intercession of former California governor Edmund "Pat" Brown was she permitted to proceed with the part.[15] As anyone familiar with the story knows—and pretty much everybody over the age of about forty is—Foster did indeed end up paying a heavy psychic price for playing Iris, though not for a reason easily foreseeable at the time.

Still, Foster has consistently described her experience working on the film as one of the highlights of her career. "When I did *Taxi Driver*, it was like the first time I ever did a role that was a little out of character," she told the *Los Angeles Times* in 1981. "I felt like I had accomplished something."[16] She has repeatedly affirmed the importance of working on the film in the decades since, perhaps most succinctly in a 2007 interview with *Entertainment Weekly*: "*Taxi Driver* was the best thing that ever happened to me."[17]

A major reason why was tutoring she received at the hands of De Niro, whose advice—and example—transformed acting from a lark into a vocation. Their major scene together, which takes place in a diner, is truly extraordinary and worthy of the Academy Award nomination Foster garnered. She glides seamlessly from worldly adolescent ("Didn't you ever hear of women's lib?" she asks in sarcastic reply to the suggestion that she belongs at home) to naive teenager (she rejects Bickle's suggestion that Sport is a killer with the assertion that he's not because he's a Libra, "which is why we get along so well"). But every once in a while, Bickle

NOT SO PRETTY PICTURE: The iconic image of Jodie Foster in *Taxi Driver* (1976). Though there were questions about whether she should be allowed to take the role, and though it proved to have unforeseen negative consequences, Foster has described it as "the best thing that ever happened to me." *(Columbia Pictures)*

says something to her expressing concern for her welfare, and her face, partially hidden by absurd green sunglasses, is momentarily but unmistakably stricken. There are also a couple of times in their scenes together when Bickle is about to give up and she tugs on his sleeve or reaches out in a way that reveals the child beneath the tough exterior, making her subsequent scene with Sport, who smoothly reassures her with his effortless lies, all the more upsetting.

Indeed, if one makes the slightly unorthodox move of viewing *Taxi Driver* from the point of view of Iris—whose very name suggests both

IRIS, SEEING: Foster listens to Robert De Niro's Travis Bickle at a diner in *Taxi Driver* (1976). She earned an Oscar nomination, and a reputation as a child prodigy, on the basis of her performance. *(Columbia Pictures)*

vision and flowering—we see that despite its antiheroic protagonist and nihilistic vision of politics, this is a movie with a moral vision. Travis Bickle is a very troubled man, and his destructive impulses, which are as likely to turn inward as outward, pull him in dangerous directions. But however awkwardly expressed, or mingled with other imperatives, there's something altruistic about his desire to rescue Iris. By contrast, there's *nothing* redemptive about Sport: he lies and exploits Iris all the more mercilessly because his mild veneer and emotional manipulation make overt violence unnecessary (and because he's obsessively guarded in dealing with his customers). Screenwriter Paul Schrader, who comes out of the Dutch Reformed Church, brings a self-conscious theological vision to his work, most obvious in the complicated relationship between Jesus and Judas in his 1988 screenplay, *The Last Temptation of Christ* (also directed by Scorsese).[18] For our purposes, the important point is that while *Taxi Driver* seems to reflect a vaguely leftist, relativistic, countercultural critique of American life common in the films of the 1970s, it is animated by a powerful vision of evil—atavistic, unexplained, palpable evil—that suffuses the city like the vapor rising up into the street in the unforgettable opening shot of the movie. This vapor corrupts Iris; it shadows Travis. But it saturates Sport and explodes in the climax of the movie. Though lacking any formal theological or philosophical framework, this notion of implacable, unexplained malice became a fixture of Jodie Foster's body of work, a vector that presses down on most of her films and gives many of them the melancholic weight that has always made her a bit unusual even as she went on to become an artist who would operate in the heart of the Hollywood mainstream.

This did not happen right away. Foster followed *Taxi Driver* with *Freaky Friday* (1976), another Disney film, her first true star vehicle. The movie, based on Mary Rodgers's classic 1972 children's novel of the same name, features Foster as a young teen who switches identities with her mother (Barbara Harris) after eating an enchanted fortune cookie, each gaining a better appreciation of the other's life (it was competently remade in 2003 with Lindsay Lohan and Jamie Lee Curtis in the daughter/mother roles). Foster followed it up with *Candleshoe* (1977), her final Disney outing, in which she plays a street waif who masquerades as the long-lost heir of an old woman. She was simultaneously emerging as a serious actor—on the strength of her work in *Taxi Driver*, but also because she was making films abroad as well. These movies are all over the map in tone and content, though alike in their relative mediocrity. Foster would be afflicted with generally inferior material from the late seventies until the late eighties. Despite this, one can begin to see a characteristic pattern emerge in the film roles she landed, most of which still reflect her mother's sensibility. And that sensibility is one of girls finding and showing strength in the face of terrible (usually male) behavior.

The most vivid early document in this regard is a Canadian-French production, *The Little Girl Who Lives Down the Lane* (1977). *Little Girl* is a strange hybrid of a movie, combining elements of the horror and thriller genres while somehow leading you to suspend your judgment about a protagonist who probably should be viewed as a monster. Foster plays Rynn, a remarkably self-sufficient early adolescent who presumably lives with her father in a remote Maine town. Yet he's not in the rental house where she lives when the landlady's son—a menacing young pedophile played by Martin Sheen—stops by on Halloween and aggressively makes his sexual interest clear. That's bad enough, but in ensuing days the land-lady herself proves to be far too nosy about her family arrangements. We learn that Rynn's father was devoted to her but terminally ill. Her mother, by contrast, was dangerously abusive, leading to a divorce in which he got custody of Rynn. Before his death he left instructions for Rynn to poison her mother with potassium cynanide in a cup of tea. The landlady comes across the body in the basement, which leads to her own death. Rynn would have been able to maintain these secrets, but the landlady's son continues to stalk her, and his subsequent discoveries culminate in sexual blackmail. So Rynn poisons him, too.

The casual cold-bloodedness of *Little Girl* retains its force decades later (the credits roll as Sheen's character quietly chokes offscreen). Foster's character shows a functional independence striking for a child her age, and her actions—or, in the case of reporting the landlady's death, inaction—reflect not only her pragmatism but behavior that seems justified in light of the malice her antagonists exhibit toward her. Significantly, legal authority in the form of a local police officer proves unable to help despite his good intentions. In an important sense, *Little Girl* is a feminist movie, in that it shows an empowered female acting effectively in her own interest. It's a grim form of feminism, though, one driven not by a sense of hope about what women may yet accomplish but rather by a belief that survival is a matter of fighting back against a hostile world by any means necessary.

The last two movies of Foster's childhood are not quite so bleak, but nevertheless portray worlds in which dangerous men and random violence pervade everyday life. In *Carny* (1980), she plays a runaway waitress who gets a job at a carnival and becomes involved in a romantic triangle between characters played by Gary Busey and Robbie Robertson (a member of the classic rock group The Band and a producer of the movie). Though the film has a contemporary setting, its core scenario is redolent of carnival road shows dating back to the nineteenth century, particularly in depicting the friction, if not hostility, that often characterized the relationship between performers and audiences. These tensions, and the ones between the two main characters, pale, however, when threatening gangsters seek to extort money from the troupe at one stop in its tour of the South. Busey's and Robertson's characters ultimately foil this effort, but not before Foster's character endures a brutal near-rape stopped only by the rapist having his throat slit. It's truly remarkable how much violence Foster characters experienced in the childhood phase of her career, and while all of it was clearly "pretend," it's hard to believe that at some level it did not seep into her psyche.

Foster's other movie of 1980, *Foxes*, is not (quite) as dark, and indeed it has a slick contemporary feel, as it was the first film directed by Adrian Lyne, who would go on to have a highly successful commercial career later in the decade. In this movie Foster again portrays a precocious teen, a chic mother hen in her posse of high school friends. She also seems more mature than her own mother, played by Sally Kellerman, who tries to navigate the new social mores of the late seventies in the aftermath of her divorce. There's plenty of casual sex and drugs in *Foxes*, whose themes anticipated the more successful *Fast Times at Ridgemont High* (1982) as well as Brat Pack movies like *The Breakfast Club* (1984). But the movie ends with a violent tragedy that leaves Foster's character bereft.

Foster turned eighteen years old in the fall of 1980. This is a treacherous time in the life of a child actor, one of difficult currents from which many careers never emerge, whether by choice or not. Foster was well aware of the uncertainties, if for no other reason than her brother Buddy's experience. Such considerations, along with a genuinely academic bent, were surely part of the reason why she accepted an offer of admission to Yale. This is not as unorthodox a decision now as it was back then, when *People* magazine described it as "the most startling career move since Garbo chose exile."[19] In an industry where momentum is nearly everything, Foster sailed into uncharted waters.

By all accounts, Foster cherishes her Yale education, where she proved to be an apt pupil and a loyal alumna.[20] But it was a very trying time in other respects. Foster never gave up her acting career entirely, squeezing screen work into compartmentalized slots like summers. But the material she got—like a 1983 television movie, *Svengali*, where she played a muse for the rakishly charming Peter O'Toole—suggested the bobbing of an actor trying to stay afloat more than a star charting her way.[21] This began to change in her final upperclassman years, when she began doing more high-profile film work, but she waged an uphill battle in forging an adult career.

The biggest challenge Foster faced, however, was the enormous shadow cast over her life by John Hinckley Jr., the troubled young man from a well-to-do family who developed an obsession with her. In some ways still a child, Foster naively parried his advances by taking his calls and trying to dissuade him from pursuing her (he went to New Haven on a few occasions, but the two never met face-to-face). A warped devotee of *Taxi Driver*, Hinckley convinced himself he could impress Foster by acting like Travis Bickle in attempting to kill the president—he tried first with Jimmy Carter in 1980 before settling on Ronald Reagan in March of 1981. In the aftermath of the unsuccessful attempt, Foster was sucked into a vortex of unwanted attention, which she tried to manage by holding a single press conference, then writing a single essay, which she insisted not be a cover story, for *Esquire* magazine in 1982. (The piece was an anguished *cri de coeur*, but she nevertheless managed to maintain a wry sense of humor, concluding with an expectation that a stranger would one day come up to her and ask, "Ain't you the girl who shot the president?") For many years, the incident was a forbidden subject; Foster canceled an appearance on the *Today* show in 1991 when she learned Hinckley's name would be mentioned in the introduction. In recent years, however, she has referenced it, freely if briefly, without obvious trauma.[22]

It's hard for anyone who hasn't experienced this kind of bizarre notoriety to gauge the adversity it imposed. Foster, moreover, had been stalked by Hinckley even before Reagan was.[23] But to focus on Hinckley is to some degree to miss the real challenges Foster faced—and to overlook the bona fide courage she has shown in the decades since.

The first indication that her ordeal was not over came within days. Appearing in an undergraduate play—adversity in its own right, as she had never been comfortable onstage and has never done live theater since—Foster was stalked again, this time by a man who planned to kill her. Though he could not bring himself to do so, he later issued a bomb threat on her dormitory, forcing its evacuation, before his apprehension by Secret Service agents in New York. In subsequent years, Foster repeatedly faced similar threats—three years later, it was a woman who got arrested for plotting to kill her—and encounters with flash photographers that ranged from annoying to frightening (one precipitating a broken clavicle). She would require a fairly elaborate infrastructure, human and otherwise, to ensure her security.[24]

Foster nevertheless proceeded with her acting career. This should not be taken for granted; it's easy to imagine another person in similar circumstances suffering some kind of breakdown or simply deciding to retreat from the public eye. Beyond that, Foster has repeatedly chosen to work on movies in which her characters are preyed upon by people with malicious intent. As I've already documented, it would be simply inaccurate to suggest that such choices can be explained entirely in terms of her personal experience; before 1981 they reflected a combination of factors that include the opportunities she was offered and her mother's guidance. It is nevertheless striking to consider how often her post-1981 movies involve people confronting and overcoming such challenges, including those posed by stalkers.

While he should not be considered the most authoritative judge of the matter, it's easy to believe Buddy Foster's assertion that the Hinckley affair changed his sister, making her a more guarded figure. That would seem to extend to Foster lending her name to political causes. Much to the consternation of gays and lesbians, for example, she has refused to discuss her romantic life (which, on the basis of what I've read, appears to be bisexual). In the tense atmosphere surrounding homosexuality in the 1980s and 1990s, this was seen by some as a damagingly closeted stance. And while in thought, speech, and action Foster is clearly a feminist filmmaker, she seems to deploy the term more descriptively than ideologically, casting her vision more in terms of art, not politics. Many eyebrows were raised in 2010–11 when Foster stood resolutely by Mel Gibson, her co-star in *The Beaver* (2011), who enjoyed little goodwill in Hollywood even before he faced domestic violence charges against his companion, later dropped.

Her interview mode involved alluding to Gibson's bad behavior while insisting on a redemptive integrity. More generally, it seems Foster has special sympathy for those in the scalding glare of publicity. In his 2011 memoir, *Stories I Only Tell My Friends*, actor Rob Lowe writes that Foster was one of the few people who reached out to him when his infamous leaked "sex tape" made headlines in the 1990s.[25]

Indeed, one might generally say that for Foster, the personal transcends the political: ideas matter less than relationships. To paraphrase a common post-Boomer line that drives women activists crazy, "She's a feminist, but…" That's not necessarily because ideas are unappealing, or even unimportant. By most reckonings, Foster is among the most cerebral figures in Hollywood. Rather, at the core of her view of the world, there will always be powerful people, usually men, who foreclose collective aspiration or institutional process. For the most part, they must be confronted alone.

Over the course of making forty-odd movies, Jodie Foster has made a few set in the past, but most take place in her lifetime (perhaps not surprisingly, the 1960s are well represented). Of that handful that can be considered genuinely historical dramas, the most important are French, like the 1984 Claude Chabrol World War II film *The Blood of Others,* or the beautifully made, yet graphically realistic, 2003 film *A Very Long Engagement*, an Audrey Tautou vehicle in which Foster has a small but arresting part as a Polish woman who becomes unwillingly enmeshed in a love triangle between two soldiers on the Western Front in the First World War. As we'll see, even her most prominent U.S. historical drama, *Sommersby* (1993), has French origins. Among Foster's first postcollegiate releases, which she also produced, was *Mesmerized* (1986), based on a real-life 1886 New Zealand case, in which Foster plays an orphan turned adolescent bride acquitted of murdering her sexually deviant husband.

Looking at these projects in the context of the movies Foster *has* made and set in the United States, there's a real shape to her choices as they delineate her vision of American history: She's a non-exceptionalist. (Not *anti*-exceptionalist, which implies an active stance and assertive statement, but *non*-exceptionalist.) There are bad people everywhere, her body of work seems to say, and bad things happen to good people at all times. Not even the land of the free and the home of brave enjoys exemption from the capricious—or not so capricious—hand of fate. What's particularly striking about this message is that it surfaces in movies set during periods that are often viewed as moments of hope, even optimism.

The outlines of this vision emerge in the one prestige project Foster undertook at Yale, Tony Richardson's *The Hotel New Hampshire* (1984), based on the 1981 novel by John Irving. As a number of observers have noted, the movie, a weird hybrid of Hollywood farce and European art-house drama, falls flat somewhere between the two.[26] Foster plays Franny Berry, the oldest daughter in a large family whose parents met in Vienna in World War II and later open a New England inn. But the father's true American Dream of success is going back to Vienna, where he opens the financially wobbly hotel of the title. Over the course of the story, Franny will endure rape at the hands of a classmate (Matthew Modine), resist the incestuous entreaties of her brother (Rob Lowe), be held hostage with the rest of the family by Marxist terrorists (among them Modine in another role and Amanda Plummer), and grapple with the tragedy of a suicidal sister who happens to be a dwarf as well as a gifted writer. If ever there was a role written to appeal to Foster's imagination, Franny, whose very name evokes that of the J. D. Salinger character she loved, was surely it. Indeed, it's a virtual compendium of the scenarios in which she'd appear for the next thirty years.

A more intriguing variation on Foster's adult sensibility surfaces in a much more modest project, *Five Corners* (1987), written by John Patrick Shanley (who also wrote screenplays for Tom Hanks and Meryl Streep movies). Set in the Bronx of 1964, *Five Corners* is vivid with a strong sense of local color. That color, however, is dark: this is not the sixties of the Beach Boys or the March on Washington, but one of urban crime and right-wing backlash. Early in the film, a high school teacher gets killed when an arrow pierces his back, a random act of violence that helps establish a tone of mordant humor. We also see the threatening figure of Heinz (John Turturro), a psychopath recently released from prison. Now that he's back, he wants to resume his grim pursuit of Linda (Foster), a pet store clerk who was only rescued from his earlier attempt to rape her by the intervention of her friend Harry (Tim Robbins), who has since become a convert to nonviolence by the example of Martin Luther King, Jr. Linda has a boyfriend, but he's no match for Heinz, who knocks Linda unconscious and takes her prisoner King Kong–style. Her friend, her boyfriend, and the police frantically track Heinz and Linda to the roof of an apartment building, where she literally rests on the edge of death. Nominally, the movie has a happy ending, although Linda is not saved by any of these men, but rather by another random act of violence. A strangely quirky yet compelling movie, *Five Corners* has an indie sensibility that anticipated the mainstream breakthrough of the movement the following year with Steven Soderbergh's *Sex, Lies, and Videotape*.

From one standpoint, it seems bizarre that Foster would choose to make a film about a crazed stalker. It seems even more bizarre that she would claim not to have realized she'd done so until the film began shooting. When the subject came up, as it did repeatedly in interviews, she reacted with barely concealed irritation. "I took this film because it's the best screenplay I've read in a long time," she told an interviewer. "I don't do films because psychologically I could learn something about myself or because the character is something I always wanted to play. A lot of people do, but that doesn't interest me as much as doing a good book. I look for good films."[27]

Fair enough. But such a response raises the inevitably subjective question about what makes a screenplay "best" or "good," and here it does not defy logic to believe that Foster defines such terms in ways that allow her to work through her experience and exorcise it artistically. Still, even if one accepts such a premise, it's clear her tastes run broader than refracted autobiography. So, for example, she took a small role as a decadent British socialite in the 1987 film *Siesta*, in which a dazed Ellen Barkin tries to figure out why she has awakened in a Spanish field wearing a bloody red dress, a movie that has since disappeared into deserved obscurity. Yet here and elsewhere, a somber subtext was apparent even in presumably upbeat stories. Foster's next movie was *Stealing Home* (1988), a conventional Hollywood tale in which a forlorn former baseball player (Mark Harmon) is inspired by the memories of his childhood babysitter, played by Foster. But these memories are prompted by her suicide, which is disclosed early in the story.

The Accused (1988) was Foster's breakthrough. It was a movie in which she got the lead only after more prominent actors turned it down, and she was forced to audition for the part, something not usually required of an established actor. *The Accused* is based on the true story of Cheryl Araujo, a waitress from New Bedford, Massachusetts, who was gang-raped at a local bar in 1983. The case was important not only because it became a local media circus in which Araujo's identity and character became matters of public discussion, but also because two men were convicted for their role in inciting the rape along with two others who actually committed it. The movie significantly changes the facts of the case by stripping its ethnic dimension: in real life, those tried for the crime were Portuguese immigrants, leading to charges of bias, despite the fact that the victim was Portuguese as well.[28] Instead, the movie inserts white college students into the largely working-class mob, simplifying the ethnic politics and replacing it with a more straightforward story of gender violation reinforced by class privilege. While this seems politically dishonest, it's also probably the only way an already difficult movie could have been made.

That said, *The Accused* does challenge its audience by giving it a relatively unsympathetic protagonist. Foster would win her first Academy Award for her performance as Sarah Tobias, a hard-bitten waitress whose evident appetite for sex and alcohol make her case a difficult one even for Kathryn Murphy, the zealous prosecutor played by Kelly McGillis (herself a real-life rape victim). Indeed, Tobias's behavior in the movie appears to have been more provocative than Araujo's. Murphy nevertheless drives a hard bargain and cuts a relatively stiff plea deal with the lawyers of the rapists. Tobias remains outraged: she wanted her day in court and would endure any backlash to get it. This leads Murphy to prosecute the secondary figures for incitement, despite her (male) boss's resistance, culminating in Tobias's testimony in open court. Foster's performance is powerful not simply for the profile in courage of her protagonist, but also—and this would increasingly become a theme of her career—for her ability to convey the terror of women facing brutal treatment, physical and otherwise. While one must not conflate the agony of Cheryl Araujo, who died a few years after her ordeal in a car crash, with that of the woman who portrayed her, there's little question that the graphic rape scene in the movie was a serious personal trial for Foster.[29] The decision to do it was a professional triumph, to be sure, but also one of solidarity with a victim and one important for calling attention to serious issues of public policy.

The Accused marked a significant personal milestone for Foster; as her entrée into the elite club of Oscar winners, it put her in the catbird seat for her next role. Characteristically, she did not cash this chit by seeking a commercial payday, but instead by taking a leading role in the next movie by Dennis Hopper, a Hollywood legend for his behavior no less than for directing movies like *Easy Rider* (1969). It proved to be a move she regretted, as Hopper lived up to his difficult reputation and was never able to complete the film, titled *Catchfire* (1990), for theatrical release. It was later issued on home video as *Backtrack* (1994). Foster plays an artist who witnesses a murder that leads the criminals involved to hire Hopper as a hit man to rub her out. He falls in love with his prey, and she ultimately with him. It was at best an unremarkable film, though one in keeping with Foster's penchant for choosing characters who find themselves in dangerous situations for reasons not of their choosing.

In her next role, however, Foster would play someone who *did* find herself in a dangerous situation of her choosing—and in doing so would achieve durable greatness.

I remember vividly the night I went to see Jonathan Demme's 1991 film *The Silence of the Lambs*. All day long I dreaded it because I've always hated horror movies, but the buzz on *Lambs* was too great to ignore. On that winter night in February, my wife and I threw a dinner party as a prelude to a trip to the movies. I was uneasy the whole time, looking ahead to the movie the way one does to a visit to the dentist.

The film begins somberly and takes a little while to get scary. The first such moment occurs when Foster's character, FBI agent in training Clarice Starling, walks down a long hallway toward the high-security cell of the psychiatrist turned cannibal, Dr. Hannibal Lecter, played by the un-blinking Anthony Hopkins. It's one of the great strengths of *Lambs* that one's sheer fascination with Lecter almost overcomes one's fear of him. If nothing else, *Lambs* is great because it—by which I mean the 1988 novel by Thomas Harris, Ted Tally's screenplay, and above all Hopkins's thrill-ing performance—utterly crushes the shopworn liberal piety that evil arises from mere dysfunction or lack of understanding on the part of those who would otherwise be good. Maybe that's true of the nominal villain of the piece, a serial murderer by the name of Buffalo Bill (Ted Levine), who skins women so that he can live out his transvestite fantasies. But in his alternatingly courteous and dismissive manner, Lecter is far more trou-bling in his cell than many criminals are outside it, because he represents a cunningly intelligent malignance that simply cannot be destroyed, only contained—temporarily.

So it is that in their first scene together, an annoyed Lecter cuts the earnest Starling down to size with slashing observations. "You know what you look like to me with your good bag and your cheap shoes? You look like a rube," he tells her. "You're not more than one generation from poor white trash, are you, Agent Starling?" As he continues his deconstruction, you watch Foster's face begin to crumple from the verbal barrage and yet somehow maintain its shape: she's already flinched, she's being toyed with, and yet she refuses to entirely surrender. She makes a lame, but nevertheless resilient, riposte to the effect that Lecter should focus his scalding insight on someone his own size.

Though Lecter/Hopkins in many ways steals the show, *Lambs* is really a Clarice/Foster movie. That's because such a powerfully credible evil character simultaneously opens the possibility of redemptive good. At a couple of points in the story, Lecter guesses that Clarice was abused by her policeman father or the rancher who temporarily served as her foster parent after she was orphaned following her father's death in the line of duty. But he is wrong. Her father, as we see in flashbacks, was a good man; so, we're told, was the rancher. So why is Starling so hell-bent on catching Buffalo Bill before he kills his next victim—who, it turns out, is the daughter of a powerful (female) Republican U.S. senator? Is Clarice motivated by ambition? Surely. But Lecter senses there's more involved, and he insists on knowing what as the price of his cooperation in capturing Buffalo Bill (whose name is an acidic parody of a mythic American figure). Starling, who has been repeatedly warned about the dangers of self-disclosure with Lecter, is desperate enough to agree to his demands.

Starling and Lecter have a series of discussions in the course of the story, the most important of which occurs about an hour into the movie. In a rapid series of quid pro quo exchanges, Lecter relinquishes tidbits of analysis in the Buffalo Bill case and then presses her on why she suddenly left the home of the rancher. Starling describes a night when she woke up to the sound of screaming and went to the barn from which it emanated. "I was so scared to look inside, but I had to," she says, a remark that also encapsulates her behavior in this grisly case. Lecter correctly speculates Starling saw the rancher engaged in the annual slaughter of the spring lambs. "First I tried to free them...but they just stood there," Starling muses, her vacant stare suggesting she's reliving that terrible moment. She grabbed one and ran. "I thought if I could just save one," she says, her hushed voice trailing off, "but he was so heavy. So heavy." She reports that she only made it a few miles (!) before she was caught. What became of the lamb, Lecter asks. "They killed him," she informs him. Lecter grasps the implications quickly: "And you think if you save poor Catherine [the senator's daughter], you could make them stop, don't you? You think if Catherine lives, you won't wake up in the dark ever again to that awful screaming of the lambs." Starling replies, "I don't know. I don't know."[30]

That night in 1991, and in multiple viewings since, I've always found Lecter's final remark breathtaking: "Thank you, Clarice. Thank you." Lecter appreciates Starling's honesty, which has characterized their relationship from the very beginning. But you get the sense that what he also appreciates is a sense of mystery. It's possible to reduce Starling's actions to a form of neurosis, an irrational belief that by following in her father's professional footsteps and apprehending a serial killer, she will somehow repair the psychic wounds of her childhood. But this only leads to the question of why her behavior takes this form and not some other, far more destructive course, which after all is the more typical response to psychic trauma. Lecter is fascinated by Starling—he etches a gorgeous pencil drawing of her holding a lamb—and he's right to be. She enlarges the world with a sense of moral possibility, one even an evil man can respect in terms of gamesmanship. In the process, Clarice enlarged Jodie Foster's career by giving us a character who's not simply forced to respond to the malice of the wide world, but who can take proactive steps in giving herself and other people a real reason to live.

This brings me to one of the most exciting moments in my cinematic life, which occurs when Starling unexpectedly finds herself in Buffalo Bill's house and decides she must descend the stairs into his dark basement alone and try to apprehend him. Foster shakes with fear, in one of the most authentic representations of terror ever committed to the screen. It has long since become a horror movie joke that characters defy all psychic logic by entering situations that will prove catastrophic, because if they don't there won't be a scary movie. This is the opposite of that: Starling knows full well she shouldn't go down those stairs, *and she does so anyway*. She simply must save Catherine, a woman she's never met. Soldiers at the front have to muster courage, but in part that's because wars create situations in which scared men have little effective chance for survival except going forward (or staying put) and hoping for the best. This, too,

LONE RANGER: Foster as the utterly terrified Clarice Starling, who nevertheless pushes forward to rescue a kidnapping victim in *The Silence of the Lambs* (1991). The sheer moral force of Foster's performance balances the film against that of Anthony Hopkins's fascinatingly evil Hannibal Lecter. *(Orion Pictures)*

is the opposite of that: courage as the decision to experience fear. Starling's descent is just the beginning; she finds herself plunged into pitch darkness while Buffalo Bill gazes upon her through night goggles. (In an eerie move, director Demme shows us Starling from his point of view, implicating us in that gaze.) But she will prevail.

There, anyway. For Hannibal Lecter has his own agenda, and while Starling and her colleagues are in hot pursuit of Buffalo Bill, he ruthlessly engineers his escape from prison. The movie ends, as its moral logic dictates, with Lecter abroad, as evil eternally is. But he can't resist a phone call to Starling at her moment of triumph. "I've no plans to call on you, Clarice," he tells her in a not entirely reassuring locution. "The world's more interesting with you in it. So you take care now to extend me the same courtesy." Starling responds by saying, "You know I can't make that promise," which of course suggests the essence of her character, someone who cannot remain passive in the presence of evil. Lecter responds with one of the movie's memorable jokes: "I do wish we could chat longer, but I'm having an old friend for dinner."

The Silence of the Lambs pulled off a rare coup, becoming one of only three movies to sweep the five major Oscars for Best Picture, Actor, Actress, Director, and Screenplay (the others were *It Happened One Night* [1934] and *One Flew Over the Cuckoo's Nest* [1975]). Never again would Foster have to recredential herself in the industry. Indeed, she consolidated her position by founding a production company, Egg Pictures, and moving into directing and producing. But while both would remain facets of her career, and while she would repeatedly claim that both were where her future lay, Foster continued to work primarily as an actor. Fortunately, as she did so, her vision widened and became more psychologically generous.

A good example is *Little Man Tate* (1991), Foster's directorial debut. Although its namesake is a precocious, Salingeresque little boy (Adam Hann-Byrd), it's not hard to see an oblique autobiographical subtext to this story about a brilliant child and the tug-of-war he engenders between two powerful women. Foster plays Dede Tate, working-class mother of the seven-year-old Fred, who loves him fiercely but lacks the resources, intellectual and otherwise, to develop his prodigious talents. Enter Jane Grierson (Dianne Wiest), who runs an institute for gifted children but shows startling deficits in nurturing them. It is to Foster's credit that she chose to tell this notably fair-minded story, which shows sensitivity to some of its specifically gendered dimensions (Harry Connick Jr. does nicely in a brief role that shows the possibilities and limits of male role models for the boy). *Little Man Tate* is also a hopeful movie in that it suggests that conflicts between adults over children may contribute positively to their development when those adults come to realize the important, if incomplete, roles they can have in the children's lives. (In this regard, *Little Man Tate* is a bit like Denzel Washington's *The Great Debaters*, a film in which an argument between two men helps forge the strong character of a civil rights leader.)

Foster followed *Little Man Tate* with a bit part in Woody Allen's *Shadows and Fog* (1992), one of the better-realized projects of that prolific director. *Shadows* is a Kafkaesque fable set in an unnamed city—think New York or London in the second quarter of the twentieth century—about a man (Allen) ordered to find a serial killer abroad on a foggy night. Mia Farrow plays a circus performer angry with her unfaithful companion (John Malkovich) who finds herself in a whorehouse whose employees include a genial prostitute played by Foster. "There's only one thing men will brave murder for," she says in a moment of wry levity with her companions. "The little furry animal between our legs." Though thoroughly Gothic in its black-and-white cinematography, the movie has an upbeat ending that gets about as close as Foster ever does to buoyancy in her movies.

Her next project, *Sommersby*, is really the only one in the Foster Hollywood canon that can truly be considered a historical epic. Given its French source material, it's a bit surprising that her co-star, Richard Gere, was executive producer, though he probably had more clout than the Francophile Foster did at the time. *Sommersby* is based on the life of Martin Guerre, a sixteenth-century man who became a source of folklore in French life and culture. Guerre, who hailed from the Basque country, fled a difficult family situation and wound up a soldier for Spain's army, in a Europe riven by religious conflict (Spain of course was arch-Catholic; Guerre hailed from a region with strong Calvinist tendencies). Years after he disappeared, the returning soldier resumed his place in the village. But suspicions grew that he was an imposter, and those suspicions grew substantially when the real Martin Guerre returned and claimed he had been robbed of his identity by a man who was really Arnaud du Tilh, nicknamed Pansette ("belly"). Pansette was eventually tried, convicted, and executed. A 1982 cinematic version of this story, starring Gérard Depardieu, was co-written by Princeton historian Natalie Zemon Davis, who later published the definitive scholarly account of the tale.[31] The inspired conceit of *Sommersby* involved taking a different period of intense warfare and ideological conflict—the American Civil War—and telling an analogous story rooted in local events and relationships.

Though nominally a conventional romance, not her typical fare, it's not hard so see why *Sommersby* appealed to Foster beyond simply establishing her as a leading lady. Though presumably a struggle between two men, it's really the woman—Bertrande de Rols in life, Laurel Sommersby in the movie—who functions as the keystone of the story. It strains credulity to believe that de Rols failed to recognize the returning soldier was not her husband, but this was nevertheless her stance as long as she could maintain it, largely because her actual marriage was an unhappy one (partly the result of Guerre's impotence, which brought their union to the brink of annulment before his departure).

Sommersby feels compelled to stack its deck—beyond simply having dreamboat Gere as the fraudulent title character—by having Sommersby champion agricultural self-sufficiency for poor farmers and hold a laughably enlightened view of race relations in the Reconstruction South. Yet there is a modicum of historical truth in his trial being presided over by a black judge (James Earl Jones), for the story is set in that brief interregnum between slavery and the imposition of a segregated Jim Crow regime. In one of his many fine performances, Jones manages to endow his character with both dignity and an implicit recognition of how fragile that dignity is. Which really goes to the heart of one of the most important meanings of the Martin Guerre saga: that in times of social upheaval, it becomes tantalizingly possible to plausibly imagine a different, better personal life.

No one makes this point better than Foster, who manages to convey it solely on the basis of her facial expressions at the start of the movie. We first see her tilling the family field, accompanied by another farmer (Bill Pullman), who is in love with her. Informed that her husband has returned from the war, she runs to the house, grabs her son, and goes inside to watch as he approaches, an excited crowd in tow. Obviously guarded—is it because she's unhappy to see him or knows he's an imposter?—she takes the boy out to the front steps, awaiting the veteran's approach. "Go say hello to your daddy," she finally says to her son, clearly too young to really remember his father, and we sense she's playing for time, not ready to embrace the man or call him a fraud. But he's playing his part to the hilt. "I'd forgotten how beautiful you are," he says, taking the hands that she had just been rubbing nervously. Foster's faint half-smile seems to suggest amusement with the performance, but after she closes her eyes and the two embrace, she opens them briefly, suggesting nervousness about where this ruse is headed.

Mrs. Sommersby nevertheless proves skillful in parrying her "husband's" advances, "reminding" him that they had not been sleeping together at the time of his departure and would not be now, either. Over time, of course, the two fall in love; the great irony of Gere's character is that his identity

HARD LOOK: Foster apprises her ostensible husband, a returning Civil War veteran, in *Sommersby* (1993). Skepticism is the default setting for most Foster characters. *(Warner Bros.)*

theft cannot disguise his irrepressible generosity. The couple's happiness is ineluctably temporary, but no less precious for that. The thin but heartfelt smile Foster gives Sommersby on the scaffold at the end of the movie suggests a joy that not even his death can take away, and the final image, of black men repairing the steeple on a damaged church, suggests that such small islands of hope become the basis of new and better worlds.

Foster followed *Sommersby* with another historical movie, this one a comic western, *Maverick* (1994), based on the TV series from the late fifties and early sixties that starred James Garner as the title character. This time Garner (who acted with Foster in the 1973 Disney feature *One Little Indian*) is Maverick's father, and the title role is filled by Mel Gibson. *Maverick* was written by a past master, William Goldman, and is exceptionally deft in pacing and plot twists that resemble a card trick, which is appropriate, since the plot concerns a set of poker-playing grifters. Foster plays Annabelle Bransford, a sexy con artist who keeps pace with a fast pack of players. Indeed, she takes the figurative trump card in the final scene of the movie, a good-natured feminist ending for a film that is by far the lightest of Foster's career, and one that she has remembered with great affection ever since. (It was during the making of this movie that she befriended Gibson, a man she cast, and stood beside, seventeen years later amid the publicity surrounding *The Beaver*.)

Maverick was a popcorn flick; Foster's other movie of 1994 was considerably more ambitious and ranks among her best performances: the title role in *Nell*, for which she received her fourth Academy Award nomination. (In a bravura turn, Foster manages the arresting task of emptying her face of expression for much of the movie.) Though this was a pedi-gree project with major talent—including Liam Neeson, his wife, Natasha Richardson, and the esteemed British director Michael Apted—*Nell* is a fairly predictable undertaking most notable for the way it once again showcases Foster's emphasis on the malignant forces that subvert the designs of even the best-intentioned people. *Nell* is the story of a young woman who has lived her whole life in the remote woods of North Carolina, insulated from contact with modern civilization (Natalie Bumppo, last of the latter-day Mohicans, you might say). She was con-ceived as a result of rape and had a twin sister who died in childhood. When her mother dies, her death is reported by an unscrupulous grocery delivery boy, and local authorities discover Nell's existence. A local doctor, played by Neeson, tries to assist her, and to do this, he enlists Richardson, a specialist in autism. They realize, however, that Nell is not mentally handicapped; her strange language results from a combination of emu-lating her stroke-stricken mother and the special language she shared with her twin. Yet their attempt to serve as surrogate parents for Nell is complicated by medical professionals who seek to institutionalize her, as well as people who wish to exploit her vulnerability. In other words, in-stitutions not only do more harm than good, they also fail to protect the vulnerable from those who operate outside and against them. After a dramatic hearing in a trial-like setting, Nell wins her freedom and can return to the wild with her new family, the Rousseau-like logic of the film finally affirmed.

Foster essentially repeated that message in a different form three years later in *Contact*, a tedious science-fiction movie in which she stars as an astronomer who teams up with Matthew McConaughey, unconvincingly cast as a theologian. They battle the skepticism—and, more importantly, the greed and hatred—of those, inside and outside their fields, who reject their fervent belief that alien life exists. The soggy New Age overtones of the film, which include the astronomer's contact with her long-dead father, suggest something of a dead end in Foster's career-long assertion that goodness and decency are locked in mortal combat with irrational malice. Fortunately, in the ensuing years, her work began to texture this paradigm and portray characters and situations with more internal com-plexity.

One good example of this is the overlooked gem of Foster's career, *Anna and the King*. Like *Last of the Mohicans*, this reality-based story has gone through many iterations over the course of the last century. Its source material is the two-volume memoir of Anna Harriette Leonowens, a Vic-torian widow who worked as a tutor in the court of the King of Siam in the 1860s, just as British imperial power was reaching its zenith. The factual accuracy of the portrait that emerges of the reform-minded Siamese ruler, Mongkut, in *The English Governess at the Siamese Court* (1870–73) has been contested, and is in any case filtered through an imperially inflected feminism.[32] Incidents in Leonowens's story received a new lease on life in 1944, when children's author Margaret Landon published *Anna and the King of Siam*, which became an evergreen novel of its genre (it was reissued in 2000 and remains in print). The novel, in turn, spawned a 1946 movie starring Rex Harrison as the King and Irene Dunne as Leonowens. The novel also led to the 1951 Rodgers and Hammerstein stage production *The King and I*, which in turn became the basis of the 1956 film version with Yul Brynner and Deborah Kerr in the lead roles. The musical has long been regarded as one of the most beloved works from Broadway's golden age, although, like its predecessors, it is marked by racism that can be truly embarrassing to watch, as in the long minstrel show sequence featuring "Asian" figures in blackface.

Given this benighted Orientalist history, it's a bit surprising that anyone would want to approach this material again, and while director Andy Tennant expressed dismay about the difficulty he encountered with the Thai government in shooting the film (most of which ended up being shot in Malaysia), he should hardly have been surprised that his motives would be questioned. In fact, his 1999 version of the story, which is more beautifully designed than any of its predecessors, recalibrates the scales in important respects. Perhaps the most important is the casting of Chinese actor Chow Yun-Fat as Mongkut, whom he endows with an incisive dignity sorely missing from previous versions. He and Anna (Foster) have very good chemistry; their evident intelligence is a source of mutual respect and attraction, even as they banter over differences in style as well as substance. In the Rodgers and Hammerstein version, there are references to Harriet Beecher Stowe and Abraham Lincoln—perhaps inevitable, given the American production and audience for the story—but in this one Mongkut cherishes a letter from President Lincoln, who has politely declined the King's assistance in the Union cause, and the monarch speaks with accuracy and clarity about the meaning of the Battle of Antietam, which takes place simultaneously with the story.

Anna and the King also recalibrates the gender politics of earlier versions. At one point, the passionate Anna intervenes to prevent the caning of one of the King's concubines, who is caught while running from court to a Buddhist monastery to join her true love. While we the viewers and even the King understand the merits of Anna's advocacy on their behalf, it is not only politically naive but counterproductive, effectively leaving him no choice but to execute the two lest he damage his credibility at a critical moment in the life of his regime.

Which represents one more layer of complexity in this telling of the story. Though substantially fictionalized, the movie depicts Mongkut as navigating complex political currents that include the imperial jockeying of Britain and France (as well as intra-imperial British tensions) and a coup attempt mounted by his own brother. Specific details aside, the message here is consistent with Foster's acting choices going back decades: destructive external forces are always lurking, ready to wreck the most promising aspirations, whether those of a Great Emancipator in the West or one in the East. Such transpolitical greed, encased in a thin veneer of ideologies that include, but are not limited to, avowed racism, become the primary barrier to peaceful unions, romantic and otherwise, in this *Anna and the King*. (One thing that doesn't change is the core chastity of the story.) But all is not lost: the King's son, sustained by the memory of his father's unique relationship with a woman as an equal, will fulfill and extend his plans to bring his nation into the modern world.

While *Anna and the King* comports with Foster's vision as a whole, it nevertheless signals some important shifts in her work. One of the most important is a more nuanced engagement with the lives of men. Though it is, of course, usually men who intimidate, terrorize, or otherwise oppress her characters, Foster movies, whether directed by her or not, have never been simple exercises in male-bashing. Still, in the twenty-first century, her projects have shown a new level of depth in their portrayal of male characters. Whether or not this has anything to do with the fact that Foster herself bore two sons in 1998 and 2001 is hard to say. She has referred to wanting to make movies her kids could see, though, and it stands to reason that she would be interested in boy stories in particular.[33]

One intriguing document in this regard is *The Dangerous Lives of Altar Boys* (2002), a small independent film in which she plays a 1970s nun who teaches at a Catholic school. The two main characters of the title belong to a posse of comic-book-obsessed students who draw graphic pictures that include sexual poses of Foster's character, Sister Assumpta. Such behavior, along with relatively mild school pranks, is for the most part portrayed as developmentally understandable, if not exactly appropriate, though Sister Assumpta is shocked and hurt when she discovers it. (In an age when the Catholic Church hierarchy has much to be ashamed about, it is bracing to see a rank-and-file nun, as well as the priest played by Vincent D'Onofrio, portrayed with real empathy, even when they're not reacting in the most productive ways). Sister Assumpta, who walks with a limp, is anxious not to be seen as a fool, which leads her to make psychological pronouncements about the boys of dubious accuracy. But her stricken look at a funeral in the final scene of the movie—Sister Assumpta appears to realize that her name bespeaks a character flaw—suggests her understanding that she has not apprehended the realities in the lives of her students, a message of muted hope in a time of disorienting social change.

Foster's other project of 2002, *Panic Room,* was one of her biggest box office successes, in part because of its terrific screenplay by veteran writer David Koepp and the typically gloomy, yet arresting, direction of David Fincher. Foster plays a divorcee with a diabetic tween daughter (Kristen Stewart) who buys a Manhattan apartment that happens to have a special high-security chamber built for the needs of the previous owner. The problem is that she's unaware that the former owner left behind a cache of millions stored in the safe of the panic room, and that the man who designed it (Forest Whitaker, who worked with Denzel Washington in *The Great Debaters*) has plans to retrieve the money, for which he has enlisted a friend (Jared Leto), who in turn recruits another (Dwight Yoakam). The robbers break into the house expecting it to be empty; mother and daughter unwittingly take refuge in precisely the place where they will be besieged. A series of psychic and logistical twists ensues, among them the need to get rid of police who sincerely want to help but whose presence on the apartment doorstep only makes matters worse (a typical Foster scenario). For our purposes, the main point is that we come to see that Whitaker's character has redeeming qualities and that he increasingly becomes besieged himself by the ruthlessness of Yoakam. Ironically, it's Whitaker, not Foster or her daughter, who ends up as the tragic figure in the story, blindsided by the very kinds of malevolence that have afflicted Foster characters going back to *Taxi Driver.*

Another new accent in this phase of Foster's career is an increasing emphasis on inner turmoil no less than external threats. In *Flightplan* (2005), she's a widow bringing her young daughter from Germany back to America to begin a new life when that daughter disappears into thin air on a plane over the Atlantic. Not only does no one know where the child is, there is doubt the child was on the plane in the first place. (*Flightplan* is a modern-day variation on the 1938 Alfred Hitchcock film *The Lady Vanishes*, which involved a train rather than a plane.) In one sense, this is standard Foster fare: women in distress fighting back hard against malicious forces, in this case, a diabolically clever terrorist who exploits 9/11 fears to his advantage. What's also typical is that authority figures like the pilot are either unable to help, or unwitting enablers of terror in their own right. The difference is that for the first time in a Foster movie, one of her

ISOLATED TOGETHER: Foster as the mother of Kristen Stewart in *Panic Room* (2002). Even when official authority is well intentioned, it's useless in a struggle with predatory men. *(Columbia Pictures)*

characters is forced to question her own sanity. Foster characters aren't always perfect, but they're almost always strong, as is this one. Even so, she can't help but be dogged by self-doubt in the face of a wall of denial, when even those not involved in the conspiracy become increasingly hostile to her "antics" and "irrationality."

With *Inside Man* (2006), Foster began edging into new territory: playing flawed people whose imperfections are not incidental to who they are, but central to our assessment of them. A character like Sarah Tobias in *The Accused* was no princess, but she did not deserve to be raped, and we would probably like her if we got to know her (there's a wonderful scene, for example, when she connects in mutual fear with a reluctant witness at her trial). Anna Leonowens of *Anna and the King* had her prejudices, but her heart is in the right place. So is Dede Tate's in *Little Man Tate*. In *Inside Man,* however, Foster's Madeleine White—her ironic name refers not to her purity of character, but rather to an absence of one—she plays a stylish, intimidating, and amoral political fixer (though one who can impose devilishly just desserts on an evil banker played by Christopher

WHITE MARBLE: Foster as the amoral Madeleine White (with Denzel Washington) in *Inside Man* (2006). In middle age, Foster's palette of characters has widened considerably. *(NBC Universal)*

Plummer). It's a supporting role; this Spike Lee movie features Denzel Washington as a police detective and Clive Owen as the lead bank robber in a memorably complex, cerebral thriller. Nevertheless, it's among the more vivid in Foster's career, and it shows her as a powerful figure functioning very successfully in a male-dominated world, which amounts to a kind of guilty pleasure in its own right.

In *The Brave One* (2007), Foster in fact becomes a criminal on the streets, albeit one of a complicated kind. She plays Erica Bain, the host of an NPR-like talk show—Foster really does have a great voice for radio— brutally attacked with her fiancé, who is killed, during a nighttime walk in Central Park. Unable to manage her grief, she buys a gun illegally and becomes a vigilante, roaming the streets of the city and killing evildoers— first those she encounters accidentally, and then those she seeks out. She's befriended by a soulful detective, played by Terrence Howard, who becomes increasingly aware of, and ambivalent about, her actions.

The Brave One is an intriguing but deeply flawed movie. It can be seen as a bookend with *Taxi Driver* in the way it resonates with classically Fosterian themes: the world is a dangerous place, even the presumably cleaned-up New York of the twenty-first century, and one in which official authority is ineffectual at best. But this time the woman "graduates" to becoming the man with the gun (Bain as the bane of evildoers, as it were) rather than the victimized bystander.

The problem is that the film's message is fatally divided. It's very clear that Foster intended *The Brave One* to be a deconstruction of the vigilante genre, in that we see a damaged woman deal with her grief in a dysfunctional way. As she explained to *Entertainment Weekly* at the time of the movie's release, "I don't believe a gun should be in the hand of a thinking, feeling, breathing human being. Americans are filled with rage/fear. And guns are a huge part of our culture. I know I'm crazy because I'm only supposed to say that in Europe. But violence corrupts absolutely. By the end, her [Bain's] transformation is complete." The interviewer noted that members of the audience tend to cheer at the climax of the film, a fact Foster calls "shameful," comparing it to those who cheered at her character's rape during a screening of *The Accused* that she attended.[34]

This is actually a misguided conflation of two very different scenarios. While such a reaction to *The Accused* is appalling in that it celebrates wanton violence against an innocent person, the rhetorical fingers of *The Brave One* press on a scale weighted toward seeing perpetrators get their comeuppance. *The Brave One* was helmed by Neil Jordan, the great Irish director, noted for his rich, independent body of work. But it was produced by action-flick impresario Joel Silver, and ultimately the moral logic of the project tips in that direction. Everyone Erica Bain shoots has it coming; we get no backstories of these people to suggest otherwise. The one person whose situation is the least bit complicated is a prostitute who gets hit by a car after Bain shoots the pimp driving it, but she may arguably be better off with that as the price of having him dead. If the movie wanted to make the point that vigilante justice is immoral, it should have done so more unambiguously. Of course, to do that would have compromised the commercial appeal of the project, whose message was plain in the image on the DVD case for the film: a tough-looking, androgynous Foster determinedly pointing a gun. So while *The Brave One* is an important document in the evolution of Foster's artistic/moral/historical vision, it is finally an unsatisfying work.

A more promising, if somewhat ironic, new direction for Foster in recent years is her attempt to show something few actors, especially successful female actors, do: weakness. Such a decision was apparently on her mind in mid-decade, because it came up a number of times in interviews. "If there's one stereotype that I have, it's that I always play strong women," she told the UK cineaste magazine *Total Film* in 2005. "I've played dumb blondes but they were strong dumb blondes. I've played bad characters but they were strong bad characters. I'm not sure I know how to play weak. I really don't know how."[35]

In the context of recent cinematic history, this is an odd confession to make. An unwritten rule in the movie business holds that audiences want strength, not weakness, and even in those cases in which weakness is depicted, the expectation is that protagonists triumph over it. The imperatives of late-twentieth-century feminism in particular put a premium on strong women characters: anything else is tantamount to betrayal. As Jane Fonda, one of the great movie stars of the modern era recently put it, "Anger was always easy. Fear was harder."[36] Foster has been a maestro of fear, one of the greatest artists of the emotion cinema has seen. But the terrors she's faced—serial killers, terrorists, rapists, et al.—have tended to be of the extreme variety. Much tougher are those of the more quotidian kind. So Foster rose to the challenge and summoned the courage to be weak.

Her first such foray, *Nim's Island* (2008), marked a return to familiar territory in that it's a children's movie, based on the 2002 novel of the same name by Canadian juvenile fiction writer Wendy Orr. Abigail Breslin plays the title character, a girl who lives on a beautiful but remote Pacific island; her widower father (Gerard Butler) is a scientist. When Dad gets shipwrecked on a seafaring expedition, Nim sends an e-mail to her favorite author, Alex Rover (Foster), an adventurer who recently queried her father about a professional matter. What Nim doesn't realize is that Rover (also played by Butler) is really just a figment in the imagination of *Alexandra* Rover, an agoraphobic woman living alone in San Francisco. Rover's desperation to help finally overcomes her desperation to avoid leaving her house. Foster's comic rendition of a fearful woman is not without pathos, and while the story vindicates a child's resourcefulness in the face of adversity, it is also affirms the power of imagination to prevail in struggles that are finally far more internal than external.

Much less satisfying is Foster's appearance in the Roman Polanski–directed *Carnage* (2011), based on French playwright Yasmina Reza's 2007 black comedy *Le Dieu du Carnage*, which won a Tony Award for Best Drama in an English-language version on Broadway in 2009. This is not simply because the two middle-aged bourgeois couples (Kate Winslet/Christoph Waltz and Foster/John C. Reilly in the cinematic version) who meet in the aftermath of their sons' scuffle on a playground are repellent people. Rather it's because the scenario we're given just seems implausible. Given the emerging frictions that emerge in their discussions at the Brooklyn apartment of Foster/Reilly, there's no way these people would remain in each other's company for the interminable eighty or so minutes that they do. Nor are Foster and Reilly believable as a married couple (she writes about antiquities and genocide; he owns a cookware supply company). The actors are all terrific; Foster in particular combines sanctimony, rage, and self-pity all too plausibly. It's hard not to admire her commitment to the performance, but harder to like it, less because it lacks heart in its own right than because of the unrelenting misanthropy—and, arguably, misogyny—that hangs like a pall over the whole movie.

Foster also directed a movie in 2011, with more complicated results. Interestingly, while few of her acting appearances focus on families, all the movies she's directed do. *Little Man Tate* has already been discussed; *Home for the Holidays* (1995), in which Foster does not appear, chronicles the life of a loving but chaotic family of adults during Thanksgiving weekend. In *The Beaver*—a severe flop for a number of reasons, among them Mel Gibson's poor reputation and its betwixt-and-between-character as a dramedy[37]—she plays Meredith Black, wife of Walter Black (Gibson), a severely depressed toy company executive who begins communicating via a beaver puppet. The couple has two sons, the older of whom is a senior in high school terrified he will end up like his father. Meredith reluctantly kicks her husband out of their home, but her resolve ebbs when Walter comes home and plays with the younger son, leading the elder boy to rebuke her for her lack of willpower. Despite her stated desire to fight for her marriage if there is any hope of preserving it, Meredith is largely a bystander—something that Foster probably could have changed if she really wanted to, but which makes sense in the logic of the story. As is so often the case in her movies, matters take a gruesome turn. It is, however, Meredith's point of view from which we see a final father-and-son reunion at the end of the film. At the end of a half century as a performer, Foster comes off as someone almost impossible to imagine: an ordinary person.

———

Though I've lived most of my life thinking I was born a little late, I still grew up believing that I was in the middle of a great world civilization. As such, I often found myself wondering what would it be like coming of age in, say, Mexico in the 1950s, or Italy in the 1890s, or Japan in the 1730s—times that, even in the histories of such storied places, don't seem that arresting. If you were a kid, I think you'd want to be an Aztec in the fifteenth century, or Japanese in the late nineteenth century, or Italian at the time of the Risorgimento—or the first century BCE. (Any turmoil, of course, would be more exciting than threatening.) But to grow up in a place that was not undergoing dramatic change or dominating the global stage seemed sad to me.

This is of course crude, imperialist thinking, though I confess it's proven durable in my psyche. I suppose it's akin to the wages of whiteness, a concept W.E.B. DuBois used to explain why oppressed white workers would never cast their lot in favor of interracial solidarity against their rapacious capitalists: at least they're not black.[38] The wages of Americanness, by contrast, are not specifically racial, though of course white people have benefited disproportionately from the psychic dividend they have conferred. But all of us who have experienced them cannot help but suspect that this dividend is soon to be cut off, and that a reckoning is at hand.

It seems quite likely to me that if the work of Jodie Foster continues to have life beyond the mortal frame of the republic, she will be seen as a distinctively American artist, perhaps in ways we can only dimly perceive now. However, for me, she's functioned—in precisely that half-conscious, ill-formed, but nevertheless discernible way that I've been at some pains to trace in the preceding chapters—as a living demonstration that you can have a full, complicated, and interesting life without caring all that much that you happen to be American. Again: she is a counterintuitive vehicle for that message, in that she herself came of age in Hollywood, the veritable cockpit of the American Dream. Perhaps that allowed her to take it for granted in a way I never did, and to become a true cosmopolitan, the way members of national elites often do. Or maybe it's simply that she's a female, and females have traditionally found their allegiances closer to home, whether or not they happen to be wives or mothers. In any case, it took an American for me to begin to imagine a post-American identity for myself and my heirs. Embarrassing, but true.

Maybe it's my turn to be the brave one.

Conclusion

Sensing the Future of History

In the sway of the seemingly eternal pendulum between reason and passion—which I'll define as a general term that includes intuition, emotion, and feeling—the temper of the early twenty-first century appears headed toward the latter, at least in the realm of popular thought. *Homo economicus*, the notion that human beings make rational choices in terms of self-interest, is in retreat. Contemporary scholars in a variety of fields from psychology to literary criticism emphasize how each individual is influenced by any number of subconscious or unconscious forces, whether in the form of biological imperatives, social influences, or the two in tandem. And we can hardly act in terms of self-interest when we don't really know what it is, either because we have conflicting desires or because we find it difficult to anticipate how we will actually feel when an imagined future arrives. In this version of our collective story, everything from racism to morality precedes consciousness, which literally rationalizes our instincts.

I should add that biology is not necessarily destiny. The technological metaphor has changed from our brains being *hard*-wired to *pre*-wired, with real, though finite, capacity for conscious environmental adaptation. Insofar as we can achieve self-knowledge and act on it productively, this version of the story goes, we need to rely less on the analytic left side of the brain and deploy it in cultivating the right—the realm of play, empathy, story, and like-minded aptitudes. Ironically, then, these writers use their powers of reason to counsel mindfulness to passion.[1]

Perhaps fittingly, it was only after I had essentially finished this book that I recognized the degree to which it has been pulled by the currents of this zeitgeist. The individual chapters are like brain scans of careers in which I trace basic patterns dyed in the color of time. These formations are part of much larger neurological operations that take place unseen and otherwise undetected inside the heads of these artists—electric signals that comprise a larger enterprise we call acting. It is precisely because it seems so unlikely that, say, Daniel Day-Lewis was consciously thinking about the frontier myth when he decided to take the role of Bill the Butcher in *Gangs of New York*, or Daniel Plainview in *There Will Be Blood*, that my ability to discern such a link—that admittedly vague but useful word scientists love to deploy when talking about genetic connections between otherwise unlikely phenomena—is so striking. You can argue with me about how strong that link is, or what it means: that's the nature of discourse, scientific and otherwise. But if you've made it this far (I say this aware that you may be reading these words of mine before others), you're willing to entertain the validity of such links.

I hardly need to say that this project grew out of a love of movies, deep admiration for the people I've chosen to write about, and confidence that love and admiration are a compelling basis for scholarship. But these artists matter to me beyond any intrinsic interest I have in their work, because I believe the historical patterns I've traced in scanning their films correspond to what's happening inside our own heads when we watch them act and may affect our understanding of how we arrived where we are in the daily act of living. History is not only a matter of thought but also a matter of feeling—or, perhaps more accurately, a complex interplay between the two.

It has long been my suspicion, without ever being able to say so succinctly or convincingly, that the historical profession has been insufficiently attentive to this interplay as it applies to the study of the past. To be sure, historians have long been aware of how emotion, intuition, and avowedly irrational forces have shaped the behavior of people in all times and places. But they seem less willing to allow for it in the production of history itself.

There are a number of (good) reasons for this. One is that the profession emerged in the late nineteenth century, when the aforementioned pendulum had swung toward empiricism, measurement, reason. At that formative moment, the prestige of science was such that a variety of fields sought to emulate it, as commonplace academic terms like "hypothesis" and "evidence" suggest. Another is that the success of the profession *as* a profession was best served by training a cadre of practitioners to develop mastery of discrete, exhaustively mapped subunits of larger fields or disciplines. In terms of creating an orderly experience for a career, master narratives were best left to, well, masters. The everyday work of historical scholarship was argument and persuasion, best achieved by forging chains of logic.

Argument, persuasion, and logic are marvelous things. Nor are they limited to the thought patterns of professional scholars: I hope it's clear that while the various master narratives of the actors in this book may be inaccurate, contestable, simplistic, or just plain wrong, they *are* reasonable. And I've tried to be reasonable myself in explaining how. It's truly frightening to consider how the life of the mind could proceed without such orderly, shared, explicit protocols.

But they're not sufficient. History is finally an art, not a science. Facts and accuracy are lifeless without a mythic dimension. Historical meaning rests on intuition, juxtaposition, suggestion, and story, at least as much as it does on explicit arguments. These are truths that actors understand intuitively (honed by a sense of craft, itself internalized as habit), and convey to their audiences the same way. Historians from Homer to Francis Parkman knew it, too. Academic historians sometimes seem to forget, which is why their work so often fails to resonate outside the academy.

I'm uncertain what all this may portend. A man of my time and place, I could only render this story, such as it is, as a piece of fairly traditional historical scholarship even as I sought to stretch its boundaries, an instinct I regard as the repository of creativity. I anticipate a day for this beloved discipline in which qualities like voice and metaphor will (again) be honored as much as argument and evidence. In any case, there's one thing I believe with as much certainty as I've ever known: the sources of history, both in terms of the records used and the modes of storytelling, will get replaced, as every regime, intellectual and otherwise, constantly does.

Maybe there's a good movie in that.

NOTES

Introduction

1. See Jim Cullen, "Daniel Day-Lewis, American Historian," *Common-Place* 7:4 (July 2007), http://www.historycooperative.org/journals/cp/vol-07/no-04/school/ [March 16, 2012]. The piece became the germ of this book.
2. Acute readers will sense a postmodernist thread underlying my train of thought here, which reflects exposure to scholars like Hayden White early in my graduate training. See, for example, *Tropics of Discourse: Essays in Cultural Criticism* (Baltimore: Johns Hopkins University Press, 1978). More specifically, some of my underlying premises as they relate to movies in particular were first articulated by Robert A. Rosenstone. His 1995 collection of essays, *Visions of the Past: The Challenge of Film to Our Idea of History* (Cambridge: Harvard University Press), is particularly suggestive. My work is somewhat different than theirs in that mine is grounded more in historical than cinematic or literary discourse, and I'm more inclined to focus on mainstream Hollywood cinema than Rosenstone, who pays particular attention to filmmakers (generally directors) who self-consciously stretch or subvert established cinematic conventions. My interest in actors in particular, and in tracing an interpretive trajectory in their body of work as a whole, takes their ideas in a somewhat different direction.
3. Rosenstone, "What You Think About When You Think About Writing a Book on History and Film," in *Visions of the Past,* 236.
4. F. Scott Fitzgerald, *The Great Gatsby* (New York: Scribner's, 1925), 6.
5. Greil Marcus, *The Doors: A Lifetime of Listening to Five Mean Years* (New York: PublicAffairs, 2011), 189.
6. James Naremore, *Acting in the Cinema,* Kindle ed. (Berkeley: University of California Press, 1988), 21, 34. For a more theoretical elaboration of the relationship between acting and movie stardom, see Richard Dyer, *Stars* (1979; London: British Film Institute/Palgrave Macmillan, 1998).
7. A formative influence on my thinking generally and in conceptualizing this project in particular, Garry Wills is among those who have explored *The Searchers* in these ways. See his chapter on film in *John Wayne's America: The Politics of Celebrity* (New York: Simon & Schuster, 1997), 251–61. See also Edward Buscombe's *The Searchers*, part of the British Film Institute series (London: BFI, 2008), particularly Buscombe's discussions of portals (natural and man-made), 63–65. In a 2010 blog post for *The Sheila Variations,* Sheila O'Malley

literally illustrates the doorway motif in the film. See "Doorways in John Ford's *The Searchers*" and related commentary at http://www.sheilaomalley.com/?p = 25214 [August 25, 2010]. Mary Rowlandson's *Sovereignty and Goodness of God* . . . is widely available online; Richard Slotkin is among the writers who has situated it as a fountainhead of the Western tradition. See *Regeneration Through Violence: The Mythology of the American Frontier, 1600–1860* (1973; Norman: University of Oklahoma Press, 2000), 102 ff.

8. Robert Kolker, *A Cinema of Loneliness*, 4th ed. (1980; New York: Oxford University Press, 2011), 15; Wills, *John Wayne's America*.

9. For more on the director-actor relationship and the ways in which an actor can be considered an auteur, see Dyer, *Stars*, 152–55.

10. This is a topic that has been grappled with by a great many scholars, but among the most important in shaping my thinking has been Robert H. Wiebe, best known for his book *The Search for Order, 1877–1920* (New York: Hill & Wang, 1966). Wiebe elaborated and extended his ideas in the capstone work of his career, *Self-Rule: A Cultural History of American Democracy* (Chicago: University of Chicago Press, 1996). At the start of that book, he notes that "we accept as simultaneously true a way in which as individuals we live alone and a way in which our lives have no meaning apart from their social environments. The history of American democracy is one expression of these twin truths and of the changing relation between them" (13).

11. I imbibed this lesson at the feet of the great Brown University historian William McLoughlin during my training as a graduate student. For a distillation of this idea, see *Revivals, Awakenings, and Reform* (Chicago: University of Chicago Press, 1978).

12. The concept of "salutary neglect" (first coined by Edmund Burke in 1775) and its revocation in the aftermath of the Seven Years War is a fixture in the historiography of the American Revolution. One scholar who has done an excellent job of tracing the connection between economic protest and political mobilization is T. H. Breen. See in particular *The Marketplace of Revolution: How Consumer Politics Shaped American Independence* (New York: Oxford University Press, 2004).

13. Americans' attachment to intensely local militias, and the headaches that attachment caused British and American military leaders trying to forge formal, cohesive military institutions, is part of a historiography that stretches across works that range from Robert Gross's *The Minutemen and Their World* (1976; New York: Hill & Wang, 2001) to David McCullough's *1776* (New York: Simon & Schuster, 2005).

14. For a survey and distillation of the Janus-faced quality of quality of the American Revolution, as captured in the Declaration of Independence, see Jim Cullen, *The American Dream: A Short History of an Idea That Shaped a Nation* (New York: Oxford University Press, 2003), chapter 2.

15. For a very good analysis of the pro-institutional tilt in American society spawned by the Second World War, see James Sparrow, *Warfare State: World War II Americans and the Age of Big Government* (New York: Oxford University Press, 2011). The literature of "consensus" that followed the war—its emergence, contours, dissipation, and legitimacy, both as a political movement and a historical construct—is vast. It received its first major articulation in the work of Richard Hofstadter in *The American Political Tradition and the Men Who Made It* (New York: Knopf, 1948). An early detailed chronicle of its rise and fall is central to Godfrey Hodgson's *America in Our Time: From World War II to Nixon—What Happened and Why* (New York: Doubleday, 1976). The best

most recent chronicle of the rise of institutional confidence and disillusionment can be found in James Patterson, *Grand Expectations: The United States, 1945–1974* (New York: Oxford University Press, 1997).

16. For a superb articulation of the institutional character of American culture in the mid-twentieth century, see Thomas Schatz, *The Genius of the System: Hollywood Filmmaking in the Studio Era* (New York: Pantheon, 1988). This system is also central to Robert Sklar's synthetic narrative *Movie-Made America: A Cultural History of American Movies* (1974; New York: Vintage, 1994).

17. The generational turn against institutional consensus is a prominent theme of Hodgson's *America in Our Time*. In *America Transformed: Sixty Years of Revolutionary Change, 1941–2001* (New York: Cambridge University Press, 2006), Richard Abrams does a fine job of isolating the particular strands I name here, whose locus was largely in the New Left, and showing how they were gradually undermined by the neoconservative challenge of the New Right. In *American Grace: How Religion Divides and Unites Us* (New York: Simon & Schuster, 2010), Robert D. Putnam and David E. Campbell chart the erosion of institutional religious cohesion—though not necessarily religiosity itself—in American life in the decades since World War II. For a broader critique of the decline in institutional commitment, see Putnam's *Bowling Alone: The Collapse and Revival of American Community* (New York: Simon & Schuster, 2000).

18. On the decline of the studio system, see Sklar, *Movie-Made America*, chapters 15–18. Mark Harris provides a granular description of this transition and how it played out in a set of films made during the 1960s in *Pictures at a Revolution: Five Movies and the Birth of the New Hollywood* (New York: Penguin Press, 2008). See also Peter Biskind, *Easy Rider, Raging Bulls: How the Sex-Drugs-and-Rock 'n' Roll Generation Saved Hollywood* (New York: Simon & Schuster, 1998). For a broader, and deeply suggestive, analysis of how the interaction of culture and technology has played out in film specifically and the mass media generally, see Tim Wu, *The Master Switch: The Rise and Fall of Information Empires* (New York: Knopf, 2011).

Chapter 1

1. The ad, which premiered on February 5, 2012, and was reportedly seen by an estimated 111 million viewers, described the nation as back on its heels at a metaphorical halftime but primed for a comeback. Some commentators saw the ad as an implicit endorsement of the Obama administration's bailout of the auto industry, even though Eastwood opposed that bailout (a stance he reaffirmed on a CNBC broadcast I saw later that week). For one discussion of the controversy, see James Stewart, "When Cars Meet Politics, a Clash," *New York Times*, February 10, 2012, accessed via nytimes.com. The ad was later satirized in a pair of bookended *Saturday Night Live* fake ads by the gifted Bill Hader: http://www.hulu.com/watch/328538/saturday-night-live-clint-eastwood-chrysler-ad [February 12, 2012].

2. Richard Schickel, *Clint Eastwood: A Biography* (1996; New York: Vintage, 1997), 370. Schickel had extensive access to Eastwood in writing this book, which makes it authoritative, though some consider it biased. Eastwood also made a number of movies for other studios, notably Universal, where he got his start and made a string of films before shifting his base of operations to Warners in the mid-1970s. In *Clint Eastwood: A Cultural Production* (Minneapolis: University of Minnesota Press, 1993), Paul Smith provides

other statistics in a chapter on Eastwood's production company, Malpaso (59 ff.). Measured in terms of cost/profit ratios (albeit on a relatively small scale compared with the big studios), Malpaso must surely be one of the most profitable production companies in Hollywood history.

3. In August of 2010, CNN ran a story about the annual "Beloit College Mindset List" for the entering Class of 2014, published to help professors understand students' cultural frames of reference. The list pointed out (item 12) that for contemporary adolescents, "Clint Eastwood is better known as a sensitive director than as Dirty Harry." http://www.cnn.com/2010/LIVING/08/18/college.mindset.list/index.html?iref=allsearch; the list itself is at http://www.beloit.edu/mindset/2014.php [November 3, 2011].

4. Pauline Kael, "Killing Time," *New Yorker*, January 14, 1974, 83.

5. In *Clint: A Retrospective* (New York: Sterling, 2010), Richard Schickel reports that some critics asserted *A Perfect World* failed at the box office because Eastwood "had sold out what they (mis)understood to be his formerly conservative principles to embrace a new identity as a lefty wuss" (219). *Million Dollar Baby* was the subject of a much more obvious and spirited debate; for one serious survey of responses to the film in the evangelical press, see the review of the movie in *Christianity Today*: http://www.christianitytoday.com/ct/2005/januaryweb-only/050113.html [November 3, 2011]. In a widely reported story, Spike Lee complained that Eastwood failed to include a single black character in either of his Iwo Jima movies; Eastwood, asserting that African Americans were not common in this arena of the Pacific theater, responded that Lee should "shut his face," leading Lee to rejoin, "We're not on a plantation." See http://www.guardian.co.uk/film/2008/jun/09/news.usa [November 2, 2011]. This was not actually the first such exchange between Lee and Eastwood. Back in 1988, Lee complained that *Bird* should have been made by a black filmmaker; Eastwood responded that Lee was welcome to make a movie about Beethoven. For more on this exchange, see Smith (who leans toward Lee), *Cultural Production*, 229–30.

6. Nixon quoted in Dennis Bingham, *Acting Male: Masculinities in the Films of James Stewart, Jack Nicholson, and Clint Eastwood* (New Brunswick: Rutgers University Press, 1994), 180.

7. Joseph Ellis, *American Sphinx: The Character of Thomas Jefferson* (1996; New York: Vintage, 1998), 252.

8. For one good examination of this point, see Daniel Boorstin, *The Lost World of Thomas Jefferson* (1948; Chicago: University of Chicago Press, 1981).

9. These and the following biographical details from Schickel, *Biography*, chapter 1.

10. Ibid., 36.

11. In a 1989 interview, Eastwood said he had seen Louis Armstrong frequently as a kid (Ric Gentry, "Clint Eastwood: An Interview," *Film Quarterly* 42:3 [Spring 1989]: 16). There seems little doubt, though, that however much he may have liked and respected Armstrong, the locus of his passion was later performers like Parker, who were closer to him generationally. In his 1993 film *In the Line of Fire*, Eastwood's character comes home from work and puts on Miles Davis's *Kind of Blue*. That character, like Eastwood himself, would have been a young man in 1959, when the album was released.

12. For one review of surprised appreciation, see http://www.undertheradarmag.com/reviews/rawhides_clint_eastwood_sings_cowboy_favorites/ [November 3, 2011].

13. In making this point, I'm developing a line of thinking suggested by the incisive British critic Christopher Frayling. See *Clint Eastwood* (London: Virgin, 1992), 68.

14. It's interesting to note that Michael Cimino, whose spendthrift ways in making *Heaven's Gate* (1980) precipitated the collapse of the entire United Artists studio, was hired by Eastwood to direct *Thunderbolt and Lightfoot* (1974). That production went off without a financial hitch.

15. Schickel, *Biography*, 231. There are any number of good reasons to hesitate before challenging the judgment of Richard Schickel, one of the finest film critics and historians of the past half century. He knows a lot, has had more access to Eastwood than any other writer, and came of age with Eastwood, with whom he shares many influences. But I think he misses something important here. Whatever context or nuance that suggested otherwise to him at the time, it is not necessarily dark or gratuitous to say that "man is really a flock animal." In any case, Schickel is not alone in his belief. Eastwood's most recent biographer, Marc Eliot, also foregrounds the notion of Eastwood as loner. See *American Rebel: The Life of Clint Eastwood* (New York: Harmony Books, 2009), introduction (Kindle ed., location 78–91).

16. Eliot, *American Rebel*, location 1192–1205.

17. See Robert Ray, *A Certain Tendency in the Hollywood Cinema, 1930–1980* (Princeton: Princeton University Press, 1985).

18. Eastwood has frequently discussed his decision to deny backstories to his characters, although perhaps the most succinct explanation came from his mentor and collaborator, Don Siegel: "The more you describe, analyse and *explain* a character, the less real he becomes. The trick is to suggest, to leave holes, problems, questions that the viewer's imagination will fill in a much more satisfying way than we could ever do" (Don Siegel, *A Siegel Film: An Autobiography* [London: Faber & Faber, 1993], 440).

19. Thompson's review appeared in the August 8 edition of the *Times*, accessed via nytimes.com. The *Variety* review, published on December 31, 1967, is available at http://www.variety.com/review/VE1117791471.html?categoryid=31&cs=1#ix zzownWUSS43 [November 2, 2011]. Paul Smith describes the interpretive confusion surrounding *Hang 'em High* and other Eastwood films of the time in *Cultural Production*, 29 ff.

20. Edward Gallafent, *Clint Eastwood: Filmmaker and Star* (New York: Continuum, 1994), 104.

21. For a more detailed reading of *Joe Kidd*'s ideological incoherence, one that emphasizes the racism of the filmmakers in their inability to decisively cast their lot with the Mexicans, see Smith, *Cultural Production*, 32–36.

22. Schickel, *Retrospective*, 127; Schickel, *Biography*, 291.

23. Robert Mazzocco, "The Supply-Side Star," *New York Review of Books*, April 1, 1982, http://www.nybooks.com/articles/archives/1982/apr/01/the-supply-side-star/?page=1 [June 2011].

24. Siegel, *Siegel Film*, 369–70.

25. Schickel, *Biography*, 279–80.

26. Siegel, *Siegel Film*, 366.

27. A point made by Fred Erisman in "Clint Eastwood's Western Films and the Evolving Mythic Hero," in Leonard Engel, *Clint Eastwood, Actor and Director: New Perspectives* (Salt Lake City: University of Utah Press, 2007), 183.

28. Richard Hutson underlines the extent to which *High Plains Drifter* is a portrait of a diseased community. See "One Hang, We All Hang," in Engel, *Clint Eastwood*, 99–118.

29. Schickel, *Biography*, 291. Wayne was generally supportive of Eastwood and had suggested they work together. But when Eastwood sent Wayne a script he thought would work, Wayne declined and added his critique of the recently released *High Plains Drifter*, which he reputedly said failed to honor the pioneer

spirit. The story that *Rio Bravo* (1959), directed by Howard Hawks, was an answer to *High Noon* is widely cited. But Garry Wills considers this dubious. See *John Wayne's America: The Politics of Celebrity* (New York: Simon & Schuster, 1997), 274–75.

30. Schickel, *Retrospective*, 114.
31. Thomas Jefferson, letter to Peter Carr, August 10, 1787, in *The Portable Thomas Jefferson*, 425.
32. Gordon Wood, "The Trials and Tribulations of Thomas Jefferson," in *Revolutionary Characters: What Made the Founders Different* (New York: Knopf, 2006), 107. The piece was first published in 1993.
33. Boorstin, *Lost World of Thomas Jefferson*, 237, 150–51.
34. For a good overview on this point, see Thomas O. Jewett, "Thomas Jefferson's Views on Women," *Early America Review* 2:2 (Fall 1997), http://www.earlyamerica.com/review/fall97/jeffersn.html [August 4, 2011].
35. Ginny Dougary, "Liz Taylor," in *OK You Mugs: Writers on Movie Actors*, ed. Luc Sante and Melissa Holbrook Pierson (New York: Vintage, 2000), 49.
36. For one example of Eastwood referring to women (this one his wife) as chicks, see Rex Reed, "No Tumbleweed Ties for Clint," in *Eastwood: Interviews*, ed. Robert E. Kapsis and Kathie Coblentz (Jackson: University of Mississippi Press, 1999), 6. Patrick McGilligan discusses Eastwood's sexual life throughout *Clint: The Life and Legend* (New York: St. Martin's Press, 2002), as does Sondra Locke in her evocatively titled *The Good, the Bad, and the Very Ugly: A Hollywood Journey* (New York: Morrow, 2002).
37. For more on Eastwood's masculinist orientation, see Bingham, *Acting Male*, 191.
38. Joan Mellen, *Big Bad Wolves: Masculinity in the American Film* (New York: Pantheon, 1977), 268; Bingham, *Acting Male*, 175; Smith, *Cultural Production*, 122. A less labored critical feminist reading of Eastwood's early work can be found in Susan Jeffords, *Hard Bodies: Hollywood Masculinity in the Reagan Era* (New Brunswick: Rutgers University Press, 1993). See especially 17–20.
39. Drucilla Cornell sees Garver as a figure haunted by remorse, emphasizing his regret over his failed relationship. She also considers the final sequence of the movie, in which we see the dead stalker, as evidence of Eastwood's effort to depict Garver's broader understanding of the consequences of his actions. But while there's no doubt of Garver's sense of compassion toward his loved one, she seems to overstate her case. See *Clint Eastwood and Issues of American Masculinity* (New York: Fordham University Press, 2009), 3.
40. Schickel, *Biography*, 292.
41. Paul Smith is one of a number of observers who see a homoerotic subtext in this movie, though, in keeping with the overall tone of his book, he tends to discount its significance. See *Cultural Production*, 143–49.
42. Dan T. Carter, "The Transformation of a Klansman," *New York Times*, October 4, 1991, accessed via nytimes.com. Dan Carter is a distant relative of Asa Carter. On the origins of the movie in *Gone to Texas*, see Schickel, *Retrospective*, 124–26.
43. Forrest (Asa) Carter, *Gone to Texas*, in *Two Westerns by Forrest Carter* (Albuquerque: University of New Mexico Press, 2004), 177. That's Forrest, by the way, as in Nathan Bedford Forrest, the celebrated Confederate cavalry commander who founded the Ku Klux Klan.
44. Michael Henry, "Interview with Clint Eastwood," in Kapsis and Koblentz, *Interviews*, 103–4, 109.

45. Schickel notes the prominence of the family theme in Eastwood's recent work in the introduction to *Clint: A Retrospective*, 31, and returns to it repeatedly in his analysis of individual movies that follow.

46. Judith Mayne, *Framed: Lesbians, Feminists and Media Culture* (Minneapolis: University of Minnesota Press, 2000), 73; Cornell, *Clint Eastwood and Issues of American Masculinity*, 4.

47. Some consider *Unforgiven* a revisionist Western, even though it isn't. Part of the issue is what one means by *revisionist*. As far as I can tell, the term has been applied to movies as far back as *The Searchers* in 1956 (some even push it back to Jimmy Stewart's Westerns under the direction of Anthony Man in the early fifties). *Revisionist* typically appears to mean a film that challenges the genre conventions of the Western. But those conventions are nothing if not elastic, and at the same time, there are certain boundaries that are never crossed (I can't think of one where everyone dies, for example, or one that is set in Rhode Island). There was much talk at the time and since of Eastwood's spaghetti Westerns being revisionist in their relatively casual, amoral air about violence, considered so different than that of the "classic" Westerns of the fifties, though Eastwood's characters were never wholly without redeeming value (the same could be said about the characters of another "revisionist" filmmaker, Sam Peckinpah).

    In a very real sense, however, *Unforgiven* does indeed revise the terms of the Western as Eastwood himself practiced it in the seventies. One important reason is that we see, in marked contrast to some of his earlier films, a string of pointed scenes that succeed in making us squirm in their intentional awkwardness. But to use *revisionism* as a term to describe both *A Fistful of Dollars* and *Unforgiven*, which would appear to have diametrically opposite positions in the way they depict gunslinging, is confusing at best.

48. For a gloss on this controversy, see Edward Buscombe, *Unforgiven* (British Film Institute Classics; London: BFI Publishing, 2004), 85–87. Susan Jeffords (*Hard Bodies*, 180–90) and Paul Smith (*Cultural Production*, 263–68) are among those who think the movie ends up glorifying the violence it supposedly critiques. While I think they have a point, I find Bingham in particular dogmatic in his consistent unwillingness to nuance in Eastwood's work.

49. In his exceptionally acute reading of the movie, Walter Metz faults the class bias in portraying Swank's family as "the worst poor white-trash stereotyping in any recent Hollywood movie." He also notes that Eastwood's character executes the decisive act in the movie and in so doing "preserves the masculine ideals of potency." See "The Old Man and the C" in Engel, *Clint Eastwood*, 215–16.

50. Bingham describes these and similar interactions in *Acting Male*, 187–90.

51. Jefferson's skepticism about organized religion is well known. "I forgot to observe," he wrote in the letter to Peter Carr cited in the epigraph of this chapter, "when speaking of the New testament that you should read all histories of Christ, as well of those whom a council of ecclesiastics have decided for us to be Pseudo-evangelists, as those they named Evangelists, because these Pseudo-evangelists pretended to inspiration as much as the others, and you are to judge their pretensions by your own reason, and not by the reason of those ecclesiastics." See Thomas Jefferson to Peter Carr, August 10, 1787 in *The Portable Thomas Jefferson*, ed. Merrill Peterson (New York: Viking, 1977), 427.

52. Wills, *John Wayne's America*, 25.

53. Richard Slotkin, *Gunfighter Nation: The Myth of the Frontier in Twentieth-Century America* (1992; New York: HarperCollins, 1993), 22.

54. Schickel, *Retrospective*, 274.

Chapter 2

1. http://xroads.virginia.edu/~hyper/turner/[November 2, 2011]. All subsequent references to the essay come from this source. On the circumstances surrounding the delivery of the address, see John Mack Faragher's introduction to *Rereading Frederick Jackson Turner: "The Significance of the Frontier in American History" and Other Essays* (New Haven: Yale University Press, 1994), 1–3. Richard White discusses the literal and figurative convergence of Turner and Cody at the Chicago Exposition in *The Frontier in American Culture: Essays by Richard White and Patricia Limerick*, ed. James R. Grossman (Berkeley: University of California Press, 1994), 7–65.
2. "Turner was, to put it mildly, ethnocentric and nationalistic. English-speaking white men were the stars of his story," notes Patricia Nelson Limerick. See *The Legacy of Conquest: The Unbroken Past of the American West* (New York: Norton, 1987), 21. Limerick makes the "f-word" observation in "The Adventures of the Frontier," her contribution to *The Frontier in American Culture*, 72. For more on her and other critiques of Turner/frontier, see *Trails: Toward a New Western History*, ed. Limerick, Clyde Milner II, and Charles E. Rankin (Lawrence: University of Kansas Press, 1991).
3. Richard Hofstadter, *The Progressive Historians: Turner, Beard, Parrington* (1968; Chicago: University of Chicago Press, 1979) 61.
4. Garry Jenkins, *Daniel Day-Lewis: The Fire Within* (London: Pan Books, 1995), 65; Lynn Hirschberg, "The New Frontier's Man," *New York Times Magazine*, November 11, 2007, accessed via nytimes.com.
5. Richard Woodward, "The Intensely Imagined Life of Daniel Day-Lewis," *New York Times,* July 5, 1992, accessed via nytimes.com.
6. Hirschberg, "The New Frontier's Man."
7. Jay Carr, "Playwright Arthur Miller Revisits Salem," *San Francisco Chronicle*, December 22, 1996, accessed via Gale/Custom Newspapers database.
8. Much of my understanding of the military frontier of northern New England comes from Mary Beth Norton, *In the Devil's Snare: The Salem Witchcraft Crisis of 1692* (2002; New York: Vintage Books, 2003). See in particular Appendix II (319–20).

    Colonial historian Neal Salisbury has questioned the degree to which Norton's argument can really explain what happened in Salem; see his review of her book in *Journal of American History* 91:1 (June 2004): 201–2, accessed via JSTOR. On other political and economic divisions in Salem, see Paul Boyer and Stephen Nissenbaum, *Salem Possessed: The Social Origins of Witchcraft* (Cambridge: Harvard University Press, 1974), esp. chapter 2.
9. Arthur Miller, *The Crucible* (New York: Dramatists Play Service, 1952), 12.
10. Norton, *In the Devil's Snare*, 21.
11. Iain Blair, "Shooting Miller's 'Crucible,' " *Bergen County Record*, November 29, 1996, accessed via ProQuest.
12. Information on Proctor comes from a variety of sources, among them Norton, *In the Devil's Snare* (esp. 70–71), and the University of Missouri/Kansas City Law School site on the Salem Witch Trials (http://www.law.umkc.edu/faculty/projects/ftrials/salem/SALEM.HTM), as well as a site operated by the University of Virginia (http://salem.lib.virginia.edu/home.html [November 2, 2011]). For a critique of Miller's portrayal of Proctor vis-à-vis the historical record, see William J. McGill, "The Crucible of History: Arthur Miller's John Proctor," *New England Quarterly* 54:2 (June 1981): 258–64, accessed via JSTOR.
13. Matthew 5:29–30; Mark 9:43–48.

14. On Cooper's family history, see Alan Taylor's magisterial *William Cooper's Town: Power and Persuasion on the Frontier of the Early American Republic* (1995; New York: Vintage Books, 1996).

15. Cooper's ethnography is murky here; he seems to conflate them with the Mohegans, who are alive and well in Connecticut; there are also Munsee Mohican in western Massachusetts. See http://www.mohican.com/ [November 2, 2011]. My thanks to Professor Elizabeth Chilton of Harvard University for this clarification.

16. Cora, we are told at one point, is the product of a marriage between Colonel Munro and a Caribbean woman of some African extraction, in effect making her mulatto—which, in the logic of a racial calculus that persisted into the twentieth century, made her tragically doomed from the start.

17. *Mohicans* was also made into a series of television productions. A syndicated 1957–58 U.S.-Canadian series was made in Hollywood and starred Lon Chaney Jr. as Chingachgook (amusingly faithful to its age of domesticity, it opens with Hawkeye coming home to his mother). An eight-part 1971 BBC series was long on acting talent but somewhat short in its production budget. *Last of the Mohicans* was also the name of a 1982 EP record by the British New Wave band Bow Wow Wow (it contained their biggest hit, "I Want Candy"). The weirdly incongruous cover depicted Mohicans-like characters inserted into a photograph modeled on the 1862 Edouard Manet painting *The Luncheon on the Grass.* A frontier in the history of Western art, I suppose.

18. Richard White, "Last of the Mohicans," in *Past Imperfect: History According to the Movies* (New York: Henry Holt, 1996), 83. White, a noted historian of Native Americans and the interracial frontier known as "the middle ground," takes a dismissive view of Mann's film, which he dubs a "well-intentioned if silly movie" in which a series of factual inaccuracies culminates in a message that all that was wrong with America was the fault of British "supercilious twits." (85) Yet this seems like a reductive reading of the film, not only because, superciliousness aside, characters like Munro and Heyward were not *solely* twits (Heywood, in an act of bravery, gives up his life for Cora, after all), but also because White seems to have difficulty accepting plausible, if arguable, propositions; for example, colonial tensions in the French and Indian War really were a factor in the coming of the Revolution, even if Mann doesn't have all his facts straight.

19. It's truly surprising how few movies, let alone good movies, have been made about the American Revolution. Perhaps the best known and remembered is John Ford's *Drums Along the Mohawk* (1939), starring Henry Fonda, which is probably the best of the lot. An improbable Cary Grant appears in *The Howards of Virginia* (1940), which usefully explores family tensions that divided families during the war. Among more recent movies, *Revolution* (1985), starring the even more improbable Al Pacino, is awful, notwithstanding the attempt at reappraisal by video re-release in 2009. As for Mel Gibson in *The Patriot* (2000), well, the less said the better. Actually, the best production I've seen about the Revolution is the HBO miniseries *John Adams* (2008), which has a sense of political and psychological complexity that outstrips any of these predecessors.

20. Woodward, "The Intensely Imagined Life of Daniel Day-Lewis."

21. William Cronon, *Nature's Metropolis: Chicago and the Great West* (1991; New York: Norton, 1992), 46–47.

22. Hofstadter, *Progressive Historians*, 163.

23. Luc Sante, *Low Life: Lures and Snares of Old New York* (1991; New York: Farrar, Straus and Giroux, 2003), 21. On the book's influence on Day-Lewis,

see *Gangs of New York: Making the Movie* (New York: Miramax Books, 2002), 58.

24. Russell Shorto, foreword to Herbert Asbury's *The Gangs of New York: An Informal History of the Underworld* (1927; New York: Vintage, 2008). Luc Sante has written of his difficulties in corroborating Asbury's stories. See *Low Life*, 380–81.

25. Asbury, *Gangs of New York*, 21.

26. The real Poole was shot, not stabbed, in 1855. See ibid., 85–90; Sante, *Low Life*, 257–59.

27. *Gangs of New York: Making the Movie*, 19–20, 24.

28. Ibid. On the financing and power struggles involved in the production of *Gangs*, see Peter Biskind, *Down and Dirty Pictures: Miramax, Sundance, and the Rise of Independent Film* (2004: New York: Simon & Schuster Paperbacks, 2005), 399–404, 464–69.

29. Ibid., 400–401.

30. Sarah Lyall, "Oscar Films: The Housewife and the Butcher; The Daniel Day-Lewis Method: A Kind of Vanishing Act," *New York Times*, March 9, 2003, accessed via nytimes.com.

31. Hirschberg, "The New Frontier's Man."

32. Edith Wharton, *The Age of Innocence,* movie tie-in ed. (1920; New York: Collier, 1993), 4–7.

33. Hirschberg, "The New Frontier's Man."

34. See Robert Ray, *A Certain Tendency in the Hollywood Cinema, 1930–1980* (Princeton: Princeton University Press, 1985), 213–25, and "It's a Wonderful Death," a essay that compares *It's a Wonderful Life* with another Scorsese film, *The Last Temptation of Christ*, in Jim Cullen, *Restless in the Promised Land: Catholics and the American Dream* (Frankin, WI: Sheed & Ward, 2001), esp. 131–34.

35. Upton Sinclair, *Oil!* (1927; New York: Penguin, 2007). We learn of Ross's background on 14. On Doheny, see Margaret Leslie Davis, *The Dark Side of Fortune: Triumph and Scandal in the Life of Oil Tycoon Edward L. Doheny* (Berkeley: University of California Press, 1998).

36. Eric Schlosser, *Fast Food Nation: The Dark Side of the All-American Meal* (New York: Houghton Mifflin, 2001).

37. Eric Schlosser, " 'Oil!' and the History of Southern California," *New York Times,* February 22, 2008, accessed via nytimes.com.

38. Timothy Noah, "What's Wrong with *There Will Be Blood*," *Slate*, January 3, 2008, http://www.slate.com/id/2181270/ [December 17, 2010]. Noah says at the outset that he had not read Sinclair's novel; I have, and I agree with him.

39. Scott Foundas, "Blood, Sweat and Tears: Paul Thomas Anderson," *L.A. Weekly,* January 16, 2008, accessed at http://www.laweekly.com/2008-01-17/film-tv/blood-sweat-and-tears/2/ [December 17, 2010].

40. See Terrence Rafferty, "The Film That Runs in the Family. Both Families, in Fact," *New York Times,* March 27, 2005, accessed via nytimes.com.

41. Frederick Jackson Turner, "The West and American Ideals," in *Rereading Frederick Jackson Turner,* 149.

Chapter 3

Epigraph: Michael Cunningham, *The Hours* (1998; New York: Picador, 2002), 12.

1. Graham Fuller, "Streep's Ahead," *Interview*, December 1998, accessed at *Simply Streep: The Meryl Streep Archives*, http://www.simplystreep.com/site/ magazines/199812interview/ [July 8, 2011]. In recent years, unofficial fan sites like this one, started by a German who goes by the name of Frederik in 1999, have become increasingly important clearinghouses of information about celebrities. But *Simply Streep* is, hands down, the best I've ever seen: comprehensive, well organized, delightfully free of trivia. It has aided my work on this chapter tremendously.

2. *Feminism* as defined at http://www.merriam-webster.com/dictionary/feminism [July 8, 2011].

3. See, for example, "Beyond Acting: Meryl Streep, Activist Mom," a description of Streep's work for the National Resources Defense Council, http://www. simplesteps.org/food/eating-well/catching-meryl-streep [July 8, 2011]. Streep discussed her contribution toward the effort to build a museum on *Ellen*, the talk show hosted by Ellen DeGeneres, on January 12, 2012; clip available on YouTube. See also the National Women's History Museum website for more information about the museum and Streep's work on behalf of it: http://www. nwhm.org. Streep discusses both her work on organically sustainable food and the museum in further detail in Vicki Woods, "Force of Nature," *Vogue*, January 2012, http://www.vogue.com/magazine/article/meryl-streep-force-of-nature/#1. [Last three citations accessed January 15, 2012.]

4. The distinction between equality feminism and difference feminism is ably sketched by poet and essayist Katha Pollitt in "Feminism at the Crossroads," in *Left, Right and Center: Voices Across the Political Spectrum,* ed. Robert Atwan and Jon Roberts (New York: Bedford, 1996), 237–44. The piece was based on a talk Pollitt gave in 1993 and originally published in *Dissent* magazine in 1994.

5. "It can be argued that, having staked out an enormous range early in her career—embodying women of various classes, periods, nationalities and personalities—Ms. Streep has settled into a narrower constellation," *New York Times* critic A. O. Scott wrote in 2010. "Who has she been, lately? A *New Yorker* writer in *Adaptation*, a magazine editor in *The Devil Wears Prada*, a radio performer in *A Prairie Home Companion* and a cookbook author in *Julie & Julia,* directed by Nora Ephron, a noted food writer before she was a filmmaker, whom Ms. Streep had already played, more or less, in *Heartburn*." See A. O. Scott, "That Unmistakable Streepness," *New York Times,* February 18, 2010, accessed via nytimes.com.

6. Friedan's submerged career in leftist politics is a central theme of Daniel Horowitz's *Betty Friedan and the Making of the Feminist Mystique: The American Left, the Cold War, and Modern Feminism* (Amherst: University of Massachusetts Press, 1998).

7. On the latter, see "Commercial Surrogacy: Feminist Perspectives," a blog post (February 22, 2010) by Thunder Fox at *Feminist Debates*, http://blog.lib.umn. edu/cgi-bin/mt-search.cgi?IncludeBlogs=11385&search=Betty%20Friedan [September 28, 2011].

8. Betty Friedan, *The Feminine Mystique* (1963; New York: Dell, 1983).

9. Christine Stansell, *The Feminist Promise: 1792 to the Present* (2010; New York: Modern Library, 2011), 205–6. Stansell also describes Friedan as "temperamental," "domineering," and "vain" (213–14).

10. Betty Friedan, *The Second Stage* (New York: Summit Books, 1981), 27.

11. Information on Streep's background can be found on the website for the PBS series *Faces of America* with Henry Louis Gates: http://www.pbs.org/wnet/ facesofamerica/profiles/meryl-streep/70/ [July 11, 2011].

12. The following biographical information comes from a variety of sources. Perhaps the most useful rendering of Streep's early life can be found in Diana Maychick, *Meryl Streep: The Reluctant Superstar* (New York: St. Martin's Press, 1984). I also consulted Nick Smurthwaite, *The Meryl Streep Story* (London: Columbus Books, 1984) and Iain Johnstone, *Streep: A Life in Film* (London: Psychology News Press, 2009).

13. For one such heartfelt testimonial, see Johnstone, *Streep*, 3.

14. Ibid., 1–2.

15. Maychick, *Meryl Streep*, 17, 19–26. Streep's yearbook photo is included as an insert in the middle of the book.

16. Ibid., 34.

17. Ibid., 35–39; Johnstone, *Streep*, 10–11.

18. Smurthwaite, *Meryl Streep Story*, 32.

19. Susan Dworkin, "Meryl Streep to the Rescue," *Ms.,* February 1979, accessed via *Simply Streep* [July 11, 2011].

20. Fonda quoted in Johnstone, *Streep*, 18. For more on "the woman's film," see Molly Haskell's chapter on the subject in her now-classic *From Reverence to Rape: The Treatment of Women in the Movies,* 2nd ed. (Chicago: University of Chicago Press, 1987), 153–87.

21. Maychick, *Meryl Streep*, 41.

22. A. Scott Berg, *Kate Remembered* (New York: Putnam, 2003), 176.

23. Bernard Weinraub, "Her Peculiar Career; Meryl Streep," *New York Times*, September 18, 1994, accessed via nytimes.com; Scott, "That Unmistakable Streepness"; John Hind, "Did I Say That?: Meryl Streep," *Guardian*, February 14, 2008, http://www.guardian.co.uk/lifeandstyle/2010/feb/14/did-i-say-that-meryl-streep; Mark Adnum, "Meryl Streep: 'Our Lady of the Accents,' " *Spiked*, February 11, 2009, http://www.spiked-online.com/site/article/6204/. On Elvis Mitchell's reaction to Streep's 2008 comment on Kael, which first appeared in the *Guardian*, see the now-defunct Independent Film Channel's website: http://www.ifc.com/blogs/indie-eye/2008/07/elvis-mitchell-pauline-kael-an.php. [All viewed July 11, 2011.]

24. Christine Spines, "Streep's the One," *Entertainment Weekly*, December 1, 2008, accessed via *Simply Streep* [July 11, 2011]; Maychick, *Meryl Streep*, 4.

25. Streep's comments in *The Making of Out of Africa*, accessed via *Simply Streep*. Streep's appearance on *Inside the Actors Studio* was accessed via YouTube [July 12, 2011].

26. Benjamin Lee, "There's Something About Meryl," *Times Live*, August 8, 2010, accessed via *Simply Streep* [July 12, 2011].

27. Friedan, *The Feminine Mystique*, 311.

28. Avery Corman, *Kramer vs. Kramer* (New York: Signet, 1977), 45, 50. Given that it's a first name given to males and females, it may be worth clarifying here that Avery Corman is a man.

29. Streep quoted in *Finding the Truth: The Making of Kramer vs. Kramer*, video accessed via YouTube [July 12, 2011].

30. Maychick, *Meryl Streep*, 87–88; Johnstone, *Streep*, 60–61.

31. Corman, *Kramer vs. Kramer,* 130.

32. Friedan, *The Feminine Mystique,* 77.

33. See the American Film Institute's 2004 Lifetime Award ceremony broadcast for Streep, for this comment and tributes by many other collaborators (available on YouTube). Jim Carrey's tribute is particularly priceless.

34. George Anthony, "A Conversation with a Natural Actress," *Marquee*, December 1983, accessed via *Simply Streep* [July 11, 2011].

35. Vincent Canby was among those with such an objection. See his review of *Silkwood* in the *New York Times*, December 14, 1983, accessed via nytimes. com.

36. The most forceful description and critique of this antifeminist current in American culture can be found in Susan Faludi, *Backlash: The Undeclared War on American Women* (New York: Crown, 1991).

37. James Naremore, *Acting in the Cinema,* Kindle ed. (Berkeley: University of California Press, 1990), 65.

38. Anthony, "Conversation with a Natural Actress."

39. Streep, *A Cry in the Dark* interview with Professor John C. Tibbets, accessed via video archive at *Simply Streep* [July 13, 2011].

40. Joy Horowitz, "That Madcap Meryl. Really!" *New York Times*, March 17, 1991, accessed via nytimes.com.

41. Streep, *Death Becomes Her* interview (1992), accessed at *Simply Streep* [July 15, 2011].

42. Glenn Plaskin, "Meryl Streep's Focus Is Work; Private Life Is Not for Sale," *Seattle Times*, September 21, 1990, accessed via *Simply Streep* [July 15, 2011].

43. *Dancing at Lughnasa* grossed about $3 million domestically, and *Music of the Heart* about $15 million. *The Matrix*, by contrast, grossed about $170 domestically and almost half a billion globally. Box office grosses on these movies can be found at the *Box Office Mojo* website: http://www.boxofficemojo. com.

44. Cunningham, *The Hours*, 50–51.

45. Kevin West, "Two Queens," *W Magazine*, May 2006, http://www.wmagazine. com/celebrities/archive/lindsay_lohan_meryl_streep [July 18, 2011].

46. Box office gross from http://boxofficemojo.com/movies/?id=mammamia.htm [January 15, 2012].

47. In a 2006 appreciation of Friedan, American Studies scholar Joyce Antler notes that Friedan "rejected religion almost entirely" early in her life, but later reclaimed her Jewish roots. Friedan encouraged Antler to stress this point by quoting Friedan's diary entries in her private papers. See "Betty Friedan: Writer, Activist, Pioneer in the Feminist Movement, 1921–2006," *Jewish Women's Archive*, http://jwa.org/weremember/friedan [February 25, 2012].

48. Streep, 1998 *Inside the Actors Studio* interview. In a 1987 profile in *Life* magazine, Streep mined a similar vein of thought. In acknowledging what her interviewer called "a kind of sotto voce spirituality," Streep says, "It's the great gift of human beings that we have this power of empathy. We can all feel like Elliott when E.T. died. We can all cry for each other. If there's hope in the future for us all, it lies in that. And it happens that actors can evoke that event between hearts . . . That's what an actor can do. That's what I want to do." Brad Darrach, "Enchanting, Colorless, Glacial, Fearless, Sneaky, Seductive, Manipulative, Magical Meryl," *Life*, December 1987, 74.

Chapter 4

1. All Ebert reviews of Washington movies come from rogerebert.com. Ebert described being moved to tears by Washington's portrayal of Rubin Carter in *The Hurricane*. He was similarly moved by the 2002 movie *Antwone Fisher*, which Washington acted in and directed, explaining this rare reaction to Charlie Rose on *The Charlie Rose Show* on December 16, 2002. The excerpt was rebroadcast on December 26, when Rose showed it to Washington when Washington was Rose's guest. "The check is in the mail," Washington joked in response.

2. Harris Poll, http://www.harrisinteractive.com/Insights/HarrisVault.aspx [February 5, 2011].

3. A. O. Scott, "Oscar's Step Toward Redemption," *New York Times,* March 21, 2002, accessed via nytimes.com. Halle Berry, who is also African American, won an Oscar for her performance in *Monster's Ball* that evening.

4. Douglas Brode, *Denzel Washington: His Films and Career* (New York: Birch Lane Press, 1997), 36.

5. Nicholas Kristof, "Blacks, Whites and Love," *New York Times,* April 24, 2005, accessed via nytimes.com.

6. Roberts quoted in Allison Samuels, "Will It Be Denzel's Day?" *Newsweek,* February 5, 2002, accessed via Gale Popular Magazines database [February 16, 2011]; Brode, *Denzel Washington,* 167–68, xxx.

7. *The Charlie Rose Show,* December 26, 2002; "Denzel Washington Says Despite Fame He Still Falls Victim to Racism," *Jet,* November 6, 1995, 23, accessed via Gale's Popular Magazines database.

8. Information about Washington's early life was gleaned from a variety of sources, the core of it from the long introduction to Brode's *Denzel Washington: His Films and Career* (xi–xxxvii). Unless otherwise specified, much of the relevant information cited can be found here.

9. Rick Lyman, "Holiday Films: Sporting Life," *New York Times*, November 14, 1999, accessed via nytimes.com.

10. Denzel Washington with Daniel Paisner, *A Hand to Guide Me* (Des Moines: Meredith Books, 2006), 11.

11. *Devil* made less than a third of what was spent to produce and market it. See Bernard Weinraub, "Dismay over Big-Budget Flops," *New York Times,* October 17, 1995, accessed via nytimes.com.

12. Porter's name alludes to a common profession for black men in the late nineteenth and early twentieth centuries, serving wealthy white men on train cars. Porters, it's also worth noting, were among the most upwardly mobile African Americans of their time.

13. DuBois's 1903 essay "The Talented Tenth" is widely available online; see, for example, http://teachingamericanhistory.org/library/index.asp?document=174 [November 2, 2011].

14. Manning Marable, *Malcolm X: A Life of Reinvention* (New York: Viking, 2011), 60–62. Marable approvingly quotes a friend of his at the time who says, "He was never no big-time racketeer or thug."

15. The uneasy state of Malcolm's marriage is discussed throughout *A Life of Reinvention.* For specific indications of infidelity, see 393, 423. He discusses Malcolm's likely homosexual activity in most detail on 66.

16. See, for example, Glenn Collins, "Denzel Washington Takes a Defiant Break from Clean-Cut Roles," *New York Times,* December 28, 1989, accessed via nytimes.com

17. Frank Lucas with Aliya King, *Original Gangster: The Real Life Story of One of America's Most Notorious Drug Lords* (New York: St. Martin's Press, 2010). Though it begins as a vivid document of black life in the South and in Harlem, the book descends into a fairly monotonous and self-serving account heavy on Lucas's thirst for material pleasures.

18. Washington, *A Hand to Guide Me,* 8, 10. (Washington cites Proverbs 22:6.)

19. In his analysis of the movie, Claiborne Carson notes that "as remembered by his son, Little was an abusive husband and father who 'savagely' beat his children, except for Malcolm" and observes that the six-year-old Malcolm had

little memory of his father's death. See Carson's essay on *Malcolm X* in *Past Imperfect: History According to the Movies*, ed. Mark C. Carnes (New York: Holt, 1996), 278. Marable depicts Earl Little as a committed Garveyite with a real attachment to Malcolm—more so than his other children—but also distracted by his political commitments and constant racial harassment. See the first chapter of *A Life of Reinvention*.

20. *Malcolm X* screenplay in Spike Lee with Ralph Wiley, *By Any Means Necessary: The Trials and Tribulations of the Making of "Malcolm X"* (New York: Hyperion, 1992), 279.

21. Much of the following analysis draws on earlier work I did on *Glory*. See Jim Cullen, *The Civil War in Popular Culture: A Reusable Past* (Washington: Smithsonian Institution Press, 1995), 158–59.

22. The story of the prodigal son can be found in the Gospel of Luke 15:11–32.

23. Douglas Brode reports that for all their temperamental differences, Spike Lee and Washington agreed that "Malcolm's story was basically about one man's search for a father figure." *Denzel Washington,* 143.

24. Washington on *The Charlie Rose Show*, February 26, 2002; Antwone Fisher and Mim E. Rivas, *Finding Fish: A Memoir* (New York: Morrow, 2001).

25. Tony Scherman, "The Great Debaters," *American Legacy*, Spring 1997, 42, PDF accessed via Wikipedia article on *The Great Debaters*.

26. "Washington Gives $1M to Wiley College," *USA Today*, December 18, 2007, http://www.usatoday.com/life/movies/2007-12-19-1179829216_x.htm [February 13, 2011].

27. See Manohla Dargis and A. O. Scott, "Hollywood's Whiteout Year: Few Blacks on Silver Screen," *New York Times*, February 13, 2011, accessed via nytimes. com. Dargis and Scott end their long piece by noting Washington's role at the nexus of class and race.

28. See, for example, Douglas J. Rowe, "Washington Looks to Stay Behind Camera," *Huffington Post,* December 24, 2007, http://www.huffingtonpost.com/huff-wires/20071224/film-denzel-washington/ [February 14, 2011].

29. Lyman, "Holiday Films: Sporting Life."

30. Brode, *Denzel Washington*, 119.

31. For more on the culture of "the good death," see Drew Gilpin Faust, *This Republic of Suffering: Death and the Civil War* (New York: Knopf, 2008).

32. The real-life version of this story is told in Sam Chaiton and Terry Swinton, *Lazarus and the Hurricane: The Freeing of Rubin "Hurricane" Carter* (1991; New York: St. Martin's Press, 1999).

33. The story of Lazarus appears in the Gospel of John, chapter 15, in which the sisters of the ailing Lazarus beg Jesus to come heal him. Jesus does not arrive in time, but nevertheless brings Lazarus back from the dead. In Genesis, Jacob abandons his first wife, Leah, for Rachel, but in verse 32 we learn that Leah has borne a son whom she names Reuben. Carter is thus comparing himself to an abandoned child who has nevertheless been given a new lease on life.

34. I base this assertion on the careful analysis of Robert Putnam and David E. Campbell in *American Grace: How Religion Divides and Unites Us* (New York: Simon & Schuster, 2010). See in particular 273–85.

35. The song was actually written by Jerry Ragovoy in 1963 and recorded in a stirring rendition by Irma Thomas in 1964. It became the Rolling Stones' first top-ten hit in the United States in 1965. We hear the Stones version at the end of the movie.

Chapter 5

1. C. A. Tripp, *The Intimate World of Abraham Lincoln* (New York: Free Press, 2005); Joshua Wolf Shenk, *Lincoln's Melancholy: How Depression Challenged a President and Fueled His Greatness* (New York: Houghton Mifflin, 2005); Adam Gopnik, *Angels and Ages: A Short Book about Darwin, Lincoln, and Modern Life* (New York: Knopf, 2009); James Lander, *Lincoln and Darwin: Shared Visions of Race, Science, and Religion* (Carbondale: Southern Illinois University Press, 2010).

2. Abraham Lincoln, "Fragments on Government," in *Lincoln: Speeches, Letters, Miscellaneous Writings,* ed. Don Fehrenbacher (New York: Library of America, 1989), 301–302.

3. Carl Sandburg, *Abraham Lincoln: The Prairie Years*, 2 vols. (New York: Harcourt, Brace, 1926), and *Abraham Lincoln: The War Years,* 4 vols. (New York: Harcourt, Brace, 1939). For an analysis of Sandburg's Lincoln biography as a document of New Deal liberalism, see Jim Cullen, *The Civil War in Popular Culture: A Reusable Past* (Washington: Smithsonian Institution Press, 1995), 29–64.

4. Writers who have paid sustained attention to Lincoln's religiosity include Garry Wills, William Miller, and Richard Carwardine. For a good brief description of his nominal Presbyterianism, see Ronald C. White, *Lincoln's Greatest Speech: The Second Inaugural* (New York: Simon & Schuster, 2002), 128 ff.

5. Abraham Lincoln, "Handbill Replying to Charges of Infidelity," in *Speeches and Writings,* 140.

6. Lincoln's strain of Calvinism is discussed in the above-mentioned sources. For a brief distillation, see Jim Cullen, *The American Dream: A Short History of an Idea That Shaped a Nation* (New York: Oxford University Press, 2003), 97–102.

7. Lincoln quoted in David Herbert Donald, *Lincoln* (New York: Simon & Schuster, 1995), 44.

8. See, for example Lerone Bennett Jr., *Forced into Glory: Abraham Lincoln's White Dream* (Chicago: Johnson Publishing, 2000); Thomas DiLorenzo, *The Real Lincoln: A New Look at Abraham Lincoln, His Agenda, and an Unnecessary War* (New York: Forum, 2002). In a recent anthology marking the 150th anniversary of the Civil War, C. Wyatt Evans notes the difficulties the modern Republican Party has in embracing Lincoln. See "The Lincoln-Obama Moment," in *Remixing the Civil War: Meditations on the Sesquicentennial*, ed. Thomas J. Brown (Baltimore: Johns Hopkins University Press, 2011), 17–36.

9. Donald, *Lincoln*, 19–20; David Gardner, *The Tom Hanks Enigma: The Biography of the World's Most Intriguing Movie Star* (London: Blake, 2007), 4–7.

10. *Saturday Night Live*, season 15, episode 13, http://snltranscripts. jt.org/89/89mmono.phtml [March 21, 2011].

11. See the respected website *Box Office Mojo* for the latest statistics: http:// boxofficemojo.com/people/chart/?id = tomhanks.htm [March 22, 2011]. Gardner cites Hanks as the leading box office star of all time (*The Tom Hanks Enigma*, xiii). Hanks has also been a longtime fixture of the Harris Poll, ranking No. 1 in 2002, 2004, and 2005; see http://www.harrisinteractive.com/ Insights/HarrisVault.aspx [February 5, 2011].

12. Kurt Andersen, "The Tom Hanks Phenomenon: How Did He Pull It Off?" *New Yorker,* December 17, 1998, accessed via kurtandersen.com [March 24, 2011].

13. Douglas Brinkley, "How Tom Hanks Became America's Historian in Chief," *Time*, March 6, 2010, accessed via Gale's Popular Magazines database [March 22, 2011].

14. "Tom Hanks: My Mum Dumped Me," *Women's Day* (Australia), June 21, 2010, accessed via Gale's Popular Magazines database [March 22, 2011]; Gardner, *The Tom Hanks Enigma*, 27. Gardner did substantial reporting on Hanks's extended family for his biography.

15. Lee Pfeiffer and Michael Lewis, *The Films of Tom Hanks* (New York: Citadel, 1996), xii.

16. Gardner gives what is probably the most detailed account of this incident in *The Tom Hanks Enigma*, 159–66.

17. Information on Hanks came from a variety of sources, most usefully distilled in Pfeiffer and Lewis, *The Films of Tom Hanks*, xiv–xv.

18. Gardner, *The Tom Hanks Enigma*, 71, 76–77.

19. Pfieffer and Lewis, *The Films of Tom Hanks*, 81–82.

20. Julie Salamon, *The Devil's Candy: The Bonfire of the Vanities Goes to Hollywood* (New York: Houghton Mifflin, 1991). The book was republished in 2002 with a new subtitle: *The Anatomy of a Hollywood Fiasco*.

21. Gardner, *The Tom Hanks Enigma*, 134.

22. Ibid., 149.

23. Salamon, *The Devil's Candy*, 3–18, 65, 128. Emphasis in original.

24. Ibid., 119; 268; 277.

25. This vision of Lincoln is elaborated most fully in Doris Kearns Goodwin, *Team of Rivals: The Political Genius of Abraham Lincoln* (New York: Simon & Schuster, 2006). The book became the basis of the 2012 movie *Lincoln,* starring Daniel Day-Lewis as Lincoln (in production as of this writing).

26. Gardner, *The Tom Hanks Enigma*, 149–50.

27. Winston Groom, *Forrest Gump* (1986; New York: Simon & Schuster, 2002).

28. See the bonus materials included with the 2007 DVD release of *That Thing You Do!* (Fox).

29. For more on the circumstances, and controversy, surrounding the Bixby letter, see Cullen, *The Civil War in Popular Culture*, 52–54.

30. John Bodnar, "Hollywood Remembers World War II: *Saving Private Ryan* and Postwar Memory in America," in *Hollywood's America: Twentieth-Century America Through Film,* ed. Steven Mintz and Randy W. Roberts, 4th ed. (Malden, MA: Blackwell-Wiley, 2010), 329–39. Bodnar's essay first appeared in the *American Historical Review* in 2001.

31. Steven Spielberg tested his friendship with Hanks by refusing to cast him in the role of the Nazi commandant played by Ralph Fiennes in *Schindler's List.* (Gardner, *The Tom Hanks Enigma*, 210). It's hard to disagree with Spielberg's decision. Even if one concedes Hanks might have tapped the vein of pure malice the role required, it's unlikely the public would have accepted him as such.

32. Quoted in Chalmers Johnson, *Dismantling the Empire: America's Last Best Hope* (New York: Metropolitan Books, 2010), 90. The late Johnson, an acute critic of American imperialism, was predictably critical of the movie. See his analysis, 87–92.

33. Gardner, *The Tom Hanks Enigma*, 286.

34. Hanks quoted in ibid., 299.

35. For more on Hanks and partisan politics, see Gardner's chapter "President Hanks?" in ibid., 249–61.

36. Marc Eliot, *Jimmy Stewart: A Biography* (New York: Harmony Books, 2007), Kindle ed., circa location 3642; James Naremore, *Acting in the Cinema,* Kindle ed. (Berkeley: University of California Press, 1988), 253.

37. Eliot discusses this in *Jimmy Stewart,* location 2020 ff.

Chapter 6

1. Foster's affection for Salinger has been widely cited. See, for example, Louis Chunovic, *Jodie: A Biography* (Chicago: Contemporary Books, 1995), 111. Foster's brother describes the influence of *Franny and Zooey* on her decision to make *Little Man Tate* in Buddy Foster and Leon Wagener, *Foster Child* (1997; New York: Signet, 1998) 246. See note 4 below, however, on its reliability as a source.
2. Hinckley's admiration for Salinger, influenced by the example of John Lennon assassin Mark David Chapman, was widely reported. For one example, see Del Quentin Wilber, *Rawhide Down: The Near Assassination of Ronald Reagan* (New York: Holt, 2011), 22.
3. Malcolm Gladwell notes this truism as a prelude to talking about the difficulties in recruiting good teachers. See "Most Likely to Succeed," *New Yorker*, December 15, 2008, http://www.newyorker.com/reporting/2008/12/15/081215fa_fact_gladwell [November 2, 2011].
4. For more on Buddy Foster's career, see his memoir (with Leon Wagener), *Foster Child: An Intimate Biography of Jodie Foster by Her Brother* (1997; New York: Signet, 1998). Though it is intelligently written and makes a real effort to be fair-minded, one is best advised to read Foster's book with a measure of skepticism, as it is clear that it was written without his sister's approval and that the adult relationship between the two is distant. I have tried to corroborate what I learned from the book with other sources. However, I have relied on it in a few cases for colorful primary source detail. Foster herself has dismissed her brother's book as motivated by greed and sour grapes, though her animus against it seems driven more by its assertions about her sexual identity than its misrepresenting the facts of her childhood. See "Foster Angry over Brother's Tell-All," CNN Interactive, May 15, 1997, http://www.cnn.com/SHOWBIZ/9705/15/foster.book/ [November 2, 2011]. Philippa Kennedy includes a chapter on Buddy Foster in *Jodie Foster: A Life on Screen* (New York: Birch Lane Press, 1996).
5. Foster ancestry as presented at http://freepages.genealogy.rootsweb.ancestry.com/~battle/celeb/foster.htm [January 17, 2012].
6. Foster, *Foster Child*, 18.
7. Kennedy, *Jodie Foster*, 6.
8. Foster, *Foster Child*, 47, 290–92; Manohla Dargis, "Forever Jodie, Forever a Pro," *New York Times,* September 9, 2007, accessed via nytimes.com. Kennedy devotes a chapter to Foster's Yale career; see *Jodie Foster*, 100–123.
9. Kennedy, *Jodie Foster*, 32.
10. Foster, *Foster Child*, 71–72; the GAF commercial can be found on YouTube.
11. Foster, *Foster Child*, 94.
12. Brandy Foster quoted in Chunovic, *Jodie*, 3.
13. Scorsese quoted in Foster, *Foster Child*, 109.
14. "The *Total Film* Interview: Jodie Foster," *Total Film*, http://www.totalfilm.com/features/the-total-film-interview-jodie-foster [November 2, 2011].
15. Kennedy, *Jodie Foster*, 39; Chunovic, *Jodie*, 29.
16. Foster quoted in Chunovic, *Jodie*, 29.
17. Karen Valby, "Jodie Foster: Unbreakable," *Entertainment Weekly*, August 31, 2007, http://www.ew.com/ew/article/0,,20054140,00.html [November 3, 2011].
18. For more on this, see Schrader's commentary on the Criterion Collection edition of *The Last Temptation of Christ*. See also the chapter on *Temptation*, "It's

a Wonderful Death," in Jim Cullen, *Restless in the Promised Land: Catholics and the American Dream* (Franklin, WI: Sheed & Ward, 2001), 109–34.

19. Lois Armstrong, "Foxy Jodie Foster," *People*, May 19, 1980. http://www.people.com/people/archive/article/0,,20076519,00.html [January 17, 2012]

20. On Foster's meticulous work as a student, see Kennedy's chapter on her Yale years, *Jodie Foster*, 100 ff. Foster's testimonials on the value of her undergraduate education stretch from her famous "Why Me?" essay in *Esquire* in December of 1982 to the speeches and visits she's made there in the twenty-first century. See, for example, her remarks during her visit there in 2009: http://www.yaledailynews.com/news/2009/apr/30/jodie-foster-85-revisits-alma-mater/ [November 3, 2011].

21. On Foster's somewhat ambiguous relationship with O'Toole, which might well have drawn serious tabloid attention, if not outrage, today, see Foster, *Foster Child*, 173–74.

22. The best full treatment of Hinckley's assassination attempt is Wilber's *Rawhide Down*; see esp. 54–58. The text of Foster's "Why Me?" essay is available in multiple forms online; one can find it collected with other Foster writings and speeches at the website *Brilliantly Jodie Foster*: http://www.freewebs.com/brilliantlyjodie/wisdombyjodie.htm [May 29, 2011]. On the *Today* show cancellation, see Richard Corliss, "A Screen Gem Turns Director," *Time*, October 14, 1981, http://www.time.com/time/magazine/article/0,9171,974023-5,00.html [May 29, 2011].

23. In *Foster Child,* Buddy Foster asserts that Hinckley was already harassing his sister during the filming of *Carny* in Georgia in 1980 (135).

24. See Jodie Foster, "Why Me?"; Buddy Foster gives the fullest account of the Foster assassination attempt in *Foster Child*, 151–53; he describes some of the security measures she was taking in the 1990s, 198–201. On the woman in the 1984 case, see Chunovic, *Jodie*, 67.

25. "There were some lasting consequences," Buddy Foster has written of the Hinckley aftermath. "Jodie became a different person afterward. She was less trusting, more cynical, and much more cautious" (*Foster Child*, 154). Philippa Kennedy usefully telescopes the controversy over Foster's sexuality in her chapter on the subject (*Jodie Foster,* 170–77). The Foster-Gibson friendship was a source of much commentary between the fall of 2010 and the spring of 2011. For one good example of Foster's thoughtful assessment of Gibson's character, listen to Kurt Andersen's interview with her on his show, *Studio 360*, on May 13, 2011: http://www.studio360.org/2011/may/13/jodie-foster-directs-beaver/[November 3, 2011]. Rob Lowe mentions Foster's support in *Stories I Only Tell My Friends: An Autobiography* (New York: Holt, 2011), 169.

26. Rob Lowe, for example, persuasively argues that *The Hotel New Hampshire* would never get major studio financing today, much less be packaged as a starring vehicle for emerging Hollywood box office idols like himself at the time. See *Stories I Only Tell My Friends*, 170.

27. Kennedy, *Jodie Foster*, 126.

28. "Frank O'Boy Speaks Out on Big Dan's Rape Case," *Taunton Daily Gazette*, May 28, 2009, http://www.tauntongazette.com/news/x313662945/Frank-O-Boy-speaks-out-on-Big-Dan-s-rape-case. The *Providence Journal* reran its coverage on the case in 1999; see "Juries Hear Big Dan Rape Case," http://www.projo.com/specials/century/month10/mass7.htm. See also "Rape Victim Remembered 25 Years Later," *Torch* (North Dartmouth, Mass.), April 3, 2008, http://www1.umassd.edu/torch/07-08/i21v54/. [All May 30, 2011.]

29. This is a subject that Foster has discussed widely. Kennedy provides a substantive discussion, *Jodie Foster*, 132–44.

30. According to the Internet Movie Database, "The filmmakers had completely prepared to go to Montana to shoot a flashback sequence depicting Clarice's runaway attempt. But after filming the dialogue between Jodie Foster and Anthony Hopkins, director Jonathan Demme realized it would be pointless to cut away from their performances and announced, 'I guess we aren't going to Montana.' " *The Silence of the Lambs* trivia, http://www.imdb.com/title/tt0102926/trivia [January 16, 2012].

31. Natalie Zemon Davis, *The Return of Martin Guerre* (Cambridge: Harvard University Press, 1983).

32. Anna Leonowens, *The English Governess at the Siamese Court, Being Recollections of Six Years in the Royal Palace at Bangkok* (1870; Kindle ed., 2006). The second volume, *The Romance of the Harem*, was published in 1873. After leaving Siam (now Thailand), Leonowens (1831–1915) spent time in New York and was part of its literary scene. She eventually settled in Canada.

33. See, for example the audio commentary accompanying the DVD release of *Nim's Island*.

34. Valby, "Jodie Foster: Unbreakable."

35. "The *Total Film* Interview—Jodie Foster."

36. Hilton Als, "Queen Jane, Approximately," *New Yorker*, May 9, 2011, 63.

37. Steven Zeitchik, "Director says film struck out in U.S. because it's a dramedy," *NewsOK,* May 20, 2011, http://newsok.com/director-says-movie-struck-out-in-the-u.s.-because-its-a-dramedy/article/3569471 [June 11, 2011].

38. For more on this, see David Roediger, *The Wages of Whiteness: Race and the Making of the American Working Class* (London and New York: Verso, 1991).

Conclusion

1. These two paragraphs represent a distillation of a series of well-publicized books I read or sampled for pleasure more than research in recent years, among them Daniel Kahneman, *Thinking, Fast and Slow* (New York: Farrar, Straus and Giroux, 2011); Daniel Gilbert, *Stumbling on Happiness* (New York: Knopf, 2006); Malcolm Gladwell, *Blink: The Power of Thinking Without Thinking* (New York: Little, Brown, 2005); Jonathan Haidt, *The Righteous Mind: Why Good People Are Divided by Politics and Religion* (New York: Pantheon, 2012); Daniel Pink, *A Whole New Mind: Why Right-Brainers Will Rule the Future,* updated ed. (New York: Riverhead, 2006); Steven Pinker, *The Blank Slate: The Modern Denial of Human Nature* (New York: Penguin, 2002); Kent Greenfield, *The Myth of Choice: Personal Responsibility in a World of Limits* (New Haven: Yale University Press, 2011); and Richard H. Thaler and Cass R. Sunstein, *Nudge: Improving Decisions About Health, Wealth, and Happiness* (New Haven: Yale University Press, 2008). For a sampling of Affect Theory across literature and other fields, see *The Affect Theory Reader*, ed. Melissa Gregg and Gregory J. Seigworth (Durham, NC: Duke University Press, 2010).

INDEX

Page numbers in *italics* denote illustrations.